Rick Steves'
PARIS
2001

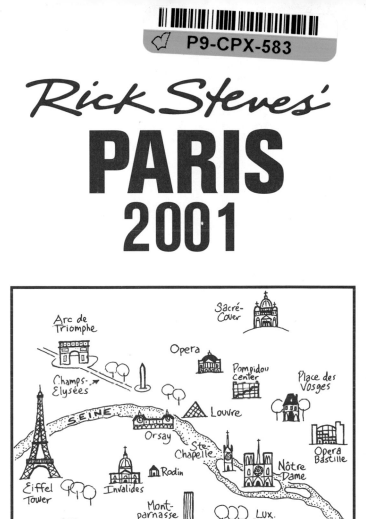

by Rick Steves, Steve Smith, and Gene Openshaw

AVALON
TRAVEL
publishing

Other ATP travel guidebooks by Rick Steves
Rick Steves' Europe 101: History and Art for the Traveler (with Gene Openshaw)
Rick Steves' Europe Through the Back Door
Rick Steves' Mona Winks: Self-Guided Tours of Europe's Top Museums
   (with Gene Openshaw)
Rick Steves' Postcards from Europe
Rick Steves' Best of Europe
Rick Steves' France, Belgium & the Netherlands (with Steve Smith)
Rick Steves' Germany, Austria & Switzerland
Rick Steves' Great Britain & Ireland
Rick Steves' Italy
Rick Steves' Scandinavia
Rick Steves' Spain & Portugal
Rick Steves' London (with Gene Openshaw)
Rick Steves' Rome (with Gene Openshaw)
Rick Steves' Phrase Books: German, Italian, French, Spanish/Portuguese, and
   French/Italian/German

Avalon Travel Publishing, 5855 Beaudry Street, Emeryville, CA 94608

Printed in the United States of America. Second printing March 2001.

Portions of this book were originally published in *Rick Steves' Mona Winks*,
© 1998, 1996, 1993, 1988 by Rick Steves and Gene Openshaw; and in *Rick Steves'
France, Belgium & the Netherlands*, © 2001, 2000, 1999, 1998, 1997, 1996 by
Rick Steves and Steve Smith.

ISBN 1-56691-237-7
ISSN 1522-3299

For the latest on Rick's lectures, guidebooks, tours, and public television series,
contact Europe Through the Back Door, Box 2009, Edmonds, WA 98020,
tel. 425/771-8303, fax 425/771-0833, www.ricksteves.com, or e-mail:
rick@ricksteves.com.

Europe Through the Back Door Editors Risa Laib, Jacquie Maupin
Avalon Travel Publishing Editor Kate Willis
Copy Editor Chris Hayhurst
Production & Typesetting: Kathleen Sparkes, White Hart Design
Cover and Interior Design: Janine Lehmann
Maps: David C. Hoerlein
Photography: pp. 68, 71, 157: David C. Hoerlein; all others by Rick Steves
Printer: Publishers Press
Front cover photo: Tour Eiffel; Paris, France; copyright © Blaine Harrington III

Distributed to the book trade by Publishers Group West, Berkeley, California

*Although the author and publisher have made every effort to provide accurate, up-to-date
information, they accept no responsibility for loss, injury, bad crêpes, or inconvenience sus-
tained by any person using this book.*

CONTENTS
paris

NUMBERS INDICATE ARRONDISSEMENTS (DISTRICTS)

1/2 MILE

INTRODUCTION

Paris—the City of Light—has been a beacon of culture for centuries. As a world capital for art, fashion, food, literature, and ideas, it stands as a symbol of all the fine things that human civilization can offer. Come prepared to celebrate rather than judge the cultural differences, to capture the romance and *joie de vivre* that Paris exudes.

Paris offers sweeping boulevards, sleepy parks, world-class art galleries, chatty crêpe stands, Napoleon's body, chic boutiques, and people watching from outdoor cafés. Climb Notre-Dame and rub shoulders with the gargoyles. Cruise the Seine, zip up the Eiffel Tower, and saunter down the Champs-Élysées. Master the Louvre and Orsay museums. Save some after-dark energy for one of the world's most romantic cities.

Sip decaf with deconstructionists in a street-side café. Step into an Impressionist painting in a tree-lined park. Get to know your hotelier on a first-name basis, then endure a rude waiter in the same restaurants that once insulted other visitors—from van Gogh and Picasso, to Hemingway and Gershwin, to Milan Kundera and Woody Allen.

This Information Is Accurate and Up-to-Date

This book is updated every year. Most publishers of guidebooks that cover a city from top to bottom can afford an update only every two or three years. Since this book is selective, covering only the places we think make the top week or two in and around Paris, we can update it each summer (we even do a winter check-up). Even with an annual update, however, things change. But if you're traveling with the current edition of this book, we guarantee you're using the most up-to-date information available (for the latest, check www.ricksteves.com/update). This book will help you have an inexpensive, hassle-free trip. Use this year's edition. Saving a few bucks by traveling on old information is not smart. If you're packing an old book, you'll learn the seriousness of your mistake...in Paris. Your trip costs at least $10 per waking hour. Your time is valuable. This guidebook saves lots of time.

Welcome to Our Paris City Guide

This book is organized in the following way:

Paris Orientation includes tourist information, public-transportation basics, and easy-to-read maps. The "Planning Your Time" section offers a suggested schedule with thoughts on how to best use your limited time.

Sights provides a succinct overview of Paris' most important sights. They're arranged by neighborhood and include ratings: ▲▲▲—Don't miss; ▲▲—Try hard to see; ▲—Worthwhile if you can make it; no rating—Worth knowing about.

The **Walks** cover five of Paris' most enjoyable neighborhoods: Historic Paris (Notre-Dame and Sainte-Chapelle), Champs-Élysées, Marais, rue Cler (near the Eiffel Tower), and Montmartre.

The **Self-Guided Museum Tours** take you through Paris' most interesting museums: Louvre, Orsay, Rodin, Marmottan, Cluny, Carnavalet, Pompidou Center, and Napoleon's Tomb.

Day Trips covers nearby sights: Versailles (includes self-guided tour), more châteaus (Vaux-le-Vicomte, Fontainebleau, Chantilly), Chartres (includes self-guided tour of cathedral), Monet's Giverny, and Disneyland Paris. Accommodations are listed for Versailles, Fontainebleau, Chartres, and Giverny.

Sleeping in Paris is a guide to our favorite budget hotels in three cozy neighborhoods, with orientation tips geared to make you feel at home.

Eating in Paris offers good-value restaurants ranging from inexpensive eateries to splurges, arranged by neighborhood, with a special section on "Grand Cafés."

Paris with Children includes our top 10 recommendations to keep your kids (and you) happy in Paris.

Shopping in Paris helps you shop painlessly and enjoyably, without letting it overwhelm your vacation or ruin your budget.

Paris at Night is a guide to entertainment and evening fun, with music, bus tours, and river cruises, plus information on how to easily translate *Pariscope* magazine, the weekly entertainment guide.

Transportation Connections covers connections by train and plane, with detailed information on Paris' two airports and six train stations, laying the groundwork for your smooth arrival and departure.

The **appendix** includes a Paris history, a climate chart,

telephone tips, French survival phrases, and a handy almanac of resources.

Throughout the book, when you see a ⊛ in a listing, it means that the sight is covered in much more depth in one of our walks or self-guided tours—a page number will tell you just where to look to find more information.

Browse through this book and choose your favorite sights. Then have a *fantastique* trip! You'll become your own guide with our self-guided walks and museum tours. Traveling like a temporary local, you'll get the absolute most out of every mile, minute, and dollar. You won't waste time on mediocre sights because, unlike other guidebooks, this one covers only the best. Since lousy, expensive hotels are a major financial pitfall, we've worked hard to assemble the best accommodations values. And, as you explore the city we know and love, we're happy you'll be meeting some of our favorite Parisian people.

Trip Costs

Five components make up your trip costs: airfare, surface transportation, room and board, sightseeing/entertainment, and shopping/miscellany.

Airfare: Don't try to sort through the mess. Find and use a good travel agent. A basic round-trip U.S.-Paris flight costs $700 to $1,100, depending on where you fly from and when.

Surface Transportation: For a typical one-week visit, allow about $50 for Métro tickets and a couple of day trips. Add an additional $70 if you opt for taxi rides to and from the airport (or save money by taking a shuttle, airport bus, or the RER).

Room and Board: You can thrive in Paris on $75 a day per person for room and board. A $75-a-day budget allows $5 for breakfast, $10 for lunch, $20 for dinner, and $40 for lodging (based on 2 people splitting the cost of an $80 double room). That's doable. Students and tightwads do it on $40 ($20 per bed, $15–20 for meals and snacks). But budget sleeping and eating require using the skills and information covered in this book (and in much greater depth in *Rick Steves' Europe Through the Back Door*).

Sightseeing and Entertainment: Get the Paris Museum and Monument Pass, which covers most sights in Paris (for more information, see Sights chapter, page 30). You'll pay about $25 for a three-day pass and $40 for a five-day pass. Without a museum pass, figure $5 to $7 per major sight (e.g., Rodin-$5, Louvre-$7), $4 for minor ones (climbing church towers), and $20 for bus tours and splurge experiences (concerts in Sainte-Chapelle). An overall average of $15 a day works for most. Don't skimp here. After all, this category directly powers most of the experiences all the other expenses are designed to make possible.

Shopping and Miscellany: Figure $3 per ice-cream cone, coffee, or soft drink. Shopping can vary in cost from nearly nothing to a small fortune. Good budget travelers find that this category has little to do with assembling a trip full of lifelong and wonderful memories.

Exchange Rate

We've priced things in this book in the local currency:

> 6.50F (French francs) = about $1.

To convert French prices to dollars, divide by six (160F = about $27).

Euro: The euro, adopted as a currency by 11 countries in Europe, won't concern you until 2002, when it materializes into actual bills and coins. In 2002, France will drop its francs and switch to euros.

Prices, Times, and Discounts

The prices in this book, as well as the hours and telephone numbers, are accurate as of late 2000. Europe is always changing, and we know you'll understand that this, like any other guidebook, starts to yellow even before it's printed.

In Europe—and in this book—you'll be using the 24-hour clock. After 12 noon, keep going—13:00, 14:00, and so on. For anything over 12, subtract 12 and add p.m. (for example, 14:00 is 2:00 p.m.).

This book lists peak-season and off-peak hours for sightseeing attractions. While discounts for sights and transportation are not listed in this book, seniors age 60 and over, students with International Student Identification Cards, and youths under 18 often get big discounts—but only when they ask.

When to Go

Late spring and fall have the best weather and the biggest crowds. Summers are generally hot and dry; if you wilt in the heat, look for the rare room with air-conditioning. It's easy to find rooms in summer, and while many French businesses close in August, the traveler hardly notices. Paris makes a great winter getaway. Airfares are cheap and the city feels lively but not touristy. The only problem—weather—is fixed by dressing correctly. Expect cold and rain, but no snow.

Red Tape, Business Hours, and Parking

You need a passport but no visa or shots to travel in France.

Most shops are open Monday through Saturday (10:00–19:00) and closed Sunday, though many small markets, *boulangeries* (bakeries), and the like are open Sunday mornings until noon. On Mondays many businesses are closed until 14:00, and often all day. Saturdays are like weekdays (but most banks are closed).

PTT (Postal, Telegraph, and Telephone) offices' hours vary, though most are open weekdays from 8:00 to 19:00 and Saturdays from 8:00 to 12:00. Stamps are also sold at the *tabac* (tobacco shop). It costs 4.40F to mail a postcard to the United States.

If you have a car, street parking is free after 19:00, on weekends, and in August. Otherwise ask your hotelier for suggestions (figure about 100F per day in a parking structure).

Banking

Bring your ATM, credit, or debit card, along with traveler's checks in dollars (never in francs, which—oddly—only a few banks will cash).

The best and easiest way to get cash in French francs is to use the omnipresent French bank machines (always open, lower fees, quick processing); you'll need a four-digit PIN (numbers only, no letters) with your Visa or MasterCard. Some ATM bankcards will work at some banks, though Visa and MasterCard are more reliable. Before you go, verify with your bank that your card will work. Bring two different cards or two copies of the same card; demagnetization seems to be a common problem. "Cash machine" in French is *distributeur automatique des billets*, or D.A.B. (day-ah-bay).

Regular banks have the best rates for cashing traveler's checks. For a large exchange, it pays to compare rates and fees. The Bank of France (Banque de France) usually offers the best rates. Banking hours vary, though most are open Tuesday through Friday 9:00 to 16:30. Some branches are open Saturday morning, and many are closed on Monday.

Post offices, train stations, and tourist offices usually change money if you can't get to a bank. Post offices (which take cash or American Express checks) give a good rate, have longer hours, and charge no fee. Banks at train stations, tourist offices, and airports offer mediocre rates.

Just like at home, credit (or debit) cards work easily at larger hotels, restaurants, and shops. Smaller businesses prefer payment in local currency. Smart travelers function with hard local cash and a major credit card.

If using traveler's checks, don't be petty about changing money. The greatest avoidable money-changing expense is having to waste time every few days returning to a bank. Change 10 days' or two weeks' worth of money, get big bills, stuff them in your money belt, and travel!

The Cultural and Language Barrier

You've no doubt heard that the French are "mean and cold and refuse to speak English." This is an out-of-date preconception that's going the same way as the "Ugly American." The French are as friendly as any other people; Parisians are no more disagreeable than New Yorkers. And, without any doubt, the French speak more English than Americans speak French. Be reasonable in your expectations: French postal clerks are every bit as speedy, cheery, and multilingual as ours are back home. The French are cold only if you decide to see them that way. Look for friendliness and give them the benefit of the doubt. The cultural fine points, not rugged Yankee individualism, are respected here.

With an understanding of French culture, you're less likely to misinterpret the French people. The French take great pride in their culture, clinging to their belief in cultural superiority despite the fact that they're no longer a world superpower. It must be tough to keep on smiling when you've been crushed by a Big Mac, Mickey-Moused by Disney, and drowned in instant coffee.

Unlike most Americans, the French value time over money. They enjoy a legislated 35-hour workweek and five weeks of paid vacation. The French wouldn't stand for just two weeks off.

Communication difficulties in France are exaggerated. To hurdle the language barrier, bring a small English/French dictionary, a phrase book (look for ours), a menu reader, and a good supply of patience. If you learn only six phrases, learn and use these: *bonjour* (good day), *pardon* (pardon me), *s'il vous plaît* (please), *merci* (thank you), *au revoir* (good-bye), and *Comment trouvez-vous mon haleine?* (How's my breath?). The French place great importance on politeness.

The French are language perfectionists—they take their language (and other languages) seriously. Often they speak more English than they let on. This isn't a tourist-baiting tactic but timidity on their part to speak another language less than fluently. Start any conversation with "*Bonjour, Madame/Monsieur. Parlez-vous anglais?*" and hope they speak more English than you speak French. In transactions, a small notepad and pen can minimize misunderstanding; have vendors write down the price.

Travel Smart

Reread this book as you travel. Buy a phone card and use it for reservations and confirmations. Enjoy the friendliness of the local people and don't let one rude person ruin your day. Ask questions. Most locals are eager to point you in their idea of the right direction. Wear your money belt and see simplicity as a virtue. Those who expect to travel smart, do. Plan ahead for banking, laundry, post-office chores, and picnics. Mix intense and relaxed periods. Every trip (and every traveler) needs at least a few slack days. Pace yourself. Assume you will return.

As you read through this book, plan your itinerary. Note the days when sights are closed. Sundays have pros and cons, as they do for travelers in the United States (special events and weekly markets, limited hours, shops and banks closed, limited public transportation, no rush hours). Saturdays are virtually weekdays. Popular places are even more popular on weekends and inundated on three-day weekends (most common in May).

French Tourist Offices in the United States

France's national tourist offices in the United States are a wealth of information. Before your trip, request any specific information such as city maps and schedules of upcoming festivals (for festivals, also see the appendix and www.ricksteves.com/festivals).

French Government Tourist Offices: For information and brochures on France, call 410/286-8310. Their web site is www.francetourism.com. You can contact their nearest office . . .

In New York: 444 Madison Avenue, 16th floor, New York, NY 10022, fax 212/838-7855, e-mail: info@francetourism.com.

In Illinois: 676 North Michigan Avenue #3360, Chicago, IL 60611, fax 312/337-6339, e-mail: fgto@mcs.net.

In California: 9454 Wilshire Bloulevard #715, Beverly Hills, CA 90212, fax 310/276-2835, e-mail: fgto@gte.net.

For the latest on Paris, visit www.pariscope.fr (in French).

Recommended Guidebooks

For most travelers, this book is all you need. But if you'd like more information, you may want to buy an additional guidebook. The Michelin Green Guide, which is somewhat scholarly, and the more readable *Paris Access* guide are both well researched. If you'll be traveling elsewhere in France, consider *Rick Steves' France, Belgium & the Netherlands 2001*.

Rick Steves' Books and Videos

Rick Steves' Europe Through the Back Door 2001 gives you budget travel tips on minimizing jet lag, packing light, planning your itinerary, traveling by car or train, finding budget beds without reservations, changing money, avoiding rip-offs, outsmarting thieves, hurdling the language barrier, staying healthy, taking great photographs, using your bidet, and lots more. The book also includes chapters on 35 of Rick's favorite "Back Doors."

Rick Steves' Country Guides are a series of seven guide-books covering the Best of Europe; France (co-written with Steve Smith); Great Britain/Ireland; Italy; Spain/Portugal; Scandinavia; and Germany/Austria/Switzerland. All are updated annually and come out in December.

Rick Steves' City Guides, updated annually (available in January), include this book and *Rick Steves' London* and *Rome*. With the sleek Eurostar train, London is just three hours from Paris. Consider combining the two cities (and books) for a great visit.

Rick Steves' Europe 101: History and Art for the Traveler (with Gene Openshaw, 2000) gives you the story of Europe's people, history, and art. Written for smart people who were sleeping in their history and art classes before they knew they were going to Europe, *101* carbonates Europe's sights.

Rick Steves' Mona Winks (with Gene Openshaw, 1998) gives you fun, easy-to-follow, self-guided tours of Europe's top 20 museums. All of the *Mona Winks* chapters on Paris are included in this Paris guidebook. But if you'd like similar coverage for the great museums in London, Amsterdam, Venice, Florence, and Rome, *Mona*'s for you.

Rick Steves' French Phrase Book & Dictionary (1999) gives you the words and survival phrases you'll need while traveling in Paris.

My television series, *Rick Steves' Europe*, airs in 2001 with 16 new shows, including one on Paris. Of the 52 earlier episodes, two cover Paris and seven half-hour shows cover other parts of France. These air throughout the country on local public television stations and the Travel Channel. They are also available as information-packed videotapes, along with my 90-minute slide-show lecture on France, Belgium, and the Netherlands (call 425/ 771-8303 for our free newsletter/catalog).

Rick Steves' Postcards from Europe (1999), my autobiographical book, packs 25 years of travel anecdotes and insights into the ulti-mate 3,000-mile European adventure. Through my guidebooks, I share my favorite European discoveries with you. *Postcards* intro-duces you to my favorite European friends.

All of my books are published by Avalon Travel Publishing (www.travelmatters.com).

Maps

The maps in this book, drawn by Dave Hoerlein, are concise and simple. Dave, who is well traveled in Paris, designed these maps to help you orient quickly and get to where you want to go painlessly. Once in Paris, simply pick up the free Paris map at your hotel and you're ready to travel.

Tours of Paris and France by Rick Steves and Steve Smith

Travel agents will tell you about all the normal tours of Paris and France, but they won't tell you about ours. At Europe Through the Back Door, we organize and lead one-week tours of Paris and longer tours (14-day and 20-day options) covering the highlights of France. The Paris tours, limited to 20 people, take place in January, March, and November when crowds and airfares are at their lowest. Our France tours depart each year from April through October, are limited to 24 people per group, and have two great guides and a big roomy bus. For details on how to travel with us, call 425/771-8303 or check www.ricksteves.com.

Transportation

Transportation concerns within Paris are limited to the subway, buses, and taxis, all covered extensively in the Orientation chapter. If you have a car, stow it. You don't want to drive in Paris. For all the specifics on transportation throughout France by train or car, see *Rick Steves' France, Belgium & the Netherlands 2001*.

Telephones, Mail, and E-mail

Make local and long-distance calls from public phones on the street. Phone cards are a breeze to use. Every country in Europe sells phone cards (good for use only in the country of purchase).

France's public phones take only cards, no coins. Buy a phone card (*une télécarte*) at any post office, train station, and most newsstands and tobacco shops (*tabac* in France). There are two denominations of phone cards in France: *une petite* costs 50F; *une grande* is 100F. When you use the card, simply take the phone off the hook, insert the card, and wait for a dial tone. The price of the call (local or international) is automatically deducted. Buy a card at the beginning of your trip and use it for dinner reservations, calling tourist information offices, and phoning home.

France's new PIN cards offer you the cheapest way to call home. With scratch-off Personal Identification Numbers, they allow you to dial from the comfort of your hotel (or anywhere) and charge the call to the card at a cheaper per-minute rate than a *télécarte*. Instructions are provided in English, and the cards are sold wherever *télécartes* are sold. KOSMOS is one of many brands. Because PIN cards are slower to use (more digits to dial) than a *télécarte*, it's quicker to make short local calls with a *télécarte* from a phone booth.

U.S.A. Direct services are no longer a good value. While it's psychologically comforting to dial an AT&T, MCI, or Sprint access number and get an operator in Atlanta, this doubles your per-minute costs for calls from Paris to the United States (and some hotels will charge a fee for calling-card calls). It's much cheaper to call home using a PIN card or French *télécarte*. A very quick call costs as little as 50 cents.

France has a dial-direct 10-digit telephone system. There are no area codes. To call to or from anywhere in France, including Paris, you dial the 10 numbers directly. All Paris numbers start with 01. (If you encounter any old eight-digit numbers in your travels, add that prefix.)

To dial out of France, you must start your call with its international code: 00. To call France from another country, start with the international access code of the country you're calling from (00 for European countries and 011 from America or Canada), dial France's country code (33), then drop the initial zero of the 10-digit local number and dial the remaining nine digits. For example, the number of a good hotel in Paris is 01 47 05 49 15. To call it from home, dial 011-33-1 47 05 49 15. For a listing of international access codes and country codes, see the appendix. Paris time is six/nine hours ahead of the east/west coast of the United States.

Mail: To arrange for mail delivery, reserve a few hotels along your route in advance and give their addresses to friends, or use American Express Company's mail services (available to anyone who has at least one Amex traveler's check). Allow 10 days for a letter to arrive. Phoning is so easy that we've dispensed with mail stops altogether.

E-mail: E-mail is catching on among hoteliers; we've added e-mail addresses for hotels whenever available. As for Internet access, we've listed several cybercafés (see pages 231 and 236).

Sleeping

A comfortable hotel in Paris costs less than a comparable hotel in London or in most major U.S. cities. It's a great hotel city. Still, you should reserve in advance to secure the best hotel for you. We like places that are clean, small, central, traditional, inexpensive, and friendly. Most places we list have at least four of these six virtues.

Paris Hotels

In this book, the price for a double room will normally range from $40 (very simple, toilet and shower down the hall) to $150 (maximum plumbing and more), with most clustering around $80. A triple and a double are often the same room, with a small double bed and a sliver single, so a third person sleeps very cheaply. Most hotels have a few singles, triples, and quads. While groups

Sleep Code

To give maximum information with a minimum of space, we use these codes to describe accommodations listed in this book. Prices listed are per room, not per person.

S = Single room (or price for one person in a double)

D = Double or Twin (French double beds can be very small)

T = Triple (generally a double bed with a single)

Q = Quad (usually two double beds)

b = Private bathroom with toilet and shower or tub

t = Private toilet only (the shower is down the hall)

s = Private shower or tub only (the toilet is down the hall)

CC = Accepts credit cards (**V** = Visa, **M** = MasterCard, **A**= American Express). If CC isn't mentioned, assume you'll have to pay cash.

* = French hotel rating system, ranging from zero to four stars.

According to this code, a couple staying at a "Db-450F, CC:V" hotel would pay a total of 450 French francs (or about $70) for a double room with a private bathroom. The hotel accepts Visa or French cash in payment.

sleep cheap, traveling alone can be expensive—a single room usually costs about the same as a double. Hotels cannot legally allow more in the room than that shown on their price list.

French receptionists are often reluctant to mention the cheaper rooms. Study the room price list posted at the desk. Understand it. You'll save about $15 on the average if you get a room with a "shower down the hall" rather than in your room; ask for a room without a shower (*sans douche*) rather than with a shower (*avec douche*). A room with a bathtub (*salle de bain*) costs $5 to $10 more than a room with a shower. A double bed (*grand lit*) is $5 to $10 cheaper than twins (*deux petits lits*). Hotels are inclined to give you a room with a tub (which the French prefer). If you prefer a double bed and a shower, you'll need to ask for it, and you'll save up to $20 (compared to the cost of a twin-bedded room with a tub). If you'll take twins *or* a double, ask for a room for two (*chambre pour deux; shambruh pur duh*) to avoid being needlessly turned away.

The French have a simple hotel rating system (zero through four stars) depending on amenities. We like the one- or two-star hotels and a few three-star hotels. More than two stars usually gets you expensive and unnecessary amenities. Unclassified hotels (no stars) can be bargains or depressing dumps. Look before you leap and lay before you pay (upon departure). Hotels in France must charge a daily tax (*taxe du séjour*) that is normally added to the bill. It varies from 3F to 6F per day depending on the number of stars the hotel has. While some hotels include it in the price list, most add it to your bill.

You'll almost always have the option of breakfast at your hotel, which is pleasant and convenient, but, at 25F to 50F, it can be much more than the price of breakfast at the corner café. While hotels hope you'll spring for their breakfast, this is optional unless otherwise noted.

Rooms are safe. Still, keep cameras and money out of sight. Towels aren't routinely replaced every day; drip-dry and conserve. If that French Lincoln-log pillow isn't your idea of comfort, American-style pillows (and extra blankets) are usually in the closet or available on request. To get a pillow, ask for "*Un oreiller, s'il vous plaît*" (un oar-ray-yay, see-voo-play). If you're planning to visit Paris in the summer, the extra expense of an air-conditioned room can be money well spent.

Making Reservations

Reserve ahead for Paris, the sooner the better. May, June, September, and October are the busiest months. If you're not sure how long you'll stay, guess long. You can always cancel the last days once there, but it's very hard to add days at the last minute. We've taken great pains to list telephone numbers with long-distance instructions (see "Telephones and Mail," above, and the appendix). Use the telephone and convenient telephone cards. Most hotels listed are accustomed to English-only speakers. A hotel receptionist will trust you and hold a room until 16:00 without a deposit, though some will ask for a credit-card number. Honor (or cancel by phone) your reservations. Long distance is cheap and easy from public phone booths. Don't let these people down—we promised you'd call and cancel if for some reason you won't show up. Don't needlessly confirm rooms through the tourist office; they'll take a commission.

To reserve from home, call, fax, e-mail, or write the hotel. E-mail is preferred when possible. Phone and fax costs are reasonable, and simple English is usually fine. To fax, use the fax form in the appendix (online at www.ricksteves.com/reservation). If you're writing, add the zip code and confirm the need and method for a deposit. A two-night stay in August would be "two nights, 16/8/01 to 18/8/01"—Europeans write the date day/month/year, and European hotel jargon uses your day of departure.

If you send a reservation request and receive a response

stating the rates and availability of rooms, this is not a confirmation. You must confirm that the rates are fine and that indeed you want the room. One night's deposit is generally required. A credit card will usually be accepted as a deposit, though you may need to send a signed traveler's check or a bank draft in the local currency. If your credit card is the deposit, you can pay with your card or cash when you arrive. If you don't show up or cancel with less than 24 hours' notice, you'll be billed for one night. Reconfirm your reservations a day in advance for safety.

Hostels
Parisian hostels charge about $20 per bed. Some require a hostel membership; the best don't. Get a hostel card before you go if you need one. Travelers of any age are welcome if they don't mind dorm-style accommodations and meeting other travelers. Travelers without a hostel card can generally spend the night for a small extra "one-night membership" fee at those places requiring membership. Cheap meals are sometimes available, and kitchen facilities are usually provided for do-it-yourselfers.

Apartments
It's easy, though not necessarily cheaper, to rent a furnished apartment in Paris. Consider this option if you're either traveling with a family or staying two weeks or longer. For listings, see the end of the Sleeping chapter (on page 245).

Eating in France
The French eat long and well. Relaxed lunches, three-hour dinners, and endless hours sitting in outdoor cafés are the norm. They have a legislated 35-hour workweek and a self-imposed 36-hour eat-week. The French spend much of their five annual weeks of paid vacation at *la table*. Local cafés, cuisine, and wines become a highlight of any French adventure—sightseeing for your palate. Even if the rest of you is sleeping in cheap hotels, let your taste buds travel first-class in Paris. (They can go coach in England.) You can eat well without going broke, but choose carefully— you're just as likely to blow a small fortune on a mediocre meal as you are to dine wonderfully for $20.

Breakfast
Petit déjeuner (peh-tee day-zhu-nay) is typically *café au lait* (coffee with hot milk), hot chocolate, or tea; a roll with butter and marmalade; and a croissant. Don't expect much variety for breakfast, but the bread is fresh and the coffee is great. While available at your hotel (25–50F), breakfasts are cheaper at the corner café. It's

entirely acceptable to buy a croissant or roll at a nearby bakery and eat it with your cup of coffee (no refills) at a café. Some hotels offer a *petit-déjeuner* buffet (about 50F) that consists of cereals, yogurts, cheeses, fruit, and breads. If the morning urge for an egg gets the best of you, drop into a café and order *une omelette* or *oeufs sur le plat* (fried eggs). You could also buy or bring plastic bowls and spoons from home, buy a box of French cereal and a small box of milk, and eat in your room before heading out for coffee. We carry fruit and a package of Vache Qui Rit (Laughing Cow) cheese to supplement the morning jelly.

Picnics

Great for lunch or dinner, French picnics can be first-class affairs and adventures in high cuisine. Be daring. Try the smelly cheeses, ugly pâtés, sissy quiches, and minuscule (usually drinkable) yogurts. Local shopkeepers are accustomed to selling small quantities of produce. Try the tasty salads to go and ask for *une fourchette en plastique* (a plastic fork).

Gather supplies early for a picnic lunch; you'll probably visit several small stores to assemble a complete meal, and many close at noon. Look for a *boulangerie* (bakery), a *crémerie* (cheeses), a *charcuterie* (deli items, meats, and pâtés), an *épicerie* or *alimentation* (small grocery with veggies, drinks, and so on), and a *pâtisserie* (delicious pastries). For fine picnic shopping, try the rue Cler neighborhood, taking the Rue Cler Walk (see page 73), and shopping as you go.

Local *supermarchés* offer less color and cost, more efficiency, and adequate quality. Department stores often have supermarkets in the basement.

If not picnicking, look for food stands and bakeries selling take-out sandwiches and drinks. For an affordable sit-down meal, try a *crêperie* or café. See "Café Culture," below.

Café Culture

French cafés (or *brasseries*) provide reasonable light meals and a refuge from museum and church overload. Feel free to order only a bowl of soup or a salad for lunch or dinner at a café. They are carefully positioned viewpoints from which to watch the river of local life flow by. It's easier for the novice to sit and feel comfortable in a café when you know the system.

Check the price list first. Prices, which must be posted prominently, vary wildly between cafés. Cafés charge different prices for the same drink depending upon where you want to be seated. Prices are posted: *comptoir* (counter/bar) or the more expensive *salle* (seated).

Your waiter probably won't overwhelm you with friendliness. Notice how hard they work. They almost never stop. Cozying up to clients (French or foreign) is probably the last thing on their minds.

The standard menu items (generally served day and night) are the Croque Monsieur (grilled cheese sandwich) and Croque Madame (Monsieur with a fried egg on top). The *salade composée* (com-po-zay) is a hearty chef's salad. Sandwiches are least expensive but plain unless you buy them at the *boulangerie* (bakery). To get more than a piece of ham (*jambon*) on a baguette, order a sandwich *jambon-crudité* (crew-dee-tay), which means garnished with lettuce, tomatoes, cucumbers, and so on. Omelets come lonely on a plate with a basket of bread. The *plat du jour* (daily special) is your fast, hearty hot plate for 50F to 70F. Regardless of what you order, bread is free; to get more, just hold up your bread basket and ask, "*Encore, s'il vous plaît.*"

To order coffee, here is the lingo:
- *un express* (uh nex-press) = shot of espresso
- *une noisette* (oon nwah-zette) = shot of espresso with a shot of milk
- *café au lait* (kah-fay oh lay) = coffee with lots of milk; also called *un grand crème* (uh grahn krem – big) or *un petit crème* (uh puh-tee krem = average)
- *un café allongé* (uh kah-fay al-own-zhay) = cup of coffee, closest to American style
- *un décaffiné* (uh day-kah-fee-nay) = decaf, and can modify any of the above drinks

Note: By law the waiter must give you a glass of tap water with your coffee if you request it; ask for "*un verre d'eau*" (uh vayre dough).

House wine at the bar is cheap (about 10F per glass, cheapest by the *pichet*, or pitcher), and the local beer is cheaper on tap (*une pression*) than in the bottle (*bouteille*). While prices include service, tip, and tax, it's polite to round up for a drink or meal well served (e.g., if your bill was 23F, leave 25F).

Restaurants

Choose restaurants filled with locals, not places with big neon signs boasting, "We Speak English." Consider your hotelier's opinion. If a restaurant doesn't post its menu (*la carte*) outside, move along.

If you want the menu, ask for *la carte* (and order à la carte like the locals do); if you ask for the *menu* (muh-noo), you'll get a fixed-price meal. This no-brainer *menu* offers three or four courses, generally a good value: You get your choice of soup, appetizer, or salad; your choice of three or four main courses with vegetables; plus a cheese course and/or a choice of desserts. Service is included, but wine or drinks are generally extra. Restaurants that offer a *menu* for lunch often charge 40F more for the same *menu* at dinner.

If you'd rather dine à la carte, ask the waiter for help deciphering the French. Go with his or her recommendations and anything *de la maison* (of the house). Galloping gourmets should bring a menu translator; the Marling Menu Master is excellent. The wines are often listed in a separate *carte des vins*.

In France an entrée is the first course and *le plat* is the main course. *Le plat* or *le plat du jour* (plate of the day) is the main course with vegetables (usually 50–80F). For a light, healthy, fast, and inexpensive option, the various salads are 40F to 60F well spent (though you are expected to order more than a salad at dinner in most restaurants—if all you want is a salad, find a café). Soft drinks and beer cost 10F to 20F, and a bottle or carafe of house wine—which is invariably good enough for Rick and Gene, if not always Steve—costs 35F to 100F. Service is always included, though it's polite to round the bill up (e.g., from 190F to 200F) if the service was good. To get a waiter's attention, simply say, "*S'il vous plaît*" (please). To alienate the same person, snap your fingers and say, "*Garçon*."

Drinks

In stores, unrefrigerated soft drinks and beer are one-third the price of cold drinks. Milk and boxed fruit juice are the cheapest drinks. Avoid buying drinks-to-go at street-side stands; you'll find them far cheaper in a shop. Try to keep a water bottle with you. Water quenches your thirst better and cheaper than anything you'll find in a store or café. We drink tap water throughout France.

The French are willing to pay for bottled water with their meal (*eau minérale*, oh mee-nay-rahl) because they prefer the taste over tap water. If you prefer a free pitcher of tap water, ask for *une carafe d'eau* (oon kah-rahf doh). Otherwise, you may unwittingly buy bottled water.

To save money when ordering beer, ask for a beer on tap (*une pression*; oon pres-yon) or a draft beer (un *demi*; uh duh-mee), which are cheaper than bottled. France's best beer is Alsatian; try Krônenburg or the heavier Pelfort. *Une panache* (pan-a-shay) is a refreshing French shandy (7-Up and beer).

To get inexpensive wine at a restaurant, order table wine in a pitcher (*un pichet*, pee-shay) rather than bottled. If all you want is a glass of wine, ask for *un verre de vin* (uh vehr duh van).

You could drink away your children's inheritance if you're not careful. The most famous wines are the most expensive, while lesser-known taste-alikes remain a bargain. If you like brandy, try a *marc* (regional brandy, e.g., *marc de Bourgogne*) or Armagnac,

cognac's cheaper twin brother. Pastis, the standard apéritif, is a
sweet anise or licorice drink that comes on the rocks with a glass
of water (cut it to taste with lots of water).

For a fun, bright, nonalcoholic drink, order *un diabolo menthe*
(7-Up with mint syrup). The ice cubes melted after the last
Yankee tour group left.

Stranger in a Strange Land

We travel all the way to Europe to enjoy differences—to become
temporary locals. You'll experience frustrations. Certain truths
that we find "God given" or "self evident," like friendly waiters,
ice in drinks, bottomless cups of coffee, hot showers, body odor
smelling bad, and bigger being better, are suddenly not so true.
One of the benefits of travel is the eye-opening realization that
there are logical, civil, and even better alternatives. Paris is an
understandably proud city. To enjoy its people you need to celebrate the differences. A willingness to go local ensures that you'll
enjoy a full dose of Parisian hospitality.

Back Door Manners

While updating our guidebooks, we hear over and over again that
our readers are considerate and fun to have as guests. Thank you
for traveling as temporary locals who are sensitive to the culture.
It's fun to follow you in our travels.

Send Us a Postcard, Drop Us a Line

If you enjoy a successful trip with the help of this book and
would like to share your discoveries, please fill out and send the
survey at the end of this book to Europe Through the Back
Door, Box 2009, Edmonds, WA 98020. We personally read and
value all feedback. Thanks in advance—it helps a lot.

For our latest travel information, tap into our Web site:
www.ricksteves.com. To check for any updates to this book,
visit www.ricksteves.com/update. Our e-mail address is
rick@ricksteves.com. Anyone is welcome to request a free
issue of our Back Door quarterly newsletter.

Judging from all the positive feedback and happy postcards
we receive from travelers who have used this book, it's safe to
assume you'll enjoy a great, affordable vacation—with the finesse
of an independent, experienced traveler.

From this point, "we" (your coauthors) will shed our respective
egos and become "I."

Thanks, and *bon voyage*!

BACK DOOR TRAVEL PHILOSOPHY
As Taught in *Rick Steves' Europe Through the Back Door*
Travel is intensified living—maximum thrills per minute and one of the last great sources of legal adventure. Travel is freedom. It's recess, and we need it.

Experiencing the real Europe requires catching it by surprise, going casual... "Through the Back Door."

Affording travel is a matter of priorities. (Make do with the old car.) You can travel—simply, safely, and comfortably—anywhere in Europe for $70 a day (allow $75 for Paris) plus transportation costs. In many ways, spending more money only builds a thicker wall between you and what you came to see. Europe is a cultural carnival, and, time after time, you'll find that its best acts are free and the best seats are the cheap ones.

A tight budget forces you to travel close to the ground, meeting and communicating with the people, not relying on service with a purchased smile. Never sacrifice sleep, nutrition, safety, or cleanliness in the name of budget. Simply enjoy the local-style alternatives to expensive hotels and restaurants.

Extroverts have more fun. If your trip is low on magic moments, kick yourself and make things happen. If you don't enjoy a place, maybe you don't know enough about it. Seek the truth. Recognize tourist traps. Give a culture the benefit of your open mind. See things as different but not better or worse. Any culture has much to share.

Of course, travel, like the world, is a series of hills and valleys. Be fanatically positive and militantly optimistic. If something's not to your liking, change your liking. Travel is addicting. It can make you a happier American, as well as a citizen of the world. Our Earth is home to 6 billion equally important people. It's humbling to travel and find that people don't envy Americans. They like us, but, with all due respect, they wouldn't trade passports.

Globe-trotting destroys ethnocentricity. It helps you understand and appreciate different cultures. Travel changes people. It broadens perspectives and teaches new ways to measure quality of life. Many travelers toss aside their hometown blinders. Their prized souvenirs are the strands of different cultures they decide to knit into their own character. The world is a cultural yarn shop. And Back Door Travelers are weaving the ultimate tapestry. Come on, join in!

ORIENTATION

Many people fall in love with Paris. Some see the essentials and flee, overwhelmed by the huge city. With the proper approach and a good orientation, you'll fall head over heels for Europe's capital city.

This orientation to the City of Light will illuminate your trip. The day plans—for visits of one to seven days—will help you prioritize the many sights. You'll tap into Paris' information sources for current events. Most important, you'll learn to navigate Paris by Métro, bus, taxi, or foot. For most travelers, the key to the city is a Métro ticket.

Arrival in Paris

For a comprehensive rundown on Paris' six train stations and two airports, see "Transportation Connections" on page 269.

Planning Your Time

Paris in One, Two, or Three Busy Days

Sights are listed in descending order of importance. If you have only one day, just do Day 1 (below); for two days, tack on Day 2. If you want to fit in Versailles on a three-day visit, try the afternoon of the second (easier) or third day.

Day 1
Morning: Follow Historic Paris Walk, featuring Île de la Cité, Notre-Dame, Latin Quarter, and Sainte-Chapelle.
Afternoon: Tour the Louvre.
Evening: Cruise Seine River or take illuminated Paris by Night bus tour.

Day 2
Morning: Follow Champs-Élysées Walk from Arc de Triomphe down the grand Champs-Élysées boulevard to Tuileries Gardens.
Midday: Tour Orsay Museum.
Afternoon: Either tour the Rodin Museum and Napoleon's Tomb or visit Versailles (take RER direct from Orsay).
Evening: Enjoy Trocadero scene and twilight ride up Eiffel Tower.

Day 3
Morning: Follow Marais Walk.
Afternoon: Stay in the Marais and tour the Pompidou Center and Jewish Art and History Museum. (Or visit Versailles.)
Evening: Take Montmartre Walk, featuring Sacré-Coeur.

Paris in Five to Seven Days without Going In-Seine
Day 1
Morning: Follow Historic Paris Walk, featuring Île de la Cité, Notre-Dame, Latin Quarter, Cluny Museum, and Sainte-Chapelle.
Afternoon: Sit in a café, go shopping, or consider visiting the nearby Pompidou Center.
Evening: Cruise Seine River or take illuminated Paris by Night bus tour.

Day 2
Morning: Tour the Louvre.
Afternoon: Follow Champs-Élysées Walk from Arc de Triomphe down the grand Champs-Élysées boulevard to Tuileries Gardens. (Reversing the morning and afternoon also works well because the Champs-Élysées Walk leaves you near the Louvre, though most have more energy for museums in the morning.)
Evening: Take Montmartre Walk, featuring Sacré-Coeur.

Day 3
Morning: Take Rue Cler Walk.
Midday: Tour Orsay Museum.
Afternoon: Tour Rodin Museum, then Napoleon's Tomb.
Evening: Enjoy a relaxed dinner on the Île St. Louis.

Day 4
Morning: Catch the RER and arrive early (9:00) at Versailles. Tour palace interior.
Afternoon: Visit Versailles' gardens, Le Hameau, and Trianon Palaces. Return to Paris with some time for shopping.
Evening: Attend a concert at Sainte-Chapelle.

Daily Reminder

Monday: These museums are closed today—Orsay, Rodin, Marmottan, Montmartre, Carnavalet, and Versailles; the Louvre is more crowded because of this, but the Richelieu wing stays open until 21:45. Many small stores don't open until 14:00. Some restaurants and banks are closed today. It's discount night at most cinemas.

Tuesday: Many museums are closed today, including the Louvre, Picasso, Cluny, and Pompidou Center, as well as the châteaus of Chantilly and Fontainebleau. The Eiffel Tower, Orsay, and Versailles are particularly busy today.

Wednesday: All sights are open, the Louvre until 21:45. The weekly *Pariscope* magazine comes out today. School is out, so many child-related sights are open (and busy).

Thursday: All sights are open (except the Sewer Tour). The Orsay is open until 21:45. Vaux-le-Vicomte hosts candle-light visits (May–Oct). Department Stores are open late.

Friday: All sights are open (except the Sewer Tour). Afternoon trains and roads leaving Paris are crowded; TGV reservation fees are higher.

Saturday: All sights are open (except the Jewish Art and History Museum). The fountains run at Versailles (July–Sept), and Vaux-le-Vicomte hosts candlelight visits (May–Oct); otherwise avoid weekend crowds at area châteaus. Department stores are busy.

Sunday: Some museums are two-thirds price all day (Louvre, Orsay, Cluny, and Picasso). The fountains run at Versailles (early April–early Oct). Most of Paris' stores are closed on Sunday, but shoppers will find relief in the lively Marais neighborhood—the Jewish Quarter—where many stores are open. Look for organ concerts at St. Sulpice and possibly other churches. The American Church usually offers a free evening concert at 18:00.

Day 5
Morning: Follow Marais Walk and tour the Carnavalet Museum.
Afternoon: Tour the Pompidou Center and/or the Jewish Art and History Museum.
Evening: Enjoy Trocadero scene and twilight ride up Eiffel Tower.

Day 6 and 7
Choose from:
Shopping and cafés
Montmartre and Sacré-Coeur (by day)
Picasso, Cluny, or Marmottan Museums
Day trip to Chartres
Day trip to Vaux-le-Vicomte and Fontainebleau
Day trip to Disneyland Paris
Evening: Night bus or boat tour (whichever you have yet to do)

Paris: A Verbal Map

Paris is split in half by the Seine River, divided into 20 *arrondissements* (proud and independent governmental jurisdictions), and
circled by a ring-road freeway (the *périphérique*). You'll find Paris
easier to negotiate if you know which side of the river you're on,
which *arrondissement* you're in, and which subway (Métro) stop
you're closest to. If you're north of the river (the top half of any
city map), you're on the Right Bank (*rive droite*). If you're south of
it, you're on the Left Bank (*rive gauche*). Most of your sightseeing
will take place within five blocks of the river.

Arrondissements are numbered, starting at Notre-Dame
(ground zero) and moving in a clockwise spiral out to the ring

road. The last two
digits in a Parisian zip
code are the *arrondisse-
ment* number. The
notation for the
Métro stop is "Mo."
In Parisian jargon,
Napoleon's tomb is
on *la rive gauche* (the
Left Bank) in the 7ème
(7th *arrondissement*),
zip code 75007, Mo:
Invalides. Paris Métro
stops are used as a stan-

PARIS ARRONDISSEMENTS

dard aid in giving directions, even for those not using the Métro.
As you're tracking down addresses, these definitions will help:
place (square), *rue* (road), and *pont* (bridge).

Tourist Information

Avoid the Paris tourist offices—long lines, short information, and a
5F charge for maps. This book, the *Pariscope* magazine (described
below), and one of the freebie maps available at any hotel are all you
need. The main tourist office is at 127 avenue des Champs-Élysées

PARIS OVERVIEW

0 KM .5 1
0 MI ¼ ½

RING ROAD PÉRIPHÉRIQUE

LA DÉFENSE

A-1 TO DE GAULLE AÉROPORT

MONTMARTRE

SACRE CŒUR

LA VILLETTE

BOIS DE BOULOGNE

ARC DE TRIOMPHE

CHAMPS ELYSEES

OPÉRA

① ②

③

PÉRIPHÉRIQUE

A-3 TO NORMANDY ROUEN

CONCORDE

LES HALLES

RIGHT BANK

PLACE DE LA RÉPUBLIQUE

PÈRE LACHAISE CEM.

RUE CLER

ORSAY MUS.

CITÉ

LOUVRE

POMPIDOU CTR.

MARAIS

SEINE

EIFFEL TOWER

INV.

RODIN MUS.

LEFT BANK

LUX. GDNS.

NÔTRE DAME

CONTRE-SCARPE

PLACE DE LA BASTILLE

④

RER TRAIN TO VERSAILLES LINE C-5

⑥ MONT-PARNASSE TOWER

PLACE D'ITALIE

⑤

BOIS DE VINCENNES

A-4 TO REIMS

A-6 TO ORLY AÉROPORT + SOUTH

TRAIN STATIONS/ GARES:

① **ST-LAZARE** TO NORMANDY

② **NORD** TO LONDON & BRUSSELS VIA EUROSTAR, TO N. EUROPE

③ **L'EST** TO E. FRANCE, S. GERMANY, SWITZERLAND, AUSTRIA

④ **LYON** TO S.E. FRANCE & ITALY

⑤ **D'AUSTERLITZ** TO S.W. FRANCE, LOIRE & SPAIN

⑥ **MONTPARNASSE** TO NORMANDY, BRITTANY, CHARTRES, TGV TO LOIRE & S.W. FRANCE

(daily 9:00–20:00, tel. 08 36 68 31 12—phone tree), but the tourist offices at the Gare de Lyon (daily 8:00–20:00, tel. 01 43 43 33 24, answered by live English-speaker), Eiffel Tower (daily May–Sept 11:00–18:00), and Louvre (Wed–Mon 10:00–19:00) are less crowded. For a complete list of museum hours and scheduled English museum tours, pick up the free *Musées, Monuments Historiques, et Expositions* booklet from any museum.

Pariscope: The *Pariscope* weekly magazine (or one of its clones, 3F at any newsstand) lists museum hours, art exhibits, concerts, music festivals, plays, movies, and nightclubs. See "Tour of *Pariscope*" on page 265.

Maps: While Paris is littered with free maps, they don't show all the streets. You may want the huge Michelin #10 map of Paris. For an extended stay, I prefer the pocket-size, street-indexed *Paris Pratique* (40F).

Bookstores: There are many English-language bookstores in Paris where you can pick up guidebooks (for nearly double their American price). A few of the best: Shakespeare & Company (daily 12:00–24:00, some used travel books, 37 rue de la Boucherie, across the river from Notre-Dame), W. H. Smith (248 rue de Rivoli, Mo: Concorde, tel. 01 44 77 88 99), and Brentanos (37 avenue de L'Opéra, Mo: Opéra, tel. 01 42 61 52 50).

American Church: The American Church is a nerve center for the American émigré community. It distributes a free, handy, and insightful monthly English-language newspaper called the *Free Voice* (with useful reviews of concerts, plays, and current events; available at around 200 locations in Paris) and an advertisement paper called *France—U.S.A. Contacts* (full of useful information for those looking for work or long-term housing). The church faces the river between the Eiffel Tower and Orsay Museum (reception open Mon–Sat 9:30–22:30, Sun 9:00–19:30, 65 quai d'Orsay, Mo: Invalides, tel. 01 40 62 05 00).

Helpful Hints

Theft Alert: Use your money belt and never carry a wallet in your back pocket or a purse over your shoulder. Thieves thrive in tourist areas and the Métro (at stations and in subway cars).

Paris Museum Pass: This worthwhile pass, covering most sights in Paris, is available at major Métro stations, tourist offices, and museums. For detailed information, see page 30.

Toilets: Carry small change for pay toilets, or walk into any sidewalk café like you own the place and find the toilet in the back. The toilets in museums are free and generally the best you'll find. Modern, super-sanitary, street-booth toilets provide both relief and a memory (2F coin required, don't leave small children inside unattended).

Getting around Paris

By Métro: Europe's best subway is divided into two systems— the Métro (for puddle jumping everywhere in Paris) and the RER (which connects suburban destinations with a few stops in central Paris). You'll be using the Métro for almost all your trips. Occasionally you'll find the RER more convenient as it makes fewer stops (like an express bus).

In Paris you're never more than a 10-minute walk from a Métro station. One ticket takes you anywhere in the system with unlimited transfers. Save 40 percent by buying a *carnet* (car-nay) of 10 tickets for 58F at any Métro station (a single ticket is 8F). Métro tickets work on city buses, though one ticket cannot be used as a transfer between subway and bus.

Key Words for the Métro and RER

- *direction* (dee-rek-see-ohn): direction
- *ligne* (leen-yuh): line
- *correspondance* (kor-res-pohn-dahns): transfer
- *sortie* (sor-tee): exit
- *carnet* (kar-nay): cheap set of 10 tickets
- *Pardon, madame/monsieur* (par-dohn, mah-dahm/mes-yur): Excuse me, lady/bud.
- *Je descend* (juh day-sahn): I'm getting off.
- *Donnez-moi mon porte-monnaie!*: Give me back my wallet!

Etiquette

- When waiting at the platform, get out of the way of those exiting their train. Board only once everyone is off.
- Avoid using the hinged seats when the car is jammed; they take up valuable standing space.
- In a crowded train, try not to block the exit. If you're blocking the door when the train stops, step out of the car and to the side, let others off, then get back on.
- Talk softly in the cars. Listen to how quietly Parisians can communicate and follow their lead.
- On escalators, stand on the right, pass on the left.

The *Mobilis* ticket (moh-bee-lee) allows unlimited travel for a single day on all bus and Métro lines (30F). If you're staying longer, the *Carte Orange* (kart oh-rahnzh) pass gives you free run of the bus and Métro system for one week (80F, ask for the *Carte Orange Coupon Vert*, supply a photo) or a month (280F, ask for the *Carte Orange Coupon Orange*, supply a photo). The weekly pass begins Monday and ends Sunday, and the monthly pass begins the first day of the month and ends the last day of that month, so midweek or midmonth purchases are generally not worthwhile. The pass prices I've listed cover only central Paris; you can pay more for passes covering regional destinations (e.g., Versailles). Passes can be purchased at any Métro station (most have photo booths) and are technically only for Parisian residents. While the purchase of these passes by tourists is rarely an issue, be aware that a ticket seller might refuse to sell you this pass. In this case you have three options: (1) say you are living in Paris for a temporary period, (2) go to another station to buy our pass, or (3) use carnets of 10 tickets instead.

To get to your destination, determine the closest "Mo" stop and which line or lines will get you there. The lines have numbers, but they're best known by their direction or end-of-the-line stop. (For example, the La Defense/Château de Vincennes line runs between La Defense in the west and Vincennes in the east.)

Once in the Métro station, you'll see blue-and-white signs directing you to the train going in your direction (e.g., "direction: La Defense"). Insert your ticket in the automatic turnstile, pass through, and reclaim and keep your ticket until you exit the system. Fare inspectors regularly check for cheaters and accept absolutely no excuses from anyone. I repeat, keep that ticket until you leave the Métro system.

Transfers are free and can be made wherever lines cross. When you transfer, look for the orange *correspondance* (connections) signs when you exit your first train, then follow the proper direction sign.

Before you *sortie* (exit), check the helpful *plan du quartier* (map of the neighborhood) to get your bearings, locate your destination, and decide which *sortie* you want. At stops with several *sorties*, you can save lots of walking by choosing the best exit.

Thieves spend their days in the Métro. Be on guard. For example, a pocket picked as you pass through a turnstile leaves you stuck on the wrong side and the thief strolling away. Any jostle or commotion (especially when boarding or leaving trains) is likely the sign of a thief or team of thieves in action.

Paris has a huge homeless population and over 11 percent unemployment; expect a warm Métro welcome by panhandlers, musicians, and those selling magazines produced by the homeless community.

By RER: The RER (Réseau Express Régionale, air-ay-air) is the suburban train system, indicated by thick lines on your subway map and identified by letters A, B, C, and so on. The RER works like the Métro but can be speedier (if it serves your destination directly) because it makes only a few stops within the city. One Métro ticket is all you need for RER rides within central Paris. You can transfer between the Métro and RER systems with the same ticket. Unlike the Métro, you need to insert your ticket in a turnstile to exit the RER system. To travel outside the city (to Versailles or the airport, for example), you'll need to buy a separate, more expensive ticket at the station window before boarding; make sure your stop is served by checking the signs over the train platform (not all trains serve all stops).

By City Bus: The trickier bus system is worth figuring out. Métro tickets are good on both bus and Métro, though you can't use the same ticket to transfer between the two systems. One ticket gets you anywhere in central Paris, but if you leave the city center (shown as section 1 on the diagram on board the bus), you must validate a second ticket. While the Métro shuts down about 00:30, some buses continue much later. Schedules are posted at bus stops. Handy bus-system maps (*plan des autobus*) are available in any Métro station and are provided in your *Paris Pratique* map book if you invest (40F).

Big system maps, posted at each bus and Métro stop, display the routes. Individual route diagrams show the exact routes of the lines serving that stop. Major stops are painted on the side of each bus. Enter through the front doors. Punch your Métro ticket in the machine behind the driver, or pay the higher cash fare. Get off the bus using the rear door. Even if you're not certain you've figured it out, do some joyriding (outside of rush hour). Lines #24, #63, and #69 are Paris' most scenic routes and make a great introduction to the city. Bus #69 is particularly handy, running between the Eiffel Tower, rue Cler (recommended hotels), Orsay, Louvre, Marais (recommended hotels), and Père Lachaise Cemetery. The handiest bus routes are listed for each hotel area recommended (see the Sleeping chapter, page 229).

By Taxi: Parisian taxis are almost reasonable. A 10-minute ride costs about 50F (versus 5.50F to get anywhere in town on the Métro). You can try waving one down (a glowing white light on the roof means it's free, an orange light means occupied), but it's easier to ask for the nearest taxi stand (*Où est une station de taxi?*; oo ay oon stah-see-ohn duh taxi) or ask your hotel to call for you. Higher rates are charged at night from 19:00 to 7:00, all day Sunday, and to either airport. There's a 6F charge for each piece of baggage. A 3F to 5F tip is generally plenty. If you call from your hotel, the meter starts as soon as the call is received. Taxis are tough to find on Friday and Saturday nights, especially after the Métro closes (around 00:30). If you need to catch a train or flight early in the morning, consider booking a taxi the night before. A typical taxi takes up to three people; groups of four need a *grand taxi*, which must be booked in advance (ask your hotel to call).

By Foot: Be careful! Parisian drivers are notorious for ignoring pedestrians. Never assume you have the right of way, even in a crosswalk. When crossing a street, keep your pace constant and don't stop suddenly. Drivers carefully calculate your speed and will miss you, providing you don't alter your route or pace.

Organized Tours of Paris

Bus Tours: Paris Vision offers handy bus tours of Paris, day and night (advertised in hotel lobbies); their "Illuminated Paris" tour is far more interesting and is explained on page 267. A better daytime bus tour for most is the hop-on hop-off double-decker bus service called **Open Deck Tours**, offering three different routes covering most of the important sights in Paris (the Paris Grand Tour offers the best introduction). Use these buses to connect the major sights (with a running commentary) and get a good city orientation tour at the same time. Expect to wait 15 to 20 minutes for a bus at each stop. Buy your tickets from the driver (1-day ticket-135F, 2-day ticket-150F, 2 buses/hrly about 10:00–18:00, you can hop off at various sights, then catch a later bus). You'll see these bright-yellow topless double-decker buses all over town—pick one up at the first important sight you visit, or start your tour at the Eiffel Tower stop (the first street on the non-river side of the tower).

Boat Tours: Several companies offer one-hour boat cruises on the Seine (best at night). The huge, mass-production **Bâteaux-Mouches** boats depart every 30 minutes from pont de l'Alma's right bank and are convenient to rue Cler hotels (40F, 20F under 14, daily 10:00–23:00, useless taped explanations in 6 languages and tour groups by the dozens, tel. 01 42 25 96 10). The much smaller and more intimate **Vedettes de pont Neuf** depart only once an hour from the center of the pont Neuf, but they come with a live guide giving explanations in French and English and are convenient to Marais and Contrescarpe hotels (50F, 25F under age 14, tel. 01 46 33 98 38). From April to October, **Bâteau-Bus** operates boats on the Seine, connecting six key stops about every 25 minutes: Eiffel Tower, Orsay/place de la Concorde, Louvre, Notre-Dame, Hôtel de Ville, and St. Germain-des-Prés. Pick up their schedule at any stop (or tourist office) and use them as a scenic alternative to the Métro. Tickets are available for single trips (20F), one day (60F), and two days (90F). Boats run from 10:00 to 19:00, until 22:00 in summer. **Paris Canal** departs twice daily for three-hour cruises between the Orsay and Parc de la Vilette; you'll cruise up the Seine then along a quiet canal through nontouristy Paris, accompanied by English explanations (100F adults, 75F ages 12–25, 55F ages 4–11, one-way departures from the Orsay at 9:30 and from Parc de la Vilette at 14:30, tel. 01 42 40 96 97).

Walking Tours: Paris Walking Tours offers a variety of excellent two-hour walks nearly daily for 60F (tel. 01 48 09 21 40, fax 01 42 43 75 51, www.pariswalkingtours.com). They focus on the Marais, Luxembourg Gardens, Opéra Garnier, Montmartre, and Hemingway's Paris. Call ahead a day or two to learn their schedule and starting point. No reservations are required. These are thoughtfully prepared, humorous, and relaxing walking tours led by British or American guides. Don't hesitate to stand close to the guide to hear. For Lost Generation fans, **Paris Literary Promenades** takes you through areas once popular with literary giants from Joyce to Beckett to Hemingway (60F, 2 hrs, late May–mid-Oct, tours depart from place de l'Odeon daily except

Wed at 14:30 and 19:00, tel. 01 48 07 80 72 or cellular 06 03 27 73 52). You can also hire a Parisian as your personal guide. Arnaud Servignat (tel. 01 42 57 03 35, fax 01 42 62 68 62, e-mail: arnotour@noos.fr) and Marianne Siegler (tel. 01 42 52 32 51) are licensed local guides who freelance for individuals and families ($150/4 hrs, $250/day).

Bike Tours: Bullfrog Bike Tours will show you Paris on two wheels at a relaxed pace (120F, 3–4-hr tours in English at 11:00 and 15:30, May–mid-Sept, no bikes or reservations needed, meet at fountain on avenue Joseph, 100 meters from Eiffel Tower in Champ de Mars park, ask about new evening tours, cellular 06 09 98 08 60, http://BullfrogBikes.com, e-mail: bullfrogbikes@hotmail.com).

PARIS SIGHTS

These sights are arranged by neighborhood for handy sightseeing. When you see a ⭐ in a listing, it means the sight is covered in much more depth in one of our walks or self-guided tours.

Paris Museum Pass: All of the sights listed in this chapter are covered by a Paris museum pass, except for the Eiffel Tower, Montparnasse Tower, Marmottan Museum, the new Jewish Art and History Museum, Jeu de Paume Exhibition Hall, and the ladies of Pigalle.

In Paris there are two classes of sightseers: those with a museum pass and those who stand in line. Serious sightseers save time and money by getting this pass. Sold at museums, main Métro stations, and tourist offices, it pays for itself in two admissions and gets you into sights with no lining up (1 day-80F, 3 consecutive days-160F, 5 consecutive days-240F; no discounts for youth). You can buy one on any day at any sight where it's valid. The pass is not activated until the first time you use it (you enter the date on the pass).

Included sights (and admission prices without the pass) you're likely to visit: Louvre (45F), Orsay (40F), Sainte-Chapelle (35F), Arc de Triomphe (40F), Napoleon's Tomb (38F), Carnavalet Museum (35F), Conciergerie (35F), Sewer Tour (25F), Cluny Museum (38F), Pompidou Center (50F), Notre-Dame towers (35F) and crypt (35F), Picasso Museum (30F), Rodin Museum (28F), and the elevator to the top of the Grand Arche de La Défense (46F). Outside Paris, the pass covers the Palace of Versailles (46F) and its Grand Trianon (25F) and Château Chantilly (43F). Tally it up— but remember, an advantage of the pass is that you skip to the front of all lines, saving hours of waiting especially in summer (though everyone must pass through the slow-moving metal-detector lines). If buying a pass at a museum with a long line, skip to the front and find the sales window. With the pass you'll pop painlessly into sights that you're walking by (even for a few minutes) that might otherwise not be worth the expense (e.g., Notre-Dame crypt, Conciergerie, Victor Hugo's House, Panthéon). The free museum and monuments directory that comes with your pass lists the latest hours, phone numbers, and specifics on what kids pay. The cutoff age for free entry varies from 5 to 18. Most major art museums let young people under 18 in for free, but anyone over age five has to pay to tour the sewers—go figure.

Museum Tips: The Louvre and many other museums are closed on Tuesday. The Orsay, Rodin, Marmottan, Carnavalet, and Versailles are closed Monday. Most museums offer reduced prices but have shorter hours on Sunday. Many sights stop admitting people 30 to 60 minutes before they close, and many begin closing rooms 45 minutes before the actual closing time. For the fewest crowds, visit very early, at lunch, or very late. Most museums have slightly shorter hours October through March. French holidays can really mess up your sightseeing plans (Jan 1, May 1, May 8, July 14, Nov 1, Nov 11, and Dec 25). The best Impressionist art museums are the Orsay and Marmottan (see our self-guided tours of these). The Orangerie, another fine Impressionist museum, is closed for renovation.

Paris Museums near the Tuileries Gardens

The Tuileries Gardens were once the private property of kings and queens. Paris' grandest public park links these museums: Louvre, Orangerie (closed), Jeu de Paume, and the Orsay.

▲▲▲**Louvre**—This is Europe's oldest, biggest, greatest, and second-most-crowded museum (after the Vatican). It's packed with Greek and Roman masterpieces, medieval jewels, Michelangelo statues, and paintings by the greatest artists from the Renaissance to the Romantics (mid-1800s).

Cost: 45F, 26F after 15:00 and on Sun, free on first Sun of month and for those under 18, covered by museum pass.

Hours: Wed through Mon 9:00 to 18:00, closed Tue, all wings open Wed until 21:45, Richelieu Wing (only) until 21:45 on Mon. Closed Jan 1, Easter, May 1, Nov 1, and Dec 25. Tel. 01 40 20 53 17 or 01 40 20 51 51 for recorded information.

Location: At Palais Royal/Musée du Louvre Métro stop. The old Louvre Métro stop called Louvre Rivoli no longer goes to the Louvre. ★ See Louvre Tour on page 85.

▲**L'Orangerie**—Closed until late 2001 or early 2002.

Jeu de Paume—This one-time home to the Impressionist art collection now located in the Orsay hosts rotating exhibits of top contemporary artists (38F, not covered by museum pass,

— MUSEUMS NEAR TUILERIES GARDENS —

Tue 12:00–21:30, Wed–Fri 12:00–19:00, Sat–Sun 10:00–19:00, closed Mon, on place de la Concorde, just inside Tuileries Garden on rue de Rivoli side, Mo: Concorde).

▲▲▲**Orsay Museum**—This is Paris' 19th-century art museum (actually, art from 1848–1914), including Europe's greatest collection of Impressionist works.

Cost: 40F, 30F for the young and old, under 18 free. English-language tours usually run daily except Sun at 11:30, cost 36F, take 90 minutes, and are also available on audioguide (30F). Tel. 01 40 49 48 48.

Hours: Tue–Sat 10:00–18:00, Thu until 21:45, Sun 9:00–18:00, closed Mon. Museum opens at 9:00 June 20–Sept 20. Last entrance is 45 minutes before closing.

Location: Directly at the RER-C stop called Musée d'Orsay; the nearest Métro stop is Solferino, three blocks south of the Orsay. From the Louvre, it's a 15-minute walk downstream to the Orsay. ✪ See Orsay Tour on page 104.

Historic Core of Paris:
Notre-Dame, Sainte-Chapelle, and More

✪ All of these sights are covered in detail in the Historic Paris Walk on page 43. Only the essentials are listed here.

▲▲**Notre-Dame Cathedral**—The 700-year-old cathedral is packed with history and tourists. Walk all around the outside, study its sculpture and windows, eavesdrop on guides, and take in a mass. Sunday masses are at 8:00, 8:45, 10:00, 11:30, 12:30, and 18:30 (cathedral-free, daily 8:00–18:45; treasury-15F, daily 9:30–17:30; ask about the free English tours, normally Wed and Thu at 12:00 and Sat at 14:30; Mo: Cité, Hôtel de Ville, or St. Michel; clean 2.70F toilets in front of church near Charlemagne's statue). ✪ See page 43.

Church Tower: Climb to the top for a great gargoyle's-eye view of the city. You get 400 steps for only 35F (entrance on outside, north tower open 9:30–17:30, closed at lunch and earlier off-season).

Crypt: The archaeological crypt is a worthwhile 15-minute stop with your museum pass (35F, 50F with Notre-Dame's tower, daily 10:00–18:00, closes at 17:00 Oct–April, enter 100 meters in front of church). You'll see Roman ruins, trace the street plan of the medieval village, and see diagrams of how early Paris grew and grew, all thoughtfully explained in English.

▲▲**Deportation Memorial (Mémorial de la Déportation)**—This memorial to the 200,000 French victims of the Nazi concentration camps draws you into their experience (free, Mon–Fri 8:30–21:45, Sat–Sun and holidays from 9:00, sometimes closes 12:00–14:00, shorter hours off-season, east tip of the island near Île St. Louis, behind Notre-Dame, Mo: Cité). ✪ See page 49.

Île St. Louis—This island behind Notre-Dame is known for its restaurants (see Eating chapter), great Bertillon ice cream (31 rue St. Louis en l'Île), and shops (along rue St. Louis en l'Île). ✪ See page 49.

Cité "Métropolitain" Stop and Flower Market—On place Louis Lepine, between Notre-Dame and Sainte-Chapelle, you'll find an early-19th-century subway entrance and a flower market (that chirps with a bird market on Sun).

▲▲▲**Sainte-Chapelle**—The triumph of Gothic church architecture is a cathedral of glass like no other. It was speedily built from 1242 to 1248 by St. Louis IX to house the supposed Crown of Thorns (35F, daily 9:30–18:30, off-season 10:00–16:30, Mo: Cité, tel. 01 48 01 91 35 for concert information). ✪ See page 54.

▲**Conciergerie**—Marie Antoinette was imprisoned here, as were 2,600 others on the way to the guillotine (35F, daily 9:30–18:30, 10:00–17:00 in winter, good English descriptions). ✪ See page 58.

▲**Samaritaine Department Store Viewpoint**—For a great, free viewpoint, take the elevator to the 9th floor and walk to the 11th-floor rooftop panorama (daily 9:30–19:00, reasonably priced café on 10th-floor terrace, supermarket in basement, Mo: Pont Neuf, tel. 01 40 41 20 20). ✪ See page 263.

Southwest Paris: Eiffel Tower Neighborhood

▲▲▲**Eiffel Tower**—It's crowded and expensive but worth the trouble. Go early (by 9:15) or late in the day (after 18:00) to avoid most crowds; weekends are worst. Pilier Nord (the north pillar) has the biggest elevator and, therefore, the fastest-moving line. The stairs (yes, you can walk up partway) are next to the Jules Verne restaurant entry.

The Tower is 1,000 feet tall (6 inches taller in hot weather), covers 2.5 acres, and requires 50 tons of paint. Its 7,000 tons of metal are spread out so well at the base that it's no heavier per square inch than a linebacker on tiptoes. Visitors to Paris may find *Mona Lisa* to be less than expected, but the Eiffel Tower rarely disappoints, even in an era of skyscrapers.

Built a hundred years after the French Revolution (and in the midst of an Industrial one), the Tower served no function but to impress. Bridge-builder Gustave Eiffel won the contest for the 1889 Centennial World's Fair by beating out such rival proposals as a giant guillotine. To a generation hooked on technology, the Tower was the marvel of the age, a symbol of progress and of man's ingenuity. To others it was a cloned-sheep monstrosity. The writer Maupassant routinely ate lunch in the Tower just so he wouldn't have to look at it.

Delicate and graceful when seen from afar, it's massive—even a bit scary—from close up. You don't appreciate the size until you walk toward it; like a mountain, it seems so close but takes forever to reach. There are three observation platforms, at 200, 400, and 900 feet; the higher you go, the more you pay. Each requires a separate elevator (and a line), so plan on at least 90 minutes if you want to go to the top and back. The view from the 400-foot-high second level is plenty.

Begin at the first floor, read the informative signs (in English) describing the major monuments, and see the entertaining free movie on the history of the Tower. Then consider a drink overlooking all of Paris at the café or at the city's best view bar/restaurant, Altitude 95 (260F meals, seatings at 19:00 and 21:00, reserve well ahead for a view table, tel. 01 45 55 20 04). Take the elevator to the second floor for even greater views and a post office. As you ascend through the metal beams, imagine being a worker, perched high above nothing, riveting this giant erector set together. On top, all of Paris lies before you, with a panorama guide. On a good day you can see for 40 miles.

Cost and Hours: It costs 24F to go to the first level,

SOUTHWEST PARIS: EIFFEL TOWER NEIGHBORHOOD

45F to the second, and 65F to go all the way for the 1,000-foot view (not covered by museum pass). On a budget? You can climb the stairs to the second level for only 18F (summers daily 9:00–24:00, off-season 9:30–23:00, Mo: Trocadero, RER: Champ de Mars, tel. 01 44 11 23 23).

The best place to view the Tower is from Trocadero Square to the north (a 10-min walk across the river, and a happening scene at night). Consider arriving at the Trocadero Métro stop then walking toward the Tower. Another great viewpoint is the long, grassy field, le Champ de Mars, to the south (after about 20:00 the *gendarmes* look the other way as Parisians stretch out or picnic on the grass). However impressive it may be by day, it's an awesome thing to see at twilight, when the tower becomes engorged with light and virile Paris lies back and lets night be on top.

▲**Paris Sewer Tour (Égouts)**—This quick and easy visit takes you along a few hundred meters of underground water tunnel. Its interesting displays and English descriptions explain the evolution of the world's longest sewer system. (If you lined up Paris' sewers, they would reach beyond Istanbul.) Don't miss the slide show, the fine WCs just beyond the gift shop, and the occasional tours in English (25F, Sat–Wed 11:00–17:00, closed Thu–Fri, where pont de l'Alma greets the Left Bank, tel. 01 47 05 10 29).

▲▲**Napoleon's Tomb and Les Invalides Army Museum**—
The emperor lies majestically dead inside several coffins under a
grand dome—a goose-bumping pilgrimage for historians. Napoleon is surrounded by the tombs of other French war heroes and
by Europe's greatest military museum in the Hôtel des Invalides.
The restored dome glitters with 26 pounds of gold (38F, 28F
ages 12–17 and students, under 12 free, daily 10:00–17:45, closes
off-season at 16:45, Mo: La Tour Maubourg or Varennes, tel.
01 44 42 37 67). ✪ See Napoleon's Tomb Tour on page 172.
▲▲**Rodin Museum**—This user-friendly museum is filled with
passionate works by the greatest sculptor since Michelangelo.
See *The Kiss, The Thinker, The Gates of Hell*, and many more (28F,
18F on Sun and for seniors and students; 5F for gardens only,
which may be Paris' best deal as many works are well displayed
in the beautiful gardens; Tue–Sun 9:30–17:45, closed Mon and
at 17:00 off-season; 77 rue de Varennes, Mo: Varennes, near
Napoleon's Tomb, tel. 01 44 18 61 10). ✪ See Rodin Museum
Tour on page 157.
▲▲**Marmottan**—In this private, intimate, less-visited museum
you'll find more than 100 paintings by Claude Monet (thanks
to his son Michel), including the *Impression: Sunrise* painting that
gave the movement its start and name (40F, not covered by
museum pass, Tue–Sun 10:00–17:00, closed Mon, 2 rue Louis
Boilly, Mo: La Muette, follow museum signs 6 blocks through
park to museum, tel. 01 42 24 07 02). Combine this fine museum
with a stroll down one of Paris' most pleasant shopping streets,
the rue de Passy (from La Muette Métro stop). ✪ See Marmottan
Tour on page 165.

Southeast Paris: Latin Quarter
✪ The Historic Paris Walk, on page 43, dips into the Latin
Quarter.
▲**Latin Quarter**—This Left Bank neighborhood, just opposite
Notre-Dame, was a center of Roman Paris. But the Latin
Quarter's touristy fame relates to its intriguing artsy, bohemian
character. This was perhaps Europe's leading university district
in the Middle Ages, when Latin was the language of higher
education. The neighborhood's main boulevards (St. Michel
and St. Germain) are lined with cafés—once the haunts of great
poets and philosophers, now the hangout of tired tourists. While
still youthful and artsy, the area has become a tourist ghetto filled
with cheap North African eateries.
▲**Cluny Museum (Musée National du Moyen Age)**—
This treasure trove of medieval art fills the old Roman baths,
offering close-up looks at stained glass, Notre-Dame carvings,

——— SOUTHEAST PARIS: LATIN QUARTER ———

fine goldsmithing and jewelry, and rooms of tapestries—the best of which is the exquisite *Lady with the Unicorn* (38F, 28F on Sun, Wed–Mon 9:15–17:45, closed Tue, near the corner of boulevards St. Michel and St. Germain, Mo: Cluny, tel. 01 53 73 78 00). ● See Cluny Museum Tour on page 186.

St. Germain-des-Près—A church was first built on this site in A.D. 452. The church you see today was constructed in 1163. The area around the church hops at night with fire-eaters, mimes, and scads of artists (Mo: St. Germain-des-Près).

▲**St. Sulpice Organ Concert**—For pipe-organ enthusiasts, this is a delight. The Grand-Orgue at St. Sulpice has a rich history, with a line of 12 world-class organists (including Widor and Dupre) going back 300 years. Widor started the tradition of opening the loft to visitors after the 10:30 service on Sundays. Daniel Roth continues to welcome guests in three languages while playing five keyboards at once. The 10:30 Sunday mass is followed by a 25-minute recital at 11:40. If you're lucky, at noon the small unmarked door will open (left of entry as you face the rear) so visitors can scamper like 16th notes up spiral stairs to a world of 7,000 pipes, where they can watch the master performing the next mass, friends warming his bench, and a committee scrambling to pull and push the 102 stops (Mo: St. Sulpice or Mabillon).

▲▲**Luxembourg Gardens**—Paris' most beautiful, interesting, and enjoyable garden/park/recreational area is a great place to watch

Parisians at rest and play. (See Paris with Children, page 258.) These private gardens are property of the French Senate (housed in the château) and have special rules governing their use (e.g., where cards can be played, where dogs can be walked, where joggers can run, when and where music can be played). The brilliant flower plantings are completely changed three times a year, and the boxed trees are brought out of the *orangerie* in May. Challenge the card and chess players to a game (near the tennis courts), or find a free chair near the main pond and take a breather. Notice any pigeons? A poor Ernest Hemingway used to hand-hunt (read: strangle) them here. Paris Walks offers a good tour of the park (see "Organized Tours," page 27). The grand neoclassical-domed Panthéon, now a mausoleum housing the tombs of several great Frenchmen, is a block away and is only worth entering if you have a museum pass. The historic cafés of Montparnasse are a few blocks from the south-west-corner exit of the park (rue Vavin, see "Les Grands Cafés de Paris," page 255). The park is open until dusk (Mo: Odéon, RER: Luxembourg). If you enjoy the Luxembourg Gardens and want to see more, visit the more elegant Parc Monceau (Mo: Monceau) and the colorful Jardin des Plantes (Mo: Jussieu or Gare d'Austerlitz, RER: Luxembourg).

Montparnasse Tower—This 59-floor superscraper is cheaper and easier to get to the top of than the Eiffel Tower, and has the added bonus of offering one of Paris' best views—since the Eiffel Tower is in it and the Montparnasse Tower isn't. Buy the photo guide to the city, then go to the rooftop and orient yourself (46F, not covered by museum pass, daily in summer 9:30–23:30, off-season 10:00–22:00, disappointing after dark, entrance on rue l'Arrivé, Mo: Montparnasse). The Tower is an efficient stop when combined with a day trip to Chartres, which begins at the Mont-parnasse train station.

Northwest Paris: Champs-Élysées, Arc de Triomphe, and Beyond

✪ Take the Champs-Élysées Walk (page 61) for a pleasant downhill stroll connecting the sights from the enduring Arc de Triomphe to the historic place de la Concorde.

▲▲**Champs-Élysées**—This famous boulevard is Paris' back-bone, with the greatest concentration of traffic. From the Arc de Triomphe down the Champs-Élysées, all of France seems to converge on place de la Concorde, the city's largest square. While the boulevard has become a bit Americanized, a walk here is a must. Take the Métro to the Arc de Triomphe (Mo: Étoile) and saunter down the Champs-Élysées (Métro stops every few blocks: Étoile, George V, FDR). ✪ See page 61.

▲▲▲**Arc de Triomphe**—Napoleon had the magnificent Arc de Triomphe commissioned to commemorate his victory at the battle of Austerlitz. There's no triumphal arch bigger (50 meters high, 40 meters wide). Many, many stairs lead to a cute museum about the arch and a grand view from the top (elevator available for disabled), even after dark (40F, June–Sept daily 9:30–23:00, Oct–May daily 9:30–22:00, Mo: Étoile, use underpass to reach arch, tel. 01 43 80 31 31). ✪ See page 61.

▲**Grande Arche de La Défense**—On the outskirts of Paris, the centerpiece of Paris' ambitious skyscraper complex (La Défense) is the Grande Arche. Built to celebrate the 200th anniversary of the 1789 French Revolution, the place is big—38 floors on more than 200 acres. It holds offices for 30,000 people. Notre-Dame Cathedral could fit under its arch. The La Défense complex is an interesting study in 1960s land-use planning. More than 100,000 workers commute here daily, directing lots of business and development away from downtown and allowing central Paris to retain its more elegant feel. This makes sense to most Parisians, regardless of whatever else they feel about this controversial complex. You'll enjoy city views from the Arche elevator (46F, daily 10:00–19:00, includes a film on its construction and art exhibits, RER or Mo: La Défense, follow signs to Grande Arche or get off 1 stop earlier at Esplanade de la Défense and walk through the interesting business complex, tel. 01 49 07 27 57).

Northeast Paris: Marais Neighborhood and More

✪ To connect the sights with a fun, fact-filled stroll leading from place de la Bastille to the Pompidou Center, take the Marais Walk on page 68.

▲▲**Pompidou Center**—Europe's greatest collection of far-out modern art is housed in the Musée National d'Art Moderne, on the top floor of this newly renovated and colorful exoskeletal building. Once ahead of its time, this 20th-century art (remember that century?) has been waiting for the world to catch up with it. After so many Madonnas and Children, a piano smashed to bits and glued to the wall is refreshing. Ride the escalator for a great city view from the café terrace on top and don't miss the free exhibits on the ground floor (50F, audioguide-25F, Wed–Mon 10:00–22:00, closed Tue, to use escalator you need a ticket for the museum or a museum pass, good mezzanine-level café is cheaper than cafés outside, Mo: Rambuteau, tel. 01 44 78 12 33).

The Pompidou Center and its square are lively, with lots of people, street theater, and activity inside and out—a perpetual street fair. Kids of any age enjoy the fun, colorful fountain (called

Homage to Stravinsky) next to the Pompidou Center. ✪ See
Pompidou Center Tour on page 130

▲▲Museum of Art and History of Judaism (Hôtel d'Aignan)—
This remarkable museum, located in a beautifully restored Marais
mansion, tells the story of Judaism throughout Europe from the
Roman destruction of Jerusalem to the theft of famous artworks
during World War II. Helpful audioguides and many English
explanations make this an enjoyable history lesson (red numbers
on small signs indicate the number you should press on your audioguide). Move along at your own speed. The museum illustrates
the cultural unity maintained by this continually dispersed population. You'll learn about the history of Jewish traditions from Bar
Mitzvahs to menorahs and see exquisite traditional costumes and
objects around which daily life revolved. Don't miss the explanation
of "the Dreyfus affair," a major event in early 1900 French politics.
You'll also see photographs of and paintings by famous Jewish
artists, including Chagall, Modigliani, and Soutine. The small
section devoted to the deportation of Jews from Paris is moving
(40F, not covered by museum pass, Mon–Fri 11:00–18:00, Sun
10:00–18:00, closed Sat, 71 rue du Temple, tel. 01 53 01 86 53).

▲Picasso Museum (Hôtel Salé)—This is the world's largest
collection of Pablo Picasso's paintings, sculptures, sketches, and
ceramics, and includes his personal collection of Impressionist
art. It's well explained in English and worth ▲▲▲ if you're a fan
(30F, Wed–Mon 9:30–18:00, closed Tue, 5 rue Thorigny, Mo:
St. Paul or Chemin Vert, tel. 01 42 71 25 21).

▲Carnavalet Museum—The tumultuous history of Paris is well
displayed in this converted Marais mansion. Explanations are in
French only, but many displays are fairly self-explanatory. You'll
see paintings of Parisian scenes, French Revolution paraphernalia,
old Parisian store signs, a small guillotine, a model of 16th-
century Île de la Cité (notice the bridge houses), and rooms
full of 15th-century Parisian furniture (35F, Tue–Sun 10:00–
17:00, closed Mon, 23 rue de Sévigné, Mo: St Paul, tel. 01 42
72 21 13). ✪ See Carnavalet Museum Tour on page 142.

Victor Hugo's House—France's literary giant lived in this house
on place des Vosges from 1832 to 1848. Inside are posters advertising theater productions of his works, paintings of some of
his most famous character creations, and a few furnished rooms
(22F, Tue–Sun 10:00–17:40, closed Mon, 6 place des Vosges).

Promenade Plantée Park—This three-kilometer narrow garden
walk, once a train track and now a joy, runs from place de la
Bastille (Mo: Bastille) along Avenue Daumesnil to Saint-Mandé
(Mo: Michel Bizot). Part of the park is elevated. At times you'll
walk along the street until you pick up the next segment. From

place de la Bastille, take avenue Daumesnil (past Opéra building) to the intersection with avenue Ledru Rollin; walk up the stairs and through the gate (free, hours vary with season, open roughly 8:00–20:00).

▲**Père Lachaise Cemetery**—Littered with the tombstones of many of the city's most illustrious dead, this is your best one-stop look at the fascinating, romantic world of "permanent Parisians." The place is confusing, but maps will direct you to the graves of Chopin, Molière, Edith Piaf, Oscar Wilde, Gertrude Stein, Heloise, and Abelard. In section 92, a series of statues memorializing World War II makes the French war experience a bit more real (helpful 10F maps at flower store near entry, across street from Métro stop, closes at dusk, Mo: Père Lachaise or bus #69).

North Paris: Montmartre
❋ Connect the sights with the Montmartre Walk on page 78.

▲▲**Sacré-Coeur and Montmartre**—This Byzantine-looking church, while only 130 years old, is impressive (daily until 23:00). One block from the church, the place du Tertre was the haunt of Toulouse-Lautrec and the original bohemians. Today it's mobbed by tourists and unoriginal bohemians, but it's still fun (go early in the morning to beat the crowds). Take the Métro to the Anvers stop (1 Métro ticket buys your way up the funicular and avoids the stairs) or the closer but less scenic Abbesses stop. A taxi to the top of the hill saves time and sweat.

Pigalle—Paris' red-light district, the infamous "Pig Alley," is at the foot of Butte Montmartre. *Ooh la la.* It's more shocking than dangerous. Walk from place Pigalle to place Blanche, teasing desperate barkers and fast-talking temptresses. In bars a 1,000F bottle of cheap champagne comes with a friend. Stick to the bigger streets, hang on to your wallet, and exercise good judgment. Cancan can cost a fortune, as can con artists in topless bars. After dark, countless tour buses line the streets, reminding us that tour guides make big bucks by bringing their groups to touristy nightclubs like the famous Moulin Rouge (Mo: Pigalle or Abbesses).

Disappointments *de* Paris
Here are a few negatives to help you manage your limited time:

La Madeleine is a big, stark, neoclassical church with a postcard facade and a postbox interior. The famous aristocratic deli behind the church, Fauchon, is elegant, but so are many others handier to your hotel.

Paris' **Panthéon** (nothing like Rome's) is another stark neoclassical edifice, filled with mortal remains of great Frenchmen who mean little to the average American tourist.

The **Bastille** is Paris' most famous nonsight. The square is there, but confused tourists look everywhere and can't find the famous prison of Revolution fame. The building's gone and the square is good only as a jumping-off point for the Marais Walk (see page 68) or Promenade Plantée Park (see page 40).

Finally, the **Latin Quarter** is a frail shadow of its characteristic self. It's more Tunisian, Greek, and Woolworth's than old-time Paris. The café life that turned on Hemingway and endeared boul' Miche and boulevard St. Germain to so many poets is also trampled by modern commercialism.

HISTORIC PARIS

WALK

From Notre-Dame to Sainte-Chapelle

paris

Paris has been the capital of Europe for centuries. We'll start where it did, on the Île de la Cité, with forays onto both the Left and Right Banks, on a walk that laces together the story of Paris: Roman, medieval, the Revolution, café society, the literary scene of the '20s, and the modern world. Allow four hours to do this three-mile walk justice.

Orientation

All sights that charge admission are covered by the Paris museum pass, which for many is a great time and money saver.

Notre-Dame: Free, daily 8:00–18:45; treasury-15F, daily 9:30–17:30; Sunday mass at 8:00, 8:45, 10:00, 11:30, 12:30, and 18:30. Leaflet with church schedule at booth inside entrance. Ask about free English tours, normally Wed and Thu at 12:00 and Sat at 14:30. The tower climb takes 400 steps and 35F—worth it for the gargoyle's-eye view of the cathedral, Seine, and city (daily 9:00–17:30, off-season closes earlier and during lunch).

Notre-Dame Archaeological Crypt: 35F, 50F with Notre-Dame's tower, daily 10:00–18:00, closes at 17:00 October–April, entry 100 meters in front of the cathedral.

Deportation Memorial: Free, Mon–Fri 8:30–21:45, Sat–Sun and holidays from 9:00, sometimes closes 12:00–14:00, shorter hours off-season.

Sainte-Chapelle: 35F, daily 9:30–18:30, off-season 10:00–16:30.
Conciergerie: 35F, daily 9:30–18:30, off-season 10:00–17:00.

NOTRE-DAME

• *Start at the Notre-Dame Cathedral on the island in the River Seine, the physical and historic bull's-eye of your Paris map (closest Métro stops are Cité, Hôtel de Ville, and St. Michel, each requiring a short walk).*

ÎLE DE LA CITÉ

On the square in front of the cathedral, stand far enough back to take in the whole facade. Look at the circular window in the center.

For centuries, the main figure in the Christian "pantheon" has been the goddess Mary, the mother of Jesus. Common people pray to her directly in times of trouble to gain comfort and to ask

her to convince God to be compassionate with them. The church is dedicated to "Our Lady" (Notre Dame), and there she is, cradling God, right in the heart of the facade, surrounded by the halo of the rose window. Though the church is massive and imposing, it has always stood for the grace and compassion of Mary, the "mother of God."

Imagine the faith of the people who built this. They

broke ground in 1163 with the hope that someday their great-great-great-great-great-great grandchildren might attend the dedication mass two centuries later. Look up the 200-foot bell towers and imagine a tiny medieval community mustering the money and energy to build this. Master masons supervised, but the people did much of the grunt work themselves for free—hauling the huge stones from distant quarries, digging a 30-foot-deep trench to lay the foundations, and treading like rats on a wheel designed to lift the stones up, one by one. This kind of backbreaking, arduous manual labor created the real hunchbacks of Notre-Dame.

• *"Walk this way" toward the cathedral, and view it from the bronze plaque on the ground marked...*

Point Zero

You're standing at the very center of France, from which all distances are measured. The "Cité" started here in the third century B.C. In 52 B.C., the Romans booted out the Parisii tribe and built their government palace at the end of the square behind you and the Temple of Jupiter where the cathedral sits. Two thousand years of dirt and debris have raised the city's altitude. The archaeological crypt nearby offers a fascinating look at the remains of the earlier city and church below today's street level.

Still facing the church, on your right is a grand equestrian statue of Charlemagne ("Charles the Great"), whose reign marked the birth of modern Europe. Crowned in A.D. 800, he briefly united much of Europe during the Dark Ages. (Maybe even greater than Charles are nearby pay toilets—the cleanest you'll find in downtown Paris.)

Before renovation, 150 years ago, this square was much smaller, a characteristic medieval shambles facing a run-down church, surrounded by winding streets and countless buildings (look at the outlines marked in the pavement of the square, showing the medieval street plan). The huge church bell towers rose above this tangle of smaller buildings, inspiring Victor Hugo's story of a deaf, bell-ringing hunchback who could look down on all Paris.

• *Now turn your attention to the church facade. Look at the left doorway and, to the left of the door, find the statue with his head in his hands.*

Notre-Dame Facade

When Christianity began making converts in Roman Paris, the Bishop of Paris was beheaded. But these early Christians were hard to keep down. St. Denis got up, tucked his head under his arm, headed north, paused at a fountain to wash it off, and continued until he found just the right place to meet his maker.

NOTRE DAME FACADE

GREAT VIEW!

← GARGOYLES

MARY IN ROSE WINDOW

28 KINGS OF JUDAH

ST. DENIS (HOLDING HEAD)

PORTAL OF MARY

LAST JUDGMENT

PORTAL OF ST. ANNE

SEINE RIVER

TOWER ENTRANCE   EXIT

ENTER

TO VIEW OF FLYING BUTTRESSES

← TO RIGHT BANK

POINT ZERO

WC →

CHARLEMAGNE STATUE →

P L A C E   D U   P A R V I S

↓ TO STE CHAPELLE

TO PLACE ST. MICHEL ↘

DCH

The Parisians were convinced of this miracle, Christianity gained ground, and a church soon replaced the pagan temple.

By the way, Christians think Montmartre (the one hill overlooking Paris) is named for this martyr (pagans think it was named after a Roman temple of Mars—Mount of Mars—which once stood here). Denis eventually died on the edge of town where the church of St. Denis was built (famous in history books as the first Gothic church, but not much to see today).

• *Now look above the central doorway, where you'll find scenes from the Last Judgment.*

Central Portal

It's the end of the world, and Christ sits on the throne of judgment (just under the arches, holding his hands up). Below him, an angel and a demon weigh souls in the balance. The good people stand to the left, looking up to heaven. The naughty ones to the right are chained up and led off to...a six-hour tour of the Louvre on a hot day. Notice the crazy sculpted demons to the right, at the base of the arch.

• *Above the arches is a row of 28 statues, known as...*

The Kings of Judah

In the days of the French Revolution (1789–1793), these Biblical kings were mistaken for the hated French kings, and Notre-Dame represented the oppressive Catholic hierarchy. The citizens stormed the church, crying, "Off with their heads!" Plop, they lopped off the crowned heads of these kings with glee, creating a row of St. Denises that wasn't repaired for decades.

But the story doesn't end there. A schoolteacher who lived nearby collected the heads and buried them in his backyard for safekeeping. There they slept until 1977, when they were accidentally unearthed. Today you can stare into the eyes of the original kings in the Cluny Museum, a few blocks away (see page 186).

• *Enter the church and find a spot to view the long, high central aisle.*

Notre-Dame Interior

Remove your metaphorical hat and become a simple bareheaded peasant, entering the dim medieval light of the church. Take a minute to let your pupils dilate, to take in the subtle, mysterious light show God beams through the stained-glass windows. Follow the slender columns up to the praying-hands arches of the ceiling and contemplate the heavens. Let's say it's dedication day for this great stone wonder. The priest intones the words of the mass that echo through the hall: "*Terribilis est locus iste*"—"This place is *terribilis*," meaning awe inspiring or even terrifying. It's a huge, dark, earthly cavern lit with an unearthly light.

This is Gothic. Taller and filled with light, this was a major improvement over the earlier Romanesque style. Gothic architects needed only a few structural columns topped by pointed arches that crisscross the columns to support the weight of the roof. This let them build higher than ever, freeing up the walls for windows. The church is designed in the shape of a cross, with the altar where the cross beams intersect.

• *Walk up to the main altar.*

The Altar

This marks the spot where mass is said and the bread and wine of communion are prepared and distributed. In olden days, there were no chairs. The church can hold up to 10,000 faithful. Join the statue of Joan of Arc (*Jeanne d'Arc*, in the right transept) in gazing up to the rose-shaped window, the only one of the three with its original medieval glass.

This was the holy spot for Romans, Christians... and even atheists. When the Revolutionaries stormed the church, they gutted it and turned it into a "Temple for the Cult of Reason." A woman dressed up like the *Statue of Liberty* held court at the altar as a symbol of the divinity of Man. France today, while nominally Catholic, remains aloof from Vatican dogmatism. Instead of traditional wooden confessional booths, notice the open, glass-walled room where modern sinners seek counseling as much as forgiveness.

Just past the altar are the walls of the choir, where more intimate services can be held in this spacious building. The aisles are lined with chapels, each dedicated to a particular saint. The faithful can pause at their favorite, light a candle as an offering, and meditate in the cool light of the stained glass. (The nearby treasury, containing lavish robes and golden relic-holders, probably isn't worth the entry fee.)

• *Amble around the ambulatory, spill back outside, and make a U-turn left. Walk to the back end of the church along the side that faces the river.*

Notre-Dame Side View

Along the side of the church, you'll notice the flying buttresses. These 50-foot stone "beams" that stick out of the church were the key to the complex architecture of Gothic. The pointed arches we saw inside caused the weight of the roof to push outward rather than down-

ward. The "flying" buttresses support the roof by pushing back inward. Gothic architects were masters at playing architectural forces against each other to build loftier and loftier churches.

Picture Quasimodo running around along the railed balcony at the base of the roof among the gargoyles. These grotesque beasts that stick out from pillars and buttresses represent souls caught between heaven and earth. They also function as rain spouts when there are no evil spirits to do battle with.

The neo-Gothic 90-meter spire is a product of the 1860 reconstruction of the dilapidated old church. Around its base are apostles and evangelists (the green men) as well as Viollet-le-Duc, the architect in charge of the work. Notice how the apostles look outward, blessing the city, while the architect (at top) looks up the spire, marveling at his fine work.

• *Behind Notre-Dame, squeeze through the tourist buses, cross the street, and enter the iron gate into the park at the tip of the island.*

Deportation Memorial (Mémorial de la Déportation)

This memorial to the 200,000 French victims of the Nazi concentration camps draws you into their experience. As you descend the steps, the city around you disappears. Surrounded by walls, you have become a prisoner. Your only freedom is your view of the sky and the tiny glimpse of the river below.

Enter the dark, single-file chamber up ahead. Inside, the circular plaque in the floor reads, "They descended into the mouth of the earth and they did not return."

The hallway stretching in front of you is lined with 200,000 lighted crystals, one for each French citizen that died. Flickering at the far end is the eternal flame of hope. The tomb of the unknown deportee lies at your feet. Above, the inscription reads, "Dedicated to the living memory of the 200,000 French Deportees sleeping in the night and the fog, exterminated in the Nazi concentration camps." Above the exit as you leave is the message you'll find at all Nazi sights: "Forgive, but never forget."

Île St. Louis

Back on street level, look across the river to the Île St. Louis. If the Île de la Cité is a tug laden with the history of Paris, it's towing this classy little residential dinghy laden only with boutiques, characteristic restaurants, and famous sorbet shops. This island wasn't developed until much later (18th century). What was a swampy mess is now harmonious Parisian architecture.

• *From the tip of the Île de la Cité, cross the bridge to the Left Bank and turn right. Walk along the river, toward the front end of Notre-Dame. Stairs detour down to the riverbank if you need a place to picnic. This side view of the church from across the river is one of Europe's great sights.*

LEFT BANK (RIVE GAUCHE)

The Left Bank of the Seine—"left" if you were floating downstream—still has many of the twisting lanes and narrow buildings of medieval times. The Right Bank is more modern and business oriented, with wide boulevards and stressed Parisians in suits. Here along the riverbank, the "big business" is books, displayed in the green metal stalls on the parapet. These literary entrepreneurs pride themselves on their easy-going business style. With flexible hours and literally no over-head, they run their businesses as they have since medieval times.

• *When you reach the bridge (pont au Double) that crosses over in front of Notre-Dame, veer to the left, across the street to a small park (square Viviani). Go through the park to the small rough-stone church of St. Julien-le-Pauvre. You'll pass Paris' oldest inhabitant, a false acacia tree ("Robinier") that may have once shaded the Sun King.*

Medieval Paris (1000–1400)

This church dates from the 12th century, and the area around it keeps the same feel. A half-timbered house stands to the right of the entrance. Many buildings in medieval times were built like this, with a wooden frame filled in with a plaster of mud, straw, and dung. Back then, the humble "half-timbered" structure would have been hidden by a veneer of upscale stucco.

Looking along nearby rue Galande, you'll see a few old houses built every which way. In medieval days, people were piled on top of each other, building at all angles, as they scrambled for this prime real estate near the main commercial artery of the day—the Seine. The smell of fish competed with the smell of neighbors in this knot of humanity.

These narrow streets would have been dirt (or mud). Origi-nally the streets sloped from here down into the mucky Seine, until modern quays cleaned that up. Many Latin Quarter lanes were named for their businesses or crafts. The rue de la Bucherie (or "Butcher Street," just around the corner, in the direction of the river) was where butchers slaughtered livestock. The blood and guts drained into the Seine and out of town.

• *At #37 rue de la Bucherie is . . .*

Shakespeare & Company Bookstore

Along with butchers and fishmongers, the Left Bank has been home to scholars, philosophers, and poets since medieval times. This funky bookstore—a reincarnation of the original shop from the 1920s—has picked up the literary torch. In the '20s it was famous as a meeting place of Paris' literary expatriate elite. Ernest Hemingway, a struggling American writer, strangled and cooked pigeons in the park and borrowed books from here to survive. Fitzgerald, Joyce, and Pound also got their English fix here.

Today it does its best to carry on that literary tradition. Struggling writers are given free accommodations upstairs in tiny, book-lined rooms with views of Notre-Dame. Downstairs, travelers enjoy the best selection of used English books in Paris. Pick up *Free Voice*, a newspaper published for today's American expatriates, and say hi to George.

• *Return to St. Julien-le-Pauvre, then turn right (west) on rue Galande, which immediately intersects with the busy rue St. Jacques (also called rue du Petit Pont). Way back in Roman times, the rue St. Jacques was the straight, wide, paved road that brought chariots racing in and out of the city. (Roman-iacs can see remains from the 3rd-century baths, along with a fine medieval collection, at the Cluny Museum, 2 blocks to the left; see tour on page 186.) Cross rue St. Jacques to the small Gothic church of St. Severin.*

St. Severin

Don't ask me why, but it took a century longer to build this church than Notre-Dame. This is flamboyant, or "flame-like," Gothic, and you can see the short, prickly spires meant to make this building flicker in the eyes of the faithful. The church gives us a close-up look at gargoyles. This weird, winged species of flying mammal, now extinct, used to swoop down on unwary peasants, occasionally carrying off small children in their beaks. Today they're most impressive in thunderstorms, when they vomit rain.

The Latin Quarter

While it may look more like the Tunisian Quarter today, this area is the Latin Quarter, named for the language you'd hear on these streets if you walked them in the Middle Ages. The university, one of the leading universities of medieval Europe, was (and still is) nearby.

A thousand years ago, the "crude" or vernacular local languages were sophisticated enough to communicate basic human needs, but if you wanted to get philosophical, the language of choice was Latin. The educated elite of Dark Ages Europe was a class that transcended nations and borders. From Sicily to Sweden, they spoke and corresponded in Latin. The most Latin thing about this area now is the beat you may hear coming from some of the subterranean jazz clubs.

Along rue St. Severin you can still see the shadow of the medieval sewer system. (The street slopes into a central channel of bricks.) In the days before plumbing and toilets, when people still went to the river or neighborhood wells for their water, flushing meant throwing it out the window. Certain times of day were flushing times. Maids on the fourth floor would holler "*Garde de l'eau!*" ("Look out for the water!") and heave it into the streets, where it would eventually wash down into the Seine.
• *At #22 rue St. Severin, you'll find the skinniest house in Paris, two windows wide. Continue along rue St. Severin to...*

Boulevard St. Michel

Busy boulevard St. Michel (or "boul' Miche") is famous as the main artery for bohemian Paris, culminating a block away (to the left), where it intersects with boulevard St. Germain. Although nowadays you're more likely to find pantyhose at 30 percent off, there are still many cafés, boutiques, and bohemian haunts nearby.

The Sorbonne—the University of Paris' humanities department—is also close, if you want to make a detour. (Turn left on boulevard St. Michel and walk two blocks. The entrance is at #47 rue des Écoles, or just gaze at the dome from the Place Sorbonne courtyard.) Founded as a theology school around the radical Peter Abelard, it became the alma mater for Thomas Aquinas, Loyola, Erasmus, and John Calvin. Children of kings and nobles were sent here to become priests, though many returned as heretics, having studied radical new secular ideas as well. Paris still is a world center for new intellectual trends.
• *Cross boulevard St. Michel. Just ahead is a tree-filled square lined with cafés and restaurants.*

Place Saint Andre des Arts

In Paris, most serious thinking goes on in cafés. (For more information, see "Les Grands Cafés de Paris," page 255.) For centuries, these have been social watering holes, where you could buy a warm place to sit and stimulating conversation for the price of a cup of coffee. Every great French writer— from Voltaire and Rousseau to Sartre and Derrida—had a favorite haunt.

Paris honors its writers. If you visit the Panthéon (a few blocks down boulevard St. Michel and to the left), you will find great French writers and scientists buried in a setting usually reserved for warriors and politicians.
• *Adjoining this square on the river side is the triangular place St. Michel, with a Métro stop and a statue of St. Michael killing a devil.*

Place St. Michel

You're standing at the traditional core of the Left Bank's artsy, liberal, hippie, bohemian district of poets, philosophers, and winos. You'll find international eateries, far-out bookshops, street singers, pale girls in black berets, jazz clubs, and—these days— tourists. Small cinemas show avant-garde films, almost always in the *version originale* (v.o.). For colorful wandering and café sitting, afternoons and evenings are best. In the morning, it feels sleepy. The Latin Quarter stays up late and sleeps in.

In less commercial times, place St. Michel was a gathering point for the city's malcontents and misfits. Here, in 1871, the citizens took the streets from the government troops, set up barricades "Les Miz"–style, and established the Paris Commune. In World War II, the locals rose up against their Nazi oppressors (read the plaques by the St. Michel fountain).

And in the spring of 1968, a time of social upheaval all over the world, young students battled riot batons and tear gas, took over the square, and declared it an independent state. Factory workers followed their call to arms and went on strike, toppling the de Gaulle government and forcing change. Eventually the students were pacified, the university was reformed, and the Latin Quarter's original cobblestones were replaced with pavement, so future scholars could never again use them as weapons.

• *From place St. Michel, look across the river and find the spire of Sainte-Chapelle church, with its weathervane angel. Cross the river on pont St. Michel and continue along boulevard du Palais.*

On your left you'll see the doorway to Sainte-Chapelle. But first, carry on another 30 meters and turn right at a wide pedestrian street, the rue de Lutece.

CITÉ "METROPOLITAIN" STOP

Of the 141 original early-20th-century subway entrances, this is one of 17 survivors now preserved as a national art treasure. (New York's Museum of Modern Art even exhibits one.) The curvy, plant-like ironwork is a textbook example of Art Nouveau, the style that rebelled against the erector-set squareness of the Industrial Age.

The flower market on place Louis Lepine is a pleasant detour. On Sundays this square chirps with a busy bird market. And across the way is the Prefecture de Police, where Inspector Clouseau of Pink Panther fame used to work, and where the local resistance fighters took the first building from the Nazis in August of 1944, leading to the allied liberation of Paris a week later.

• *Pause here to admire the view. Sainte-Chapelle is a pearl in an ugly architectural oyster, part of a complex of buildings that includes the Palace of Justice (to the right of Sainte-Chapelle, behind the iron and bronze gates).*

Return to the entrance of Sainte-Chapelle. You'll need to pass through a metal detector to get into Sainte-Chapelle. (It's best to leave your Uzi at the hotel.) Walk through the security scanner. Toilets are ahead on the left. The line into the church may be long. (Museum passholders can go directly in.) Enter the humble ground floor . . .

SAINTE-CHAPELLE

Sainte-Chapelle, the triumph of Gothic church architecture, is a cathedral of glass like no other. It was built in 1248 for St. Louis IX (France's only canonized king) to house the supposed Crown of Thorns. Its architectural harmony is due to the fact that it was completed under the direction of one architect and in only five years— unheard of in Gothic times. Recall that Notre-Dame took over 200.

The exterior is ugly. But those fat buttresses are all the support needed to hold up the roof, opening up the walls for stained glass. The design clearly shows an Old Regime approach to worship. The basement was for staff and more common folks. Royal Christians worshiped upstairs. The paint job, a 19th-century restoration, helps you imagine how grand this small, painted, jeweled chapel was. (Imagine Notre-Dame painted like this . . ..)

• *Climb the spiral staircase to the Haute Chapelle. Leave the rough stone of the earth and become enlightened.*

The Stained Glass

Fiat lux. "Let there be light." Christianity, like many religions, intuitively recognized the sun as the source of life on earth. Light shining through stained glass was a symbol of God's grace shining down to earth, and Gothic architects used their new technology to turn dark stone buildings into lanterns of light. For me, the glory of Gothic shines brighter here than in any other church.

There are 15 separate panels of stained glass, with more than 1,100 different scenes, mostly from the Bible. In medieval times,

SAINTE-CHAPELLE

JESUS'
PASSION SCENES

ALTAR

CAMPAIGN OF
HOLOPHERNES

ST.
LOUIS'
PEEK·A·
BOO
WINDOW

MORE
MOSES

LIFE
OF
MOSES

STAINED GLASS

CAIN
CLUBBING
ABEL

BUTTRESSES

HELENA IN
JERUSALEM

SPIRAL
STAIRCASE

SPIRAL
STAIRCASE

50 FEET

DCH

ENTER
BELOW
(INTO LOWER CHAPEL)

TO
W.C.

scenes like these helped teach Bible stories to the illiterate.
These cover the entire Christian history of the world, from the
Creation in Genesis (first window on the left), to the coming of
Christ (over the altar), to the end of the world (the round "rose"-
shaped window at the rear of the church). Each individual scene
is interesting, and the whole effect is overwhelming.

Let's look at a single scene. Head toward the altar to the
fourth big window on the right. Look at the bottom circle, second
from the left. It's a battle scene (the campaign of Holophernes)
showing three soldiers with swords slaughtering three men.
The background is blue. The men have different colored clothes—

red, blue, green, mauve, and white. Notice some of the details. You can see the folds in the robes, the hair, facial features... and look at the victim in the center—his head is splotched with blood!

Craftsmen made glass (which is, essentially, melted sand), coloring it by mixing in metals like cobalt (blue) or copper (green). Then they'd assemble pieces of different colored glass to make, say, the soldier in blue with a green shield (upper right). The pieces were held together by lead. Details like the folds in the robes (see the victim in white, lower left) came by either scratching on the glass or by baking in imperfections. It was a painstaking process of finding just the right colors, fitting them together to make a scene... and then multiplying by 1,100. (Note: The sun lights up different windows at different times of day. Overcast days give the most even light. On bright sunny days, some sections are glorious while others look like a sheet of lead.)

Other scenes worth a look:

1) Cain clubbing Abel (first window on the left, second row of circles, far right—Cain is in red).

2) The life of Moses (second window, the bottom row of diamond panels). First panel shows baby Moses in a basket, placed by his sister in the squiggly brown river. Next, he's found by the pharaoh's daughter. Then, he grows up. And finally, he's a man, a prince of Egypt on his royal throne.

3) In the next window (third on left) you'll see various scenes of Moses. He's often given "horns" because of a medieval mistranslation of the Biblical description of his "aura" of holiness.

4) Over the altar are scenes from Jesus' arrest and crucifixion. Stand at the stairs in front and look over the altar and through the canopy to find Jesus being whipped (left), Jesus in purple being crowned with thorns (right), Jesus in yellow carrying his cross (a little above), and, finally, Jesus on the cross being speared by a soldier (above, left).

It takes 13 tourists to build a Gothic church: six columns, six buttresses, and one steeple.

5) Helena, the mother of Constantine—the first

Christian Roman emperor, travels to Jerusalem to find the Crown of Thorns and Crucifixion cross (first window to the right, lowest level).

If you can't read much into the individual windows, you're not alone. The medieval worshiper was a stained-glass speed-reader, and we're the illiterate ones. (For some tutoring, a little book with color photos is on sale downstairs with the postcards.)

The altar was raised up high (notice the staircase for the priest to the right) to better display the relic around which this chapel was built—the Crown of Thorns. This was the crown put on Jesus when the Romans were torturing and humiliating him before his execution. King Louis was convinced he'd found the real McCoy and paid three times as much money for it as was spent on this entire chapel. Today the supposed Crown of Thorns is kept in the Notre-Dame Treasury and shown only on Good Friday.

Notice the little private viewing window in the wall to the right of the altar. Louis was both saintly and shy. He liked to be able to go to church without dealing with the rigors of public royal life. Here he could worship still dressed in his jammies.

Lay your camera on the ground and shoot the ceiling. Those pure and simple ribs growing out of the slender columns are the essence of Gothic structure.

Palais de Justice

As you walk around the church exterior, look down and notice how much Paris has risen in the 800 years since Sainte-Chapelle was built. You're in a huge complex of buildings that has housed the local government since ancient Roman times. It was the site of the original Gothic palace of the early kings of France. The only surviving medieval parts are Sainte-Chapelle and the Conciergerie prison.

Most of the site is now covered by the giant Palais de Justice, home of France's supreme court, built in 1776. "*Liberté, Egalité, Fraternité*" over the doors is a reminder that this was also the headquarters of the Revolutionary government. Here they doled out justice, condemning many to torture in the Conciergerie

downstairs or to have their
heads removed by "Monsieur
de Paris"—the guillotine.

• *Now pass through the big iron
gate to the noisy boulevard du
Palais and turn left (toward
the Right Bank).*

*On the corner is the site of
the city's oldest public clock
(1334). While the present clock
is Baroque, it still manages to
keep accurate time.*

Paris' City Palace in 1650, with
Sainte-Chapelle, the Conciergerie, and Pont
Neuf (then 30 years old) in the background.

*Turn left onto quai d'Horologe and walk along the river. The
round medieval tower just ahead marks the entrance to the Conciergerie.
Even if you don't pay to see the Conciergerie, you can visit the courtyard
and lobby. Step past the serious-looking guard into the courtyard.*

Conciergerie

The Conciergerie, a former prison and place of torture, is a
gloomy place. Kings used it to torture and execute failed assassins.
The leaders of the Revolution put it to similar good use. The
tower next to the entrance, called "the babbler," was named
for the painful sounds that leaked from it.

Look at the stark printing above the
doorways. This was a no-nonsense revolutionary time. Everything, including letter-
ing, was subjected to the test of reason.
No frills or we chop 'em off.

Marie-Antoinette was imprisoned here.
During a busy eight-month period in the
Revolution, she was one of 2,600 prisoners
kept here on their way to the guillotine.

The interior (requires ticket), with its
huge vaulted and pillared rooms, echoes with
history but is pretty barren. You can see Marie-Antoinette's cell,
with a collection of Marie-Antoinette mementos. In another room,
a list of those made "a foot shorter at the top" by the guillotine
includes ex-King Louis XVI, Charlotte Corday (who murdered
Marat in his bathtub), and the chief Revolutionary who got a taste
of his own medicine—Maximilien Robespierre.

• *Back outside, wink at the flak-vested guard (but no jokes about your
Uzi), turn left, and continue your walk along the river. Across the river
you can see the rooftop observatory of the Samaritaine department store,
where we'll end this walk. At the first corner, veer left into a sleepy triangular square called "place Dauphine."*

Place Dauphine

It's amazing to find such coziness in the heart of Paris. This city of 2 million is still a city of neighborhoods, a collection of villages. The French Supreme Court building looms behind like a giant marble gavel. Enjoy the village-Paris feeling in the park. You may see lawyers on their lunch break playing *boules.*

• *Walk through the park to the statue of Henry IV, who in 1607 inaugurated the Pont Neuf. (If you need a romantic hideaway in the midst of this megacity, take the steps down into the park on the tip of the island and dangle your legs over the prow of this concrete island.) From the statue, turn right onto the old bridge. Walk to the little nook halfway across.*

Pont Neuf

The Pont Neuf, or "new bridge," is now Paris' oldest. Its 12 arches span the widest part of the river. The fine view includes the park on the tip of the island (note Seine boats), the Orsay, and the Louvre. These turrets were originally for vendors and street entertainers. In the days of Henry, who originated the promise of "a chicken in every pot," this would have been a lively scene.

• *The first building you'll hit on the Right Bank is the venerable old department store Samaritaine. Go through the door, veer left, and catch the elevator to the ninth floor. Climb two sets of stairs to the panorama. (Don't confuse the terrace level with the higher, better panorama. Light meals are served on the terrace. Public WCs on fifth and ninth floors.)*

THE REST OF PARIS

From the circular little crow's nest of the building, ponder the greatest skyline in Europe. Retrace the walk you just made, starting with Notre-Dame and Sainte-Chapelle. Then spin counterclockwise (or run down the stairs to hop on the Métro) and check out the rest of Paris:

The **Pompidou Center**, the wild and colorful rectangular tangle of blue and white pipes and tubes, is filled with art that makes this building's exterior look tame. See page 130.

Sacré-Coeur is a neo-Romanesque church topping Montmartre. This is an atmospheric quarter after dark, its streets filled with strolling tourists avoiding strolling artists. ✪ See Montmartre Walk, page 78.

The **Louvre** is the largest building in Paris, the largest palace in Europe, and the largest museum in the Western world. ✪ See Louvre Tour, page 85.

Stretching away from the Louvre, the **Tuileries Gardens**, place de la Concorde, and the Champs-Élysées lead to the Arc de Triomphe. The gardens are Paris' "Central Park," filled with

families at play, cellists in
the shade, carousels, pony
rides, and the ghost of
Maurice Chevalier.

The gardens overlook the
grand **place de la Concorde**,
marked by an ancient obelisk,
where all of France seems to
converge. It was "guillotine
central" during the Revolu-
tion and continues to be a place of much festivity.

Europe's grandest boulevard, the **Champs-Élysées**, runs uphill
from place de la Concorde about a mile to the Arc de Triomphe.
While pretty globalized, and with rich-and-single aristocrats more
rare than ever, it's still the place you're most likely to see Sylvester
Stallone. ✪ See Champs-Élysées Walk, page 61.

Napoleon began constructing the magnificent **Arc de
Triomphe** in 1806 to commemorate his victory at the battle
of Austerlitz. It was finished in 1836, just in time for the
emperor's funeral parade. Today it commemorates heroes
of past wars. There's no triumphal arch bigger (50 meters
high, 40 meters wide). And, with 12 converging boulevards,
there's no traffic circle more thrilling, either on foot or behind
the wheel. See page 61.

Paris, the capital of Europe, is built on an appropriately monumental plan, with an axis that stretches from the Louvre, up the
Champs-Élysées, past the Arc de Triomphe, all the way to the
modern Grande Arche among the skyscrapers at **La Défense**. (Find
the faint shadow of this arch, just above the Arc de Triomphe.)

The **Orsay Museum**, the train-station-turned-art-museum,
is just beyond the Louvre on the Left Bank. See page 104.

The body of Napoleon lies under the gilded dome. The giant
building is **Les Invalides**, designed to house his wounded troops.
Today it houses a fine military museum. See page 172. The
Rodin Museum is nearby. See page 157.

The **Eiffel Tower** is a thousand-foot exclamation point built
as a temporary engineering stunt to celebrate the 100th anniversary
of the French Revolution. Paris decided to let it be an exception
to a downtown building code that allows the skyline to be broken
only by a few prestigious domes and spires. See page 34.

The 52-story **Montparnasse Tower**, a city in itself
(5,000 workers, 700 feet high) reminds us that, while tourists
look for hints of Louis and Napoleon, work-a-day Paris looks
to the future.

CHAMPS-ÉLYSÉES
WALK

paris

Leaving Paris without strolling the Champs-Élysées is like walking out of a great restaurant before dessert. This is Paris at its most Parisian: monumental sidewalks, stylish shops, grand cafés, and glimmering showrooms. This walk covers about three miles and takes three hours if done completely. The Arc de Triomphe (open daily until 23:00 in summer) and Champs-Élysées are best at night. Métro stops are located every three blocks on the Champs-Élysées (zhahn-zay-lee-zay).

Start by taking the Métro to the Arc de Triomphe. At the Métro stop Charles de Gaulle Étoile, follow *sortie* Champs-Élysées/Avenue Friedland to "access Arc de Triomphe" signs. Exit at the top of the Champs-Élysées and face the Arc de Triomphe. Underground WCs are on the left side of Champs-Élysées, and an underground walkway leading to the arch should be in front of you on the right side of the Champs-Élysées.

Ascend the **Arc de Triomphe** via the 230 steps or the elevator if you're disabled—sorry, no discount for walkers (40F, daily June–Sept 9:30–23:00, Oct–May 9:30–22:00, skip the line if you have a pass or don't want to go to the top of the arch, Mo: Étoile, tel. 01 43 80 31 31).

A small museum near the top explains its history; the exhibits are in French, but there's a good video in English. Begun in 1806, the arch was intended to honor Napoleon's soldiers, who, in spite of being vastly outnumbered by the Austrians, scored a remarkable victory at the battle of Austerlitz. Napoleon died prior to its completion. But it was finished in time for his funeral procession to pass underneath carrying his remains from exile in St. Helena home to Paris. Today the Arc de Triomphe is dedicated to the glory of all French armies.

From the rooftop viewpoint, get your bearings with the

CHAMPS-ÉLYSÉES WALK

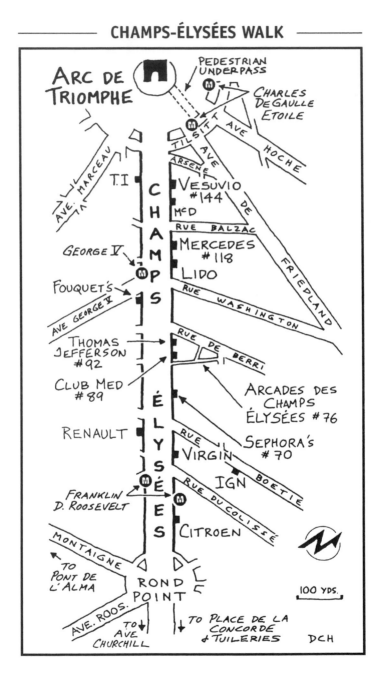

circular orientation tables. Opposite the Champs-Élysées, the avenue Grande Armée leads to the skyscraper ghetto of the La Défense suburb. Notice what a contrast they make to the regular height of buildings closer to the arch. French President Mitterand had the huge white **Grande Arche de La Défense** built as a centerpiece of this mini-Manhattan (see the Sights chapter, page 39). It's part of the huge axis capped by the arch you're standing on and the Louvre. The wide boulevard lined with grass and trees a little to your left is avenue Foch (named after a WWI hero) and is the best address to have in Paris (the shah of Iran and Aristotle Onassis had homes here). The Bois de Boulogne is the big green park at the end of avenue Foch. While the arch was under construction, the land below you was a rural forest, looking much like the Bois de Boulogne.

Walk to the Champs-Élysées side and scan the cityscape of downtown Paris. Notice the uniform height and symmetry. The beauty of Paris—basically a flat basin with a river running through it—is man-made. The key to this beauty is the relationship between the width of its grand boulevards and the uniformity in the height and design of the buildings. To the right, the rude **Montparnasse Tower** looks lonely out there, standing like the box the Eiffel Tower came in. It served as a wake-up call in the early 1970s to preserve the building height restriction and strengthen urban design standards.

The 12 boulevards that radiate from the Arc de Triomphe were part of Baron Haussmann's master plan for Paris: the creation of a series of major boulevards, intersecting at diagonals with monuments (like the Arc de Triomphe) as centerpieces of those intersections. His plan did not anticipate the automobile—obvious when you watch the traffic scene below. As you gaze down at what appears to be a chaotic traffic mess, watch how smoothly it really functions. Cars entering the circle have the right of way; those in the circle must yield. Motorcycles are fair game. Pedestrians are used as target practice. Still, there are plenty of accidents, often caused by tourists who don't understand the rules of the game. Tired of related disputes, insurance companies split the fault and damages of any Arc de Triomphe accidents 50-50.

Look straight down the **Champs-Élysées**. The first street was built at the lower end in the early 1600s by Queen Marie de Medici, a short extension of her Tuileries Gardens. It soon became the place to cruise in your carriage. (It still is today—traffic can be jammed up even at midnight.) One hundred years later, it was extended uphill to where you are now.

Like its Roman ancestors, this arch has served as a parade gateway for triumphal armies (French or foe) and important ceremonies. From 1941 to 1944, a large swastika flew from here as Nazis goose-stepped down the Champs-Élysées. Allied troops marched triumphantly under this arch in August 1944.

Descend the arch and stand on the bronze plaque at the foot of the **Tomb of the Unknown Soldier** (from World War I). Daily at 18:30 the flame is rekindled and new flowers set in place. On the columns you'll see lists of battle victories and officers (with a line under the names of those who died in battle).

Still facing the Tomb of the Unknown Soldier, turn right and walk to the front of the arch's massive column to see its most famous sculpture. *The Departure of the Volunteers*, or *La Marseillaise*, is a rousing effort to rally the troops by what looks like an ugly reincarnation of Joan of Arc. On the right side of this column, a scene a little over halfway up the arch shows Napoleon's confident pose as he oversees his victory at Austerlitz.

Walk out to the traffic circle and look down the Champs-Élysées. Plan your walking attack from here. The Louvre is the building at the very end of the avenue through the Tuileries Gardens. You'll turn right off the Champs-Élysées about halfway there. Notice how the left sidewalk is more popular with pedestrians. While the left side is most interesting, cross over at least once for the exhilarating view from the center of the avenue's 10 lanes. The **tourist information office** is immediately on the right at #127. Le Drugstore (next door) has a small grocery store in the back.

Cross back under the tunnel to the top of the Champs-Élysées. The *nouveau* Champs-Élysées is a revitalized avenue with new street benches, lamps, broader sidewalks, and an army of green-suited workers with small machines designed to keep Paris' most famous avenue spic-and-span.

Start your descent. The first tiny street you cross, rue de Tilsitt, is part of a shadow ring road—an option for drivers who'd like to avoid the chaos of the arch, complete with stoplights. Be careful of speedy cars on these cross streets as you descend.

On the first block down, stop by Café Vesuvio (#144, reasonable prices) to enjoy fine views of the arch with its rooftop bristling with tourists. The Big Macs for sale next door are just as popular among the French as they are at home.

At the Mercedes showroom (#118), you can pick up your new sedan and a leather jacket and purse to match.

Next to the Mercedes showroom is the famous **Lido**, Paris' largest cabaret—check out the photos, video, and prices. These sensational shows pull out every stop for floor customers. Moviegoing on the Champs-Élysées is also popular. Check to see if there are films you recognize, then look for the showings (*seances*); if there is a "v.o." (*version originale*) next to the time, the film will be in its original language.

Now cross the boulevard where the elegant avenue George V (home to several 4-star hotels and the Crazy Horse Saloon) spills into the Champs-Élysées. **Fouquet's café-restaurant**, under the orange awning, serves the most expensive shot of espresso I found in Paris (29F), but the setting is tops. Since the early 1900s, Fouquet's has been a favorite of French actors and actresses. The welcome mat of golden plaques honors winners of France's Oscarlike film awards, the Cesars (see "Les Grands Cafés de Paris," page 255).

Cross back to the lively side. At #92 a wall plaque marks the place Thomas Jefferson lived while minister to France (1785). A plaque just below marks the spot where Robert Birlinger died fighting the Germans during the liberation of Paris in August 1944.

Nearby are several **arcades**. My favorite is the Arcade des Champs-Élysées, at #76. This refuge of the belle epoque seems out of place today. Wander in.

Just down *les Champs*, glide down Sephora's ramp at #74 into a vast hall of cosmetics and **perfumes** (Mon-Sat 10:00-24:00). The young woman at the wheel of scents will explain how it works. Grab a black basket and join the frenzy. Halfway down on your left in red flashing numbers are the current prices of perfumes (*cours des parfums*) in cities throughout the world. Notice that Paris is hardly the cheapest.

The English **pharmacy** is open until midnight at the corner on rue Boetie, and map lovers can detour one block down this street to the Institut Geographique National, France's version of the National Geographic Society (Mon–Sat 9:30–19:00).

Virgin Megastore sells a world of **music** one block farther down the Champs-Élysées. The Disney and Quicksilver stores are reminders of global economics—the French love these stores as much as Americans do.

Near the bottom of the Champs-Élysées, Renault and Citroen showrooms glare across the avenue, each offering late-night cafés and restaurants. (Renault also has an **antique car museum**, fun for kids and car lovers.)

At the Rondpoint the shopping ends and the park begins. This leafy circle is always colorful, lined with flowers or seasonal decorations (thousands of pumpkins at Halloween, hundreds of trees at Christmas).

Now it's decision time. You have three options: 1) You can continue straight (by Métro or foot) to reach place de la Concorde and the Tuileries Gardens; 2) A hard right turn here takes you back to the river and pont de l'Alma, down Paris' most exclusive shopping street, the avenue Montaigne, where you need an appointment to buy a dress; 3) You can finish the walk with me.

To continue, walk a block past Rondpoint, then turn right on avenue Churchill and walk between the glass- and steel-domed **Grand and Petit Palais** exhibition halls, built for the 1900 World's Fair. Today these examples of the "can do" spirit of the early 20th century host a variety of exhibits (details at tourist offices or in *Pariscope*). Impressive temporary exhibits fill the huge Grand Palais (drop in to see what's on; not covered by museum pass), while the Petit Palais (left side) houses a permanent collection of 19th-century paintings by Delacroix, Cézanne, Monet, and others (covered by museum pass).

Cross the river on **pont Alexandre**, eyeing the golden dome of Les Invalides. Les Invalides was built by Louis XIV as a veteran's hospital for his battle-weary troops (see Napoleon's Tomb Tour on page 172); in the Esplanade des Invalides, possibly the largest slice of accessible grass in Paris, soccer balls and Frisbees fill the air.

This exquisite bridge, spiked with golden statues and ironwork lamps, was built to celebrate a turn-of-the-century treaty between France and Russia. Like the two palaces just passed, it's a fine example of belle epoque exuberance. Notice the elegant street lamps on the railing. The barges under the bridge are some of over 2,000 houseboats on the Seine.

At the end of the bridge, turn left and follow the Seine past the Air France bus terminal and Ministry of Foreign Affairs (#37) to the Greek temple–like **Assemblée Nationale** (at the next bridge). France's 600 members of parliament convene here. If the gates are open, climb to the top of the steps for a fantastic view over the place de la Concorde.

From here, **pont de la Concorde** leads to place de la Concorde. The bridge, built of stones from the Bastille prison (which was demolished by the Revolution in 1789), symbolizes that, with good government, *concorde* (harmony) can come from chaos. Walk to the far (right) side of the bridge and begin crossing it. Stand near the center of the bridge and gaze upriver. Using a clock as a compass, the L'Orangerie (closed for renovation) is at 10:00 and the tall building with the skinny chimneys (at 11:00) is the architectural caboose of the sprawling Louvre Palace. The park between is the Tuileries Gardens. The thin spire of Sainte-Chapelle is dead center at 12:00, with the twin towers of Notre-Dame to its right. The Orsay Museum is closer on the right (just this side of the next bridge), opposite the Tuileries.

Leaving the bridge, you'll cross a freeway underpass similar to the one at pont de L'Alma, three bridges downstream, where Princess Diana lost her life in the tragic 1997 car accident.

Continue to the **place de la Concorde**, the 21-acre square with the obelisk. Walk to the island in the center from the crosswalk on the far side of the square. During the Revolution, this was the place de la Revolution. Over 1,300 heads lost their bodies here during the Reign of Terror.

The guillotine sat here. A bronze plaque on the Arc de Triomphe side of the obelisk memorializes the place where Louis XVI and Marie-Antoinette, among many others, were made a foot shorter on top. Three worked the guillotine: One managed the blade, one held the blood bucket, and one caught the head, raising it high to the roaring crowd.

Look for **Le Crillon**, Paris' most exclusive hotel, one of the twin buildings that guards the entrance to rue Royale (which leads to the Greek-style Basilique de la Madeleine). Eleven years before the king lost his head on this square, Louis XVI met with Benjamin Franklin in this hotel to sign a treaty recognizing the United States as an independent country. (The American embassy is located next door.) For an affordable splurge, consider high tea at Le Crillon; see "Les Grands Cafés de Paris," page 255.

The 3,200-year-old **obelisk of Luxor** now forms the center-piece of place de la Concorde. It was carted here from Egypt in 1829, a gift to the French king. The gold pictures on the obelisk tell the story of its incredible journey.

The obelisk also forms a center point along a line locals call the "royal perspective." From this straight line (Louvre—Obelisk—Arc de Triomphe—Grand Arche de la Défense) you can hang a lot of history. The Louvre symbolizes the old regime (divine-right rule by kings and queens). The obelisk and place de la Concorde symbolize the people's revolution (cutting off the king's head). The Arc de Triomphe calls to mind the triumph of nationalism (victorious armies carrying national flags under the arch). And the huge modern arch in the distance, surrounded by the headquarters of multinational corporations, heralds a future where business entities are more powerful than nations.

The beautiful **Tuileries Gardens** lead through the iron gates to the Louvre (with a public WC just inside on the right). If high tea at Le Crillon isn't your cup of tea, pull up a chair next to the pond or find one of the cafés in the gardens.

MARAIS
WALK

paris

This walk takes you through one of Paris' most characteristic quarters, the Marais, and finishes in the Beaubourg neighborhood. When in Paris, you naturally want to see the big sights, but to experience Paris you need to visit a vital neighborhood.

The **Marais** neighborhood contains more pre-Revolutionary lanes and buildings than anywhere else in town and is more atmospheric than touristy. It's medieval Paris. This is how much of the city looked until, in the mid-1800s, Napoleon III had Baron Haussmann blast out the narrow streets to construct broad boulevards (wide enough for the guns and ranks of the army, too wide for revolutionary barricades), creating modern Paris.

This walk is about three miles long. Allow two hours, and add another hour if you visit the Carnavalet Museum. Paris Walks offers in-depth guided tours of this area (see "Organized Tours," page 27).

Start by riding the Métro to the Bastille stop. At **place de la Bastille**, there are more revolutionary images in the Métro station murals than on the square. Exit the Métro following signs to rue Saint Antoine (not the signs to rue Saint Antoine du Faubourg). Ascend onto a noisy square dominated by the bronze **Colonne de Juillet** (July Column). Victims of the revolutions of 1830 and 1848 are buried in a vault 55 meters below this gilded statue of liberty. The actual Bastille, a royal fortress-then-prison that once symbolized old-regime tyranny and now symbolizes the Parisian emancipation, is long gone. While only a brick outline of the fortress' round turrets survives (under the traffic where rue Saint Antoine hits the square), the story of the Bastille is indelibly etched into the city's psyche.

For centuries the Bastille was used to defend the city (mostly from its own people). On July 14, 1789, the people of Paris

MARAIS WALK

stormed the prison, releasing its seven prisoners and hoping to find arms. Instead, they found heads. They demolished the brick fortress and decorated their pikes with the heads of a few bigwigs. By shedding blood, the leaders of the gang made sure it would be tough to turn back the tides of revolution. Ever since, the French have celebrated July 14 as their independence day—Bastille Day.

The flashy, glassy-gray, and controversial **Opéra-Bastille** dominates (some say overwhelms) the square. Designed by the Canadian architect Carlos Ott, this grand Parisian project was opened with great fanfare by François Mitterrand on the 200th Bastille Day, July 14, 1989. The Opéra follows in the footsteps of other "grand projects" like the Louvre's pyramid, the Grande Arche at La Défense, and the Pompidou Center. (For opera ticket information, see page 267.)

Turn your back to the statue and, passing the Banque de France on your right (good rates, long lines, opposite a fine

map of the area), head down rue Saint Antoine about four
blocks into the Marais.

Leave rue Saint Antoine at #62 and turn right through two
elegant courtyards of **Hôtel de Sully** (open until 19:00, fine bookstore inside, 62 rue Saint Antoine). Originally a swamp (*marais*)
during the reign of Henry IV, it became the hometown of the
French aristocracy. In the 17th century, big shots built their private
mansions (*hôtels*), like this one, close to Henry's place des Vosges.
Hôtels that survived the revolution now house museums, libraries,
and national institutions. The aristocrats may be gone, but the
Marais—which, until recently, was a dumpy bohemian quarter—
is today a thriving, trendy, real community and a joy to explore.

To get to the **place des Vosges** park, continue through Hôtel
de Sully (if it's closed, backtrack to rue de Biraque to reach place des
Vosges). The small door on the far right corner of the second courtyard pops you out into one of Paris' finest squares (closes at dusk).
Walk to the center, where Louis XIII sits on a horse surrounded by
locals enjoying their community park. Children frolic in the sand-
box, lovers warm benches, and pigeons guard their fountains while
trees shade this retreat from the glare of the big city. Henry IV built
this centerpiece of the Marais in 1605. As hoped, this turned the
Marais into Paris' most exclusive neighborhood. **Victor Hugo**
lived at #6, and you can visit
his house (22F, Tue–Sun
10:00–17:40, closed Mon,
corner closest to the Bastille,
see page 40). Walk behind
Louis' horse to the arcade.
Follow it left past art galleries and antique shops
onto the boutique-filled rue
des Francs Bourgeois.

To see impressive vestiges of Philippe Auguste II's 12th-
century defensive wall, detour from our walk and follow this
route: Turn left on rue de Turenne, cross rue St. Antoine,
continue down rue St. Paul, then make a right on rue Charlemagne. The wall is two blocks down on your left and shows
the limit of the developed city in the late 1100s.

To continue our original walk, return to rue des Francs Bourgeois via rue de Sévigné, where you'll see the Musée Carnavalet.

The **Carnavalet Museum**, which focuses on the history of
Paris, is housed inside a Marais mansion (35F, Tue–Sun 10:00–
17:00, closed Mon, 23 rue de Sévigné). ✪ See Carnavalet
Tour on page 142.

Go another block along rue des Francs Bourgeois (peeking

through the gate on the right) and turn left at the post office. (The **Picasso Museum**, described on page 40, is up 1 block to the right: 30F, Wed–Mon 9:30–18:00, closed Tue, 5 rue Thorigny). Go right onto rue Rosiers, which runs straight for three blocks through Paris' Jewish Quarter, lively every day except Saturday.

The **Jewish Quarter** is lined with colorful shops and kosher eateries. Check out Jo Goldenberg's delicatessen/ restaurant (first corner on left, #7 rue Rosiers, scene of a terrorist bombing in darker times). You'll be tempted by kosher pizza and plenty of 25F falafel-to-go joints (*emporter* = to go). Rue Rosiers dead-ends into rue du Vieille du Temple. Turn right.

Frank Bourgeois is waiting at the corner postcard/print shop. Turn left on rue des Francs Bourgeois, which leads past the national archives (peek inside the courtyard) and turns into rue Rambuteau, then continue for several blocks on rue Rambuteau. As you approach the Pompidou Center, you'll pass within a few doors of the new **Jewish Art and History Museum**—to the right on rue du Temple (40F, not covered by museum pass, Mon–Fri 11:00–18:00, Sun 10:00–18:00, closed Sat, 71 rue du Temple, see page 40).

The pipes and glass of the newly renovated **Pompidou Center** mark your exit from the Marais and reintroduce you to our century. Pass that huge building on your left to join the fray in front of the center (also called the Centre Beaubourg). Survey this popular spot from the top of the sloping square. Tubular escalators lead up to a great view and the modern art museum (50F, Wed–Mon 10:00–22:00, closed Tue). ★ See Pompidou Center Tour on page 130.

The Pompidou Center follows with gusto the 20th-century architectural axiom "form follows function." To get a more spacious and functional interior, the guts of this exoskeletal building are draped on the outside and color coded: vibrant red for people lifts,

 cool blue for air-conditioning, eco-green for plumbing, don't-touch-it yellow for electrical stuff, and white for bones (compare the Pompidou Center to another exoskeletal building, Notre-Dame). Enjoy the adjacent *Homage to Stravinsky* fountain. Jean Tingley designed this as a tribute to the composer: Every fountain represents one of his hard-to-hum scores. For low-stress meals try **Le Mélodine**, a self-service cafeteria at the Rambuteau Métro stop, or the fun **Dame Tartine**, which overlooks the *Homage to Stravinsky* fountain and serves a young clientele and good, cheap meals.

With your back to the Pompidou Center's escalators, walk the cobbled pedestrian mall, crossing the busy boulevard Sebastopol to the ivy-covered pavilions of **Les Halles**. Paris' down-and-dirty central produce market of 800 years was replaced by a glitzy but soulless shopping center in the late 1970s. The mall's most endearing layer is its grassy rooftop park. The Gothic Saint Eustache church overlooking this contemporary scene has a famous 8,000-pipe organ. The Louvre and Notre-Dame are not far away. The mall is served by Paris' busiest Métro hub (Chatelet–Les Halles).

RUE CLER
WALK

The Art of Parisian Living

paris

Paris is changing fast, but a stroll down this street puts you into a thriving traditional Parisian neighborhood.

Shopping for groceries is an integral part of daily life here. Parisians shop almost daily for three good reasons: Refrigerators are small (expensive electricity, tiny kitchens), produce must be fresh, and it's an important social event. Shopping is a chance to hear about the butcher's vacation plans, see photos of the florist's new grandchild, relax over *un café*, and kiss the cheeks of friends (twice for regular acquaintances, three times for friends you haven't seen in a while).

Rue Cler—traffic-free since 1984—offers plenty of space for tiny stores and their shoppers to spill into the street. It's an ideal environment for this ritual to survive and for you to explore. The street is lined with all the necessary shops—wine, cheese, chocolate, bread—as well as a bank and a post office. And the shops of this community are run by people who've found their niche: boys who grew up on quiche, girls who know a good wine.

If you wish to learn the fine art of living Parisian-style, rue Cler provides an excellent classroom. And if you wish to assemble the ultimate French picnic, there's no better place. This is the only walking tour in this guidebook you should start hungry.

(Do this walk when the market is open and lively: Tue–Sat 8:30–13:00 or 17:00–19:00, Sun 8:30–12:00, dead on Mon).

1. Bakery: Start your walk where the pedestrian section of rue Cler does, at rue de Grenelle (Mo. École Militaire). The corner bakery is typical of a newer breed of bakeries with space in the corner for coffee drinkers and fast-fooders. The almond croissants here are famous among locals. Like locals, we'll buy our baguette later to avoid damaging the slender loaves.

RUE CLER WALK

2. Café Roussillon: This café across the street is typical. Drinks at the always-active bar (*comptoir*) are about half the price of drinks at the tables. The "*tickets restaurant*" and "*cheque déjeuner*" decals on the door advertise that this café accepts lunch checks. In France, an employee lunch subsidy program is an expected perk. Employers issue checks (worth about 30F or $5) for the number of days an employee works in a month. Few workers bring sack lunches. A good lunch is sacred.

3. Top Halles Produce: Fresh produce is trucked in each morning from the huge Rungis market near Orly Airport. Rungis' location, outside of town, is handy for small farmers bringing in their goods. Notice the lack of bags (paper or plastic?). Most locals bring their own.

Parisians shop with their nose. Try it. Insist on quality. Smell the cheap Spanish strawberries. Then smell the French Gariguette. Find the herbs. Is today's delivery in? *Ooh la la*, look at the price of those melons. What's the country of origin? It must be posted. If they're out of season, they come from Guadeloupe. Many people buy only French products.

The Franprix across the street is a small Safeway type store. Opposite Hôtel Leveque is Asie Traiteur. Fast Asian food to go is popular in Paris. These shops—about as common as bakeries now—are making an impact on Parisian eating habits.

4. Butcher: Next to Asie Traiteur is the Triperie/Boucherie. Look for things you may want to avoid in restaurants: *rognons* (kidneys), *foie* (liver), *coeur de boeuf* (heart of beef). Next door is fish, brought in daily from ports on the English Channel, just 100 miles away. Across the street is a wine shop. Next to that, smell the...

5. Fromagerie: A long, narrow, canopied cheese table brings the *fromagerie* into the street. Wedges, cylinders, balls, and miniature hockey pucks all powdered white, grey, and burnt marshmallow—it's a festival of mold. Much of the street cart is devoted only to the goat cheeses. *Ooh la la* means you're impressed. If you like cheese, show greater excitement with more *la*s. *Ooh la la la la*. My local friend held the stinkiest glob close to her nose, took an orgasmic breath, and exhaled, "Yes, it smells like zee feet of angels." Try it.

Step inside and browse through some of the 400 different types of French cheese. Behind the heavy plastic curtains in the back room are *les meules*, the big, 170-pound wheels of cheese (250 gallons of milk go into each wheel). The "hard" cheeses are cut from these. Don't eat the skin of these big ones...they roll them on the floor. But the skin on the smaller cheeses—the Brie,

the Camembert—is part of the taste.
"It completes the package."

At dinner tonight you can take the
cheese course just before or as the
dessert. On a good cheese plate you
have a hard cheese (like Emmenthaler),
a flowery cheese (maybe Brie or
Camembert), a blue, and a goat.

6. Tarte Julie: Perhaps the most
tempting storefront on rue Cler is Tarte
Julie's. The front windows are filled
with various pies. The shop's classy old
storefront is a work of art that survives from the previous occu-
pant. The inset stones and glass advertise horse meat: *Boucherie
Chevaline*. The decorated front, from the '30s and signed by the
artist, would fit in a museum. But it belongs right here. And
everyone knows this is a place for a fine tart, not horse meat.

7. Droguerie Ménage and More: This French drugstore
sells everything but drugs. It's the classic kitchen/hardware store
where you buy corkscrews, brooms, knives, and so on.

Wander on past the flower shop, pharmacy (in France the
first diagnosis and prescription is made by the pharmacist—if it's
out of his league, he'll recommend a doctor), rotisserie (quarter
of a roasted chicken with a salad and a drink to go?), and another
wine shop. In France, when invited to dinner, it's bad style to
bring a bottle of wine. The host cooks with a particular wine in
mind. Bring flowers or chocolates instead.

8. Butcher: At Coucheries Coucaud, sort through pigeons, quail,
and rabbit. Hoist a duck and check the feet; they should be rough
and calloused—an indication that they weren't stuck in an industrial
kennel but ran wild on a farm. While Americans prefer beef, pork,
and chicken, the French eat more rabbit, lamb, duck, and horse.

9. Crêperie and More: Almost next door you'll find the
smallest, friendliest business on rue Cler, the Crêperie. Savory
crêpes come with ingredients we'd put in an omelet (cheese, ham,
mushrooms, and so on). They're called *galettes*, and the pancake is
made from buckwheat flour. Dessert crêpes are made of wheat flour
and come with everything you might enjoy on your ice-cream
sundae. The Café du Marché, on the corner, is the best place to sit
and enjoy the rue Cler action. For a reasonable meal, grab a chair
and the waiter will prop the chalky menu listing the *plat du jour*

(blue plate special) on an empty chair. The shiny, sterile Leader Price grocery store (across the street) is a French Costco selling bulk items. Because storage space is so limited in most Parisian apartments, bulk purchases are unlikely to become a big deal here.

10. Charcuterie J. Ragut:

Across the street, a *charcuterie* sells mouthwatering deli food to go (try their homemade potato chips). Because kitchens are so small, these gourmet delis are handy, allowing hosts to concentrate on the main course and buy beautifully prepared side dishes to complete a fine dinner. Notice the system: Pay the cashier and return with the receipt to pick up your food.

11. Boulangerie:

Locals debate the merits of rue Cler's rival *boulangeries*. It's said that a baker cannot be both a good bread man and a good pastry man: When you do good bread, you have no time to do good pastry. The baker at the rue Grenelle bakery (stop #1) specializes in pastry. The bread suffers. Here, the baker does good bread. He has a man who does the tasty little pastries for him.

12. Le Lutin Gourmand Chocolats Confiseries:

Corinne recently took over the shop from a woman who kept this neighborhood in fine chocolates for 30 years. The wholesalers want you to take the new products, but she keeps the old traditional candies, too. "The old ladies, they want the same sweets they had 80 years ago."

Corinne dips and decorates her chocolates in the back, where the merchants used to live. As was the tradition in rue Cler shops, the merchants lived and produced in the back and sold in the front.

Rue Cler ends at the post office. The École Militaire Métro stop is just around the corner. If you bought a rue Cler picnic, you'll find benches and gardens nearby. From the post office, avenue la Motte Picquet leads to two fine parks: Turn left for Les Invalides or right for the Eiffel Tower. *Bon appétit!*

MONTMARTRE
WALK

While most tourists make the almost obligatory trek to the top of Paris' touristy Montmartre, eat an overpriced crêpe, and marvel at the view, the neighborhood has a fascinating charm and history missed by most and uncovered with this short walk. To avoid the crowds, arrive in the morning by 9:30. If crowds don't get you down, come for the sunset and stay for dinner. I've included several restaurants on this tour. This walk is best done under clear skies—the views can be sensational. There are four sights you can enter on this tour: the Basilica of Sacré-Coeur (daily until 23:00), the church of St Pierre, the Dalí Museum (daily 10:00–18:00), and the Montmartre Museum (Tue–Sun 11:00–18:00, closed Mon).

You'll walk about two miles, up and down, on this 90-minute, 12-stop tour. To avoid the climb, either take the funicular (described below) or catch a taxi (about 70F from the Eiffel Tower or Bastille to Sacré-Coeur) and begin the tour at the church on top. And wear your money belt!

To reach Sacré-Coeur by Métro, get off at Anvers. When you exit the Métro, look up the only real hill in Paris. The peeling and neglected Elysées Montmartre theater across the street is the oldest cancan dance hall in Paris and sets the stage for this area in transition (it's a rowdy rock-and-roll dance hall today). From artists to Arabs, people have always moved to this area for cheap rent. It still feels neglected, though some urban gentrification is underway as young professionals restore neglected apartments and hotels renovate for a more upscale clientele.

Walk two blocks up rue de Steinkerque (the street to the right of Elysées Montmartre) through waves of tourists and past cheap clothing and souvenir shops (inexpensive postcards) to the grassy parkway below the white Sacré-Coeur church. Hike toward the church or ride the funicular (costs 1 Métro ticket, to the left, past the merry-go-round). The best view is just below the last flight of stairs.

1. Sacré-Coeur Church and View: From Paris' highest point (427 feet), the City of Light fans out at your feet. The big triangular roof on your left is the Gare du Nord train station; the golden dome out there on the right is Les Invalides. The colorful Pompidou Center is straight ahead, and the domed Panthéon lies just beyond to the right, on Paris' only other (and far smaller) butte. The Montparnasse ("Awful") Tower is farther off to the right, and the skyscrapers beyond define the southern limit of central Paris. Now walk up to the church.

The Sacré-Coeur ("Sacred Heart") **church**, with its onion domes and bleached-bone pallor, looks ancient but was built only a century ago by Parisians chastened by German invaders. Otto von Bismark's Prussian army laid siege to Paris for over four months in 1870. Things got so bad for residents that urban hunting for dinner (to cook up cats and dogs) became accepted behavior. The church was erected as a "praise the Lord anyway" gesture after France's humiliation by Germany.

The five-dome Romano-Byzantine basilica took 40 years to build. The church is dedicated to the "sacred heart" of Jesus, which enables Him to understand human needs and feelings. The contrast between the brilliant white exterior and the sooty interior is jarring. Explore the impressive mosaics, especially of Christ with his sacred heart, above the altar. Walk clockwise around the ambulatory behind the altar. Notice the colorful mosaic stations of the cross as you walk behind the altar on your right. Between stations VII and VIII, rub St. Peter's bronze foot and look up to the ceiling.

For an unobstructed panoramic view of Paris, climb 262 feet up the tight and claustrophobic spiral stairs to the top of the **dome** (15F, daily June–Sept 9:00–19:00, off-season 10:00–18:00, access is outside church and downstairs to the right, especially worthwhile if you have kids with excess energy). Skip the crypt (15F); it's just a big empty basement.

• *Leaving the church, turn right and follow the tree-lined street with the view to your left. At rue St. Eleuthere turn right and walk uphill to the Church of St. Pierre (at top on right).*

2. Church of St. Pierre: Originally a headquarters for nuns, the church is one of Paris' oldest—some say Dante prayed here. Older still are the four grey columns inside that may have stood in a temple of Mercury and Mars in Roman times (2 flank the entrance and 2 are behind the altar.) The name "Montmartre" comes from the Roman "Mount of Mars," though later generations, thinking

MONTMARTRE WALK

SACRE COEUR

IIII = STAIRS
300 YARDS

CEMETERY

RUE ST-VINCENT

RUE DES SAULES →

R. CORTOT

RUE

LEPIC

RUE DE ORCHAMPT

RUE RAVIGNAN

NORVINS

PLACE DE TERTRE

SACRE COEUR

FUNICULAR →

N

BLVD.

Blanche

M

DE

FINISH
↓
PLACE PIGALLE

Pigalle

CLICHY

ROCHECHOUART

Anvers

M

RUE DE STEINKERQUE →

DCH

START →

① SACRE COEUR
② ST. PIERRE
③ PLACE DU TERTRE
④ DALI MUSEUM
⑤ MONTMARTRE MUSEUM
⑥ VINEYARD

⑦ LAPIN AGILE
⑧ BATEAU LAVOIR
⑨ MOULIN DE LA GALETTE

⑩ VAN GOGH'S HOUSE
⑪ MOULIN ROUGE
⑫ PIG ALLEY

of their beheaded patron St. Denis, preferred a less pagan version, "Mount of Martyrs."

In front of the church, the Café and Cabaret La Boheme remind visitors that the community was a haunt of the bohemian crowd in the 19th and early 20th centuries. The artist-filled place du Tertre awaits.

3. Bohemian Montmartre—Place du Tertre: In 1800 a

wall separated Paris from this village on the hill. You had to pay a toll to get in. Montmartre was a mining community (the local gypsum was the original plaster of Paris) where the wine flowed cheap and easy. Life here was a working-class festival of cafés, bistros, and dance halls. Painters came here for the ruddy charm, the light, and the low rents. In 1860 Montmartre was annexed in to the growing city of Paris. The "bohemian" ambience survived and attracted sophisticated Parisians ready to get down and dirty in the belle epoque of cancan.

Lined with cafés and filled with artists, hucksters, and tourists, the scene mixes charm and kitsch in ever-changing proportions. The place du Tertre artists, who at times outnumber the tourists, are the great-great-grandkids of the Renoirs, van Goghs, and Picassos who once roamed here—poor, carefree, seeking inspiration, and occasionally cursing a world too selfish to bankroll their dreams.

The Syndicat d'Initiative across the square is a tourist office (daily 10:00–19:00). Find it, then turn left and walk along the square.

4. Dalí Museum: Is place du Tertre too surreal? Escape downhill, walking past the Patachou restaurant (great views from its backyard tables, 180F dinner *menu*) into the tiny place du Calvaire for a great view.

Not surreal enough? Turn right, walking past the café Chez Plumeau, and visit the Salvador Dalí Museum. The museum— a beautifully lit black gallery with the right music—offers a walk through statues, etchings, and paintings by Dalí. Don't miss the printed interview on the exit stairs (40F, not covered by museum pass, daily 10:00–18:00, well described in English, 11 rue Poulbot).

Exit the museum to the right, and follow rue Poulbot as it curves to the rue Norvins, the spine and main tourist drag of the community (you'll pass the Butte en Vigne restaurant at #5 rue Poulbot—decent 60F plats du jour and 98F *menus*). Turn left down rue Norvins and walk 20 steps to the crossroads with rue des Saules. The venerable *boulangerie* on the left (dating from 1900) is one of the last surviving bits of the old-time community. From here we'll side trip three blocks down the backside of the *mont*, then return to carry on past the *boulangerie*.

From the boulangerie, walk to the Auberge de la Bonne Franquette on rue des Saules (allow 90F for lunch, 160F for dinner, classic Montmartre ambience and good French onion soup). Stop at its doorway and notice the dome of Sacré-Coeur rising above the rooftops. Painters such as Maurice Utrillo (1883–1955) captured views like this, making the neighborhood famous. Utrillo, the son of a free-spirited single mom, grew up in Montmartre's streets. He fought, broke street lamps, and haunted the cafés and bars, buying drinks with masterpieces.

5. Montmartre Museum: Follow rue des Saules downhill into the less-touristed backside of Montmartre. A right up rue Cortet (just before Maison Rose restaurant) leads up an exclusive street with vine-covered homes to the Montmartre Museum, at #12. Utrillo once lived here with his mom. (Composer Erik Satie lived at #16.) The museum fills eight rooms in this creaky 17th-century manor house with paintings, posters, old photos, music, and memorabilia recreating the traditional cancan and caberet Montmartre scene (25F, not covered by

museum pass, Tue–Sun 11:00–18:00, closed Mon, reasonably well described in English).
• *Return to the rue des Saules and walk downhill past the Maison Rose restaurant one block to Paris' last remaining vineyard.*

6. Clos Montmartre Vineyard: What originally drew artists
to Montmartre was its country charm. With vineyards, wheat fields, windmills, animals, and a village tempo of life, it was the perfect escape from grimy Paris. Today's vineyard is off-limits to tourists except for the annual grape-harvest fest (first Saturday in October), when a thousand costumed locals bring back the boisterous old days and the vineyard's annual production of 300 liters is auctioned off to support local charities.
• *Continue downhill to the foot of the vineyard.*

7. Lapin Agile Cabaret: The faded poster above the door
gives the place its name. A rabbit (*lapin*) makes an agile leap into a pot while balancing a bottle of wine. This was the village's hot spot. Picasso and other artists and writers would gather for "performances" that ranged from serious poetry, dirty limericks, sing-alongs, and parodies of the famous to anarchist manifestos. Once they tied a paintbrush to the tail of the owner's donkey and entered the "abstract painting" that resulted in the Salon— it won critical acclaim and sold for a nice price.

You now have two options. Most will want to walk back up the rue des Saules to the bakery at the top of the hill, where we'll continue our walk. If you have a reserve of energy, 20 extra minutes, and want and see more of Montmartre (including Renoir's home), walk up the rue des Saules and turn right at la Maison Rose. Follow rue de l'Abbreuvoir onto the small walkway at the curve, and you'll pass Renoir's home, at #6. Walk down the steps at the walkway's end then stroll up through the small park (notice the *boules* court). Turn left at the top of the park onto rue Junot, which turns into rue Norvins. The bakery is at the top of rue Norvins.
• *Once reunited at the bakery, we all go downhill (along place Jean Baptiste Clement), hugging the buildings on our left—don't curve right on rue Lepic. Turn right on rue Ravignan and follow it to the "TIM Hôtel." Next door, at 13 place Emile-Goudeau, is Bâteau-Lavoir.*

8. Bâteau-Lavoir, Picasso's Studio: Modern art was
born here in this humble artists' abode, where as many as 10 artists lived and worked. The fading photos in the window show Picasso and the studio where he and his friends Georges Braque and Juan Gris revolutionized art. Sharing paints, ideas, and girlfriends,

they created art, such as Picasso's *Demoiselles d'Avignon*, that shocked the world. Modigliani and the poet Apollinaire also lived here. The original studio burned down in 1970. Picasso wrote, "I know one day we'll return to Bâteau-Lavoir. It was there that we were really happy—where they thought of us as painters, not strange animals."

• *Walk back uphill one short block, turn left on rue d'Orchampt, squirt out the end, and (at rue Lepic and rue d'Orchampt) come face-to-face with a wooden windmill. (Le Montagnard restaurant is uphill 1 block at 102 rue Lepic, offering cozy, country-elegant dining at fair prices.)*

9. Moulin de la Galette:

Only two windmills (*moulins*) remain on a hill that was once dotted with them. Originally, they pressed grapes and crushed stones. When the gypsum mines closed and vineyards became apartments, this one turned into a popular outdoor dance hall. Renoir's *Bal du Moulin de La Galette* (at the Orsay) shows it in its heyday—a sunny Sunday afternoon in the leafy gardens, with ordinary folk dancing, eating, and laughing. Some call it the quintessential Impressionist painting.

• *Rue Lepic winds down the hill. The green-latticed building to your right was part of the Moulin de la Galette. Continue past the main entry of Moulin de la Galette down rue Lepic to the rue Durantin. At this intersection look down rue Tourlaque one block to the building with the tall brick-framed windows and heavy Mansart roof. Toulouse-Lautrec lived here. Continue down rue Lepic and, at # 54, find ...*

10. Van Gogh's House:

In the two short years (1886–1888) he stayed here with his brother, Vincent van Gogh transformed from a gloomy Dutch painter of brown and grey peasant scenes into an inspired visionary with wild ideas and Impressionist colors.

• *Follow the rue Lepic downhill as it makes a hard right just past #42 and continue to place Blanche; check out the horse butcher at #30 as you descend. Notice the happy horses on the price stickers. This leg of the rue Lepic is little changed from when Vincent lived here. Enjoy that notion for the delightful last stretch of rue Lepic before it hits the big street and a big change. On busy place Blanche is the ...*

11. Moulin Rouge:

Ooh la la! The new Eiffel Tower at the 1889 World's Fair was nothing compared to the sight of pretty cancan girls spreading their legs at the newly opened "Red Windmill." The nightclub seemed to sum up the belle epoque, the age of elegance, opulence, sophistication, and worldliness. On most nights, you'd see a small man in a sleek black coat, checked pants, a green scarf, and a bowler hat peering through his pince-nez glasses at the dancers and making sketches of them—Henri de Toulouse-Lautrec. Perhaps he'd order an absinthe, the dense green liqueur that was the toxic muse for so many great and forgotten artists. Toulouse-Lautrec's sketches of dancer Jane Avril and comic La Goulue hang in the Orsay. Walk in and mull over the photos, show options, and prices.

12. Pig Alley: The stretch of boulevard de Clichy from place Blanche eastward (toward Sacré-Coeur) to place Pigalle is the den mother of all iniquities. Plaster of Paris from the gypsum found on this mount was loaded sloppily at place Blanche . . . the white place. Today, sex shops, peep shows, live sex shows, and hotdog stands line the busy boulevard de Clichy. Dildos abound.

Although raunchy now, the area has always been the place where bistros had tax-free status, wine was cheap, and prostitutes roamed free. WWII GIs nicknamed Pigalle "Pig Alley."

End your tour at the place Blanche Métro stop (if you want to skip the raunchiness) or hike through Pigalle, escaping home from the fine Art Nouveau Métro stop, Pigalle.

LOUVRE TOUR

Paris walks you through history in three world-class museums—the Louvre (ancient world to 1850), the Orsay (1850–1914, including Impressionism), and the Pompidou (20th-century to today). Start your art-yssey at the Louvre. The Louvre's collection—more than 30,000 works of art—is a full inventory of Western civilization. To cover the entire collection in one visit is in-Seine. We'll enjoy just three of the Louvre's specialties—Greek sculpture, Italian painting, and French painting.

Orientation

Cost: 45F, 26F after 15:00 and on Sun, free on first Sun of month and for those under 18, covered by museum pass. Tickets good all day; reentry allowed.

Hours: Wed–Mon 9:00–18:00, closed Tue. Open Wed until 21:45. On Mon, part of the museum (the Richelieu wing) is open until 21:45. Galleries start closing 30 minutes early. Closed Jan 1, Easter, May 1, Nov 1, and Dec 25. Crowds are worst on Sun, Mon, Wed, and mornings. Save money by visiting in the afternoon.

Getting There: The Métro stop Palais Royal/Musée du Louvre is closer to the new entrance than the stop called Louvre Rivoli.

There is no grander entry than through the pyramid, but metal detectors create a long line at times. There are several ways to avoid the line. Museum-pass holders can use the group entrance in the pedestrian passageway between the pyramid and rue de Rivoli (facing the pyramid with your back to the Tuileries Gardens, go to your left, which is north; under the arches you'll find the entrance and escalator down). Otherwise, you can enter the Louvre underground from the Carrousel shopping mall, which is connected to the museum. Enter the mall at 99 rue de Rivoli (the door with the red awning) or directly from the Métro

THE LOUVRE–A BIRD'S EYE VIEW

N R I G H T   B A N K

METRO: PALAIS ROYAL
MUSÉE DU LOUVRE

RUE DE RIVOLI

TUILERIES GARDENS

RICHELIEU

ARC DU CARROUSEL

FRENCH + NORTHERN

PEDESTRIAN PASSAGEWAY

FRENCH

METRO: LOUVRE RIVOLI

RUE DE COLIGNY

SULLY
COUR CARRÉE

Entrance →

AXIS VIEW

TUILERIES PALACE (DESTROYED 1852)

LOUIS XIV

ITALIAN + FRENCH

GREEK

RUE L'AMIRAL

DCH

DENON

WINGED VICTORY

CAFES

QUAI DU LOUVRE

PONT ROYAL

CARROUSEL

SEINE   RIVER

DES ARTS

QUAI   VOLTAIRE

L E F T   B A N K

←--TO ORSAY MUSEUM
(15 MIN WALK)

❶ ENTRY TO UNDERGROUND MALL
VIA RESTAURANT CLUSTER

TO
LATIN QUARTER
(15 MIN WALK) →

stop Palais Royal/Musée du Louvre (exit following signs to "Musée du Louvre").

Information: Pick up the free *Louvre Handbook* in English at the information desk under the pyramid as you enter. Tel. 01 40 20 51 51, recorded info tel. 01 40 20 53 17, www.louvre.fr.

Checkrooms: The coat check does not take bags. The bag check is separate from the coat check and may have a much shorter line.

Photography: Photography without a flash is allowed.

Cuisine Art: The underground shopping mall has a dizzying assortment of good-value eateries (up the escalator near the inverted pyramid). There's also a post office, handy tourist office, SNCF train office, glittering boutiques, and the Palais-Royal Métro entrance. Stairs at the far end take you right into the Tuileries Gardens, a perfect antidote to the stuffy, crowded rooms of the Louvre.

Length of Our Tour: Two hours.

Louvre Tours: The 90-minute English-language tours leave six times daily except Sun (35F, tour tel. 01 40 20 52 09). Clever 30F digital audioguides (after ticket booths, at top of stairs) give you a directory of about 130 masterpieces, allowing you to dial a rather

dull commentary on included works as you stumble upon them.
I recommend the free, self-guided tour described below.
Starring: *Venus de Milo*, *Winged Victory*, *Mona Lisa*, Raphael,
Michelangelo, and the French painters.

Surviving the Louvre

Pick up the map at the information
desk under the pyramid as you
enter. The Louvre, the world's
largest museum, fills three wings
in this immense U-shaped palace.
The north wing (Richelieu) houses
French, Dutch, and Northern art.
The east wing (Sully) houses the
extensive French painting collection.

For this tour we'll concentrate on the Louvre's south
wing (Denon), which houses the superstars: ancient Greek sculpture, Italian Renaissance painting, and French neoclassical and
Romantic painting.

Expect changes. The Louvre is in flux for several years as
they shuffle the deck. If you can't find a particular painting, ask
a guard where it is. Point to the photo in your book and ask,
"Où est?" (oo ay).

THE TOUR BEGINS—
GREEK STATUES (600 B.C.–A.D. 1)

Every generation defines beauty differently. For Golden Age
Greeks, beauty was balance, combining opposites in just the

right proportions. They thought that the
human body—especially the female
form—embodied the order they saw in the
universe. In the Louvre, we'll see a series
of "Venuses" throughout history. Their
different poses and gestures tell us about
the people that made them. We'll see how
the idea of beauty (as balance) began in
ancient Greece, how it evolved into Hellenism (tipping the balance from stability
to movement), and then how it resurfaced
in the Renaissance, 2,000 years later.

• *From inside the big glass pyramid, you'll see signs to the three wings.
Head for the Denon wing.*

*Escalate up one floor. After showing your ticket, take the first left
you can, climbing a set of stairs to the brick-ceilinged Salle (Room) 1:
"La Grece preclassique." Enter prehistory.*

——— PRE-CLASSICAL GREECE ———

Pre-Classical Greece

These statues are noble but crude. The Greek Barbie dolls (3000 B.C.) are older than the pyramids, as old as writing itself. These pre-rational voodoo dolls whittle women down to their life-giving traits. Farther along, a woman (*Dame d'Auxerre*) pledges allegiance to stability. Another (*Core*) is essentially a column with breasts. A young naked man (*Couros*) seems to have a gun to his back—his hands at his sides, facing front, with sketchy muscles and a mask-like face. "Don't move."

The early Greeks who admired such statues found stability more attractive than movement. Like their legendary hero, Odysseus, the Greek people had spent generations wandering, war-weary, and longing for the comforts of a secure home. The noble strength and sturdiness of these works looked beautiful.

• *Exit Salle 1 at the far end and climb the stairs one flight. At the top, veer 10-o'clock left, where you'll soon see* Venus de Milo *rising above a sea of heads. As you approach her, turn right into Salle 7 (Salle du Parthenon), where you'll find two carved panels from the Parthenon on the wall.*

Golden Age Greece

The great Greek cultural explosion that changed the course of history happened in a 50-year stretch (around 450 B.C.) in Athens, a Greek town smaller than Muncie, Indiana. They dominated the ancient world through brain, not brawn, and the art shows their love of rationality and order.

In a sense, we're all Greek. Democracy, mathematics, theater, philosophy, literature, and science were practically invented in ancient Greece. Most of the art that we'll see in the Louvre either came from Greece or was inspired by it.

Parthenon Frieze (Fragment de la Frise des Panathenees), c. 440 B.C.

These stone fragments once decorated the exterior of the greatest Athenian temple, the Parthenon. The right panel shows a half-man/half-horse creature sexually harassing a woman. It tells the story of how these rude centaurs crashed a party of humans. But the Greeks fought back and threw the brutes out, just as Athens (metaphorically) conquered its barbarian neighbors and became civilized.

The other relief shows the sacred procession of young girls who marched up the hill every four years with an embroidered veil for the 40-foot statue of Athena, the goddess of wisdom. The maidens, carved in only a few inches of stone, are amazingly realistic—more so than anything we saw in the pre-Classical period. They glide along horizontally (their belts and shoulders all in a line), while the folds of their dresses drape down vertically. The man in the center is relaxed and realistic. Notice the veins in his arm.

Greeks of the Golden Age valued the golden mean—that is, balance. The ideal person was well rounded—an athlete and a bookworm, a lover and a philosopher, a realtor who plays the piano, a warrior and a poet. In art, the balance between timeless stability and fleeting movement made beauty. The maidens' pleated dresses make them look as stable as fluted columns, but their arms and legs step out naturally—the human form is emerging from the stone.

• *Now seek the Goddess of Love. You'll find her floating above a sea of worshiping tourists. It's been said that, among the warlike Greeks, this was the first statue to unilaterally disarm.*

Venus de Milo (Aphrodite), c. 100 B.C.

The *Venus de Milo* (or Goddess of Love from the Greek island of Milos) created a sensation when it was discovered in 1820. Europe

GREEK STATUES

1 - Parthenon Frieze
2 - Venus de Milo
3 - Borghese Gladiator
4 - Melpomene, Muse of Tragedy
5 - Roman detour
6 - **Winged Victory**

was already in the grip of a classical fad, and this statue seemed to sum up all that ancient Greece stood for. The Greeks pictured their gods in human form, telling us they had an optimistic view of the human race.

Most "Greek" statues are actually later Roman copies. This is a rare Greek original. This "epitome of the Golden Age" was actually

sculpted three centuries later, though in the style of the earlier.

Venus de Milo is a harmonious balance of opposites. Venus is stable, resting her weight on one leg (called *contrapposto*, or "counterpose"), yet her other leg is slightly raised, ready to take a step. This slight movement sets her whole body in motion, though she remains perfectly still.

Split *Venus* down the middle (left and right) and see how the two halves balance each other. As she lifts her left leg, her right shoulder droops down. And as her knee points one way, her head turns the other. The twisting pose gives an S-curve to her body (especially noticeable from the back view) that the Greeks and succeeding generations found beautiful.

Other opposites balance as well, like the rough-cut texture of her dress (size 14) that sets off the smooth skin of her upper half. She's actually made from two different pieces of stone plugged together at the hips (the seam is visible). The face is realistic and anatomically accurate, but it's also idealized, a goddess, too generic and too perfect. This isn't any particular woman but Everywoman— all the idealized features that the Greeks found beautiful.

What were her missing arms doing? Several archaeologists' theories are on a plaque nearby. Some say her right arm held her dress while her left arm was raised. Others say she was hugging a man statue or leaning on a column. I say she was picking her navel.

• *This statue is interesting and different from every angle. Remember the view from the back—we'll see it again later. Orbit* Venus. *Make your reentry to Earth as you wander among Greek statues. Try to find even one that's not* contrapposto. *Oh yes, there is one.*

Borghese Gladiator (Guerrier Combattant, Dit Gladiateur Borghese)

We see a fighting gladiator at the peak of action. He blocks a blow with the shield that used to be attached to his left arm while his right hand, weighted with an early version of brass knuckles, prepares to deliver the counterpunch. His striding motion makes a diagonal line from his left foot up his leg, along the body and out the extended arm. It's a dramatic, precariously balanced pose.

This is the motion and emotion of Greece's Hellenistic Age, the time after the culture of Athens was spread around the Mediterranean by Alexander the Great (c. 325 B.C.).

The earlier Golden Age Greeks might have considered this statue ugly. His rippling, knotted muscles are a far cry from the more restrained Parthenon sculptures and the soft-focus beauty of *Venus*. And the statue's off-balance pose leaves you hanging, like an unfinished melody. But Hellenistic Greeks loved these cliff-hanging scenes of real-life humans struggling to make their mark. The artist himself made his mark, signing the work proudly on the tree trunk: "Agasias of Ephesus, son of Dositheos, did this."

• *Before heading upstairs to the* Winged Victory, *find the "Antiquités romaines" and take a . . .*

Roman Detour

The Romans were great conquerors but bad artists. Fortunately for us, they had a huge appetite for Greek statues and made countless copies. They took the Greek style and wrote it in capital letters—like the huge statue of Melpomene, holding the frowning mask of tragic plays.

One area the Romans excelled in was realistic portrait busts, especially of their emperors, who were worshiped as gods on earth. Stroll among the Caesars and try to see the man behind the public persona—Augustus, the first emperor, and his wily wife, Livia; Nero ("Neron"), who burned part of his own city; Hadrian, who popularized the beard; crazy Caligula; the stoic Marcus Aurelius; Claudius of "I" fame; and the many faces of the ubiquitous Emperor Inconnu.

The Roman rooms also contain sarcophagi and an impressive mosaic floor. Weary? Relax with the statues in the Etruscan Lounge.

• *Now ascend the staircase, making a U-turn up to the...*

Winged Victory of Samothrace (Victoire de Samothrace)

This woman with wings, poised on the prow of a ship, once stood on a hilltop to commemorate a great naval victory. Her clothes are windblown and sea-sprayed, clinging to her body like the winner of a wet T-shirt contest. (Notice the detail in the folds of her dress around the navel, curving down to her hips.) Originally her right arm was stretched high celebrating the victory like a Super Bowl champion, waving a "we're-number-one" finger.

This is the *Venus de Milo* gone Hellenistic—a balance of opposites that produces excitement, not grace. As *Victory* strides forward, the wind blows her and her wings back. Her feet are firmly on the ground, but her wings (and missing arms) stretch upward. She is a pillar of vertical strength while the clothes curve and whip around her. These opposing forces create a feeling of great energy, making her the lightest two-ton piece of rock in captivity.

In the glass case nearby is *Victory*'s open right hand, discovered in 1950, a century after the statue itself was unearthed. Also in the case is *Victory*'s finger. When the French discovered this was in Turkey, they negotiated with the Turkish government for rights to it. Considering all the other ancient treasures the French had looted from Turkey in the past, the Turks thought it only appropriate to give France the finger.

• *Enter the octagonal room to the left as you face the* Winged Victory, *with Icarus bungee-jumping from the ceiling. Bench yourself under a window and look out toward the pyramid.*

FRENCH HISTORY
The Louvre as a Palace

The Louvre, a former palace, was built in stages over several centuries. On your right (the east wing) was the original medieval fortress. Next, another palace, the Tuileries, was built 500 yards to the west—in the open area past the pyramid and past the triumphal arch. Succeeding kings tried to connect these two palaces, each one adding another section onto the long, skinny north and south wings. Finally, in 1852, after three centuries of building, the two palaces were connected, creating a rectangular Louvre. Soon after that, the Tuileries Palace burned down during a riot, leaving the U-shaped Louvre we see today.

The glass pyramid was designed by the American architect I. M. Pei. Many Parisians hated the pyramid, like they used to hate another new and controversial structure 100 years ago—the Eiffel Tower.

The plaque above the doorway to the Apollo Gallery (Galerie d'Apollon) explains that France's Revolutionary National Assembly (the same people who brought you the guillotine) founded this museum in 1793. What could be more logical? You behead the king, inherit his palace and art collection, open the doors to the masses, and, Voilà! You've got Europe's first public museum. Major supporters of the museum are listed on the walls—notice all the Rothschilds.

• *Enter the Apollo Gallery ("Galerie d'Apollon").*

Apollo Gallery

The Apollo Gallery gives us a feel for the Louvre as the glorious home of the French kings (before Versailles). Imagine a chandelier-lit party in this room, drenched in stucco and gold leaf, with tapestries of leading Frenchmen and paintings with mythological and symbolic themes.

In the glass case at the far end, you'll find the crown jewels. There's the jewel-studded crown of Louis XV;

the 140-carat Regent Diamond, worn by Louis XV, Louis XVI, and Napoleon; and the dragon-shaped 107-carat Côte de Bretagne Ruby. You'll also see the pearl-and-diamond earrings worn by Napoleon's wife, Josephine, and the golden crown of the pinheaded Empress Eugenie.

In another glass case is the cameo crown of that great champion of democracy, Napoleon—we'll see this crown in a painting later.

The inlaid tables made from marble and semiprecious stones and many other art objects show the wealth of France, Europe's number one power for two centuries.

• *The Italian collection ("Peintures Italiennes") is on the other side of the Winged Victory. Cross to the other side and pause at the two fresco paintings on the wall to the left.*

ITALIAN RENAISSANCE

A thousand years after Rome fell, plunging Europe into the Dark Ages, the Greek ideal of beauty was "reborn" in 15th-century Italy. This was the Renaissance, the cultural revival of ancient art.

In these two frescoes by the Italian Renaissance artist Botticelli, we see echoes of ancient Greece. The maidens, with

their poses, clear sculptural lines, and idealized beauty, are virtual *Venus de Milo*s with clothes. The Renaissance was a time of great optimism, exploration, and liberation, and here we see it in its fresh-faced springtime.

The key to Renaissance painting was realism, and for the Italians "realism" was spelled "3-D." Painters were inspired by the realism and balanced beauty of Greek sculpture.

• *The Italian collection—including* Mona Lisa—*is scattered throughout the next few rooms (Salles 3 & 4), in the long Grand Gallery, and in adjoining rooms. To see the paintings in chronological order may require a little extra shoe leather. When in doubt, show the photo to a guard and ask, "Où est, s'il vous plaît?" (It rhymes.)*

Medieval and Early Italian Renaissance (1300–1500)

Painting a 3-D world on a 2-D surface is tough, and after a millennium of Dark Ages, artists were rusty. Living in a religious age, they painted mostly altarpieces full of saints, angels, Madonnas-and-bambinos, and crucifixes floating in an ethereal gold-leaf heaven. Gradually, though, they brought these other-worldly scenes down to earth.

Painters like Giotto, Fra Angelico, and Uccello broke Renaissance ground by learning to paint realistic, 3-D humans. They placed them in a painted scene with a definite foreground, background, and middle ground to create the illusion of depth. Composition was simple but symmetrically balanced in the Greek style—two angels to the left, two to the right, and so on. Art was a visual sermon, appreciated for its moral message, not its beauty.

• *The long Grand Gallery displays Italian Renaissance painting, some masterpieces, some not.* Mona Lisa *is in a room about halfway down on the right.*

The Grand Gallery

The Grand Gallery was built in the late 1500s to connect the old palace with the Tuileries Palace. From the doorway look to the

far end and consider this challenge: I hold the world's record for the Grand Gallery Heel-Toe-Fun-Walk-Tourist-Slalom—end to end in one minute 58 seconds, two injured. Time yourself—it's a good break, if a bit of a detour. Along the way, notice some of these features of Italian Renaissance painting:

1) Religious: Lots of Madonnas, children, martyrs, and saints.
2) Symmetrical: The Madonnas are flanked by saints, two to the left, two to the right, and so on.
3) Realistic: Real-life human features are especially obvious in the occasional portrait.
4) Three-Dimensional: Every scene gets a spacious setting with a distant horizon.
5) Classical: You'll see some Greek gods and classical nudes, but even Christian saints pose like Greek statues, and Mary is a "Venus" whose face and gestures embody all that was good in the Christian world.

THE GRAND GALLERY

STAIRS DOWN
TO SLAVES

WC

CAFÉ

GRAND

SEINE RIVER

ITALIAN RENAISSANCE

GRAND GALLERY

COURT YARD

SALON DES ETATS

COURT YARD

SALON CARREÉ

ROMAN MOSAIC BELOW

APOLLO GALLERY

SALLE DENON

FRENCH ROMANTICISM
(SALLE MOLLIEN)

1 - BOTTICELLI frescoes
2 - Early Italian
3 - High Renaissance: LEONARDO, RAPHAEL
4 - MONA LISA
5 - High Renaissance: TITIAN, RAPHAEL, etc.

6 - VERONESE: Marriage at Cana
7 - DAVID: Coronation of Napoleon
8 - INGRES: La Grande Odalisque
9 - GERICAULT: Raft of the Medusa
10 - DELACROIX: Liberty Leading the People

FRENCH NEOCLASSICISM
(SALLE DARU)

DCH

Mantegna—*St. Sebastian*

This isn't the patron saint of porcupines. St. Sebastian was a Christian martyr, although here he looks more like a classical Greek statue. Notice the *contrapposto* stance (all of his weight resting on one leg) and the Greek ruins scattered around him. His executioners look like ignorant medieval brutes bewildered by this enlightened Renaissance man. Italian artists were beginning to learn how to create human realism and earthly beauty on the canvas. Let the Renaissance begin.

Italian High Renaissance (1500–1600)

The two masters of Renaissance grace and balance were Raphael and Leonardo da Vinci.

Leonardo was the consummate Renaissance man. Musician, sculptor, engineer, scientist, and sometimes painter, he combined knowledge from all areas to create beauty. If he were alive today, he'd create a Unified Field theory in physics—and set it to music.
• *Look for the following masterpieces by Leonardo and Raphael in the Grand Gallery.*

Leonardo da Vinci—*Virgin, Child, and St. Anne (La Vierge, l'Enfant Jesus, et Sainte Anne)*

Three generations—grandmother, mother, and child—are arranged in a pyramid form with Anne's face as the peak and the lamb as the lower right corner. Within this balanced structure, Leonardo sets the figures in motion. Anne's legs are pointed to our left. (Is Anne *Mona*? Hmm.) Her daughter Mary, sitting on her lap, reaches to the right. Jesus looks at her playfully while turning away. The lamb pulls away from him. But even with all the twisting and turning, this is still a placid scene. It's as orderly as the geometrically perfect universe created by the Renaissance god.

There's a psychological kidney punch in this happy painting. Jesus, the picture of childish joy, is innocently playing with a lamb—the symbol of his inevitable sacrificial death.

The Louvre has the greatest collection of Leonardos in the world—all five of them. Don't miss the neighboring *Madonna of the Rocks* and his androgynous *John the Baptist*.

Raphael—*La Belle Jardinière*

Raphael (roff-eye-ELL) perfected the style Leonardo pioneered. This Madonna, Child, and John the Baptist is also a balanced pyramid with hazy grace and beauty. Mary is a mountain of maternal tenderness (the title translates as "The Beautiful Kindergarten Teacher"), eyeing her son with a knowing look. Jesus looks up innocently, standing *contrapposto* like a chubby Greek statue.

With Raphael, the Greek ideal of beauty reborn in the Renaissance reached its peak. His work spawned so many imitators who

cranked out sickly sweet generic Madonnas that we often take
him for granted. Don't. This is the real thing.

While the *Jardinière* has an idealized beauty, Raphael could
deliver photo-realism, too. See his portrait of black-hatted,
clear-eyed Balthazar Castiglione.

• *Have a seat and prepare for the* Mona Lisa *mob scene. Best to read
ahead here. Then follow the crowds and signs to* Mona Lisa *in the
Salle des Etats.*

Leonardo da Vinci—*Mona Lisa*

Leonardo was already an old man when François I invited him to
France. Determined to pack light, he took only a few paintings

with him. One was a portrait of a Lisa del
Giocondo, the wife of a wealthy Florentine
merchant. When he arrived, François
immediately fell in love with the painting,
making it the centerpiece of the small collection of Italian masterpieces that would,
in three centuries, become the Louvre
museum. He called it *La Gioconda*. We
know it as a contraction of the Italian for
"my lady Lisa"—*Mona Lisa*.

Advance warning: *Mona* may disap-
point you. She's smaller than you'd expect,
darker, engulfed in a huge room, and hidden behind a glaring
pane of glass. So, you ask, "Why all the hubbub?" Let's take a
closer look. Like any lover, you've got to take her for what she is,
not what you'd like her to be.

The famous smile attracts you first. Leonardo used a hazy
technique called *sfumato*, blurring the edges of *Mona*'s mysterious
smile. Try as you might, you can never quite see the corners of
her mouth. Is she happy? Sad? Tender? Or is it a cynical super-
model's smirk? Every viewer reads it differently, projecting his
own mood onto *Lisa*'s enigmatic face. *Mona* is a Rorschach
inkblot... so how are you feeling?

Now look past the smile and the eyes that really do follow
you (most eyes in portraits do) to some of the subtle Renaissance
elements that make this work work. The body is surprisingly
massive and statuelike, a perfectly balanced pyramid turned
at an angle so that we can see its mass. Her arm is resting lightly
on the chair's armrest almost on the level of the frame itself,
like she's sitting in a window looking out at us. The folds of
her sleeves and her gently folded hands are remarkably realistic
and relaxed. The typical Leonardo landscape shows distance
by getting hazier and hazier.

The overall mood is one of balance and serenity, but there's also an element of mystery. Her smile and long-distance beauty are subtle and elusive, tempting but always just out of reach, like strands of a street singer's melody drifting through the Métro tunnel. *Mona* doesn't knock your socks off, but she winks at the patient viewer.

• *Near* Mona *look for . . .*

Titian—*Pastoral Symphony (Le Concert Champêtre)*

Venus enters the Renaissance in this colorful work by Titian the Venetian (they rhyme). The nymph turning toward the well at left is like a Titian reconstruction of the *Venus de Milo*, but what a difference! The Greek Venus was cold and virginal, but these babes are hot, voluptuous, sensual. The two couples are "making music," if you catch my drift.

The three figures on the grass form a pyramid, giving the scene a balanced, classical beauty, but this appeals more to the senses than to the mind. The golden glow of the skin, the ample flesh, and the hazy outlines became the standard of female nudes for centuries. French painters, especially, learned from Titian's rich colors and sensual beauty.

• *The huge canvas at the far end of the Salle des États is . . .*

Veronese—*Marriage at Cana*

Stand 10 steps away from this enormous canvas to where it just fills your field of vision, and suddenly . . . you're in a party! Pull up a glass of wine. This is the Renaissance love of beautiful things gone hog-wild. Venetian artists like Veronese painted the good life of rich, happy-go-lucky Venetian merchants.

In a spacious setting of Renaissance architecture we see colorful lords and ladies decked out in their fanciest duds, feasting on a great spread of food and drink while the musicians fuel the fires of good fun. Servants prepare and serve the food, jesters play, and animals roam. In the upper left, a dog and his master look on. A sturdy line-backer in yellow pours wine out of a jug, while nearby a ferocious cat battles a lion. The man in white samples some wine and thinks, "Hmm, not bad." The wedding couple at the far left is almost forgotten.

Believe it or not, this is a religious work showing the wedding celebration where Jesus turned water into wine. And there's Jesus in the dead center of 130 frolicking figures, wondering if maybe wine coolers might not have been a better choice. With true Renaissance optimism, Venetians pictured Christ as a party animal, someone who loved the created world as much as they did.

Now, let's hear it for the band! On bass—the bad cat with the funny hat—Titian the Venetian! And joining him on viola—Crazy Veronese!

• *Exit behind the* Marriage at Cana *into the Salle Denon. The dramatic Romantic room is to your left, and the grand neoclassical room is to your right. They feature the most exciting French canvases in the Louvre. In the neoclassical room, kneel before the largest canvas in the Louvre.*

FRENCH PAINTING—NEOCLASSICAL (1780–1850)

J. L. David—*The Coronation of Napoleon*

France's last kings lived in a fantasy world, far out of touch with the hard lives of their subjects. The people revolted, and this decadent world was decapitated—along with the head of state, Louis XVI. Then, after a decade of floundering under an inefficient revolutionary government, France was united by a charismatic, brilliant, temperamental upstart general who kept his feet on the ground, his eyes on the horizon, and his hand in his coat—Napoleon Bonaparte.

Napoleon quickly conquered most of Europe and insisted on being made emperor (not merely king) of this "New Rome." He staged an elaborate coronation ceremony in Paris. The painter David (dah-veed) recorded it for posterity.

We see Napoleon holding aloft the crown—the one we saw in the Apollo Gallery. He has just made his wife, Josephine, the empress, and she kneels at his feet. Seated behind Napoleon is the pope, who journeyed from Rome to place the imperial crown on his head. But Napoleon felt that no one was worthy of the task. At the last moment, he shrugged the pope aside, grabbed the crown, held it up for all to see... and crowned himself. The pope looks p.o.'d.

The radiant woman in the gallery in the background center wasn't actually there. Napoleon's mother couldn't make it to see her boy become the most powerful man in Europe, but he had her painted in anyway. (There's a key on the frame telling who's who in the picture.)

The traditional place of French coronations was the ultra-Gothic Notre-Dame cathedral. But Napoleon wanted a setting that would reflect the glories of Greece and the grandeur of Rome. So interior decorators erected stage sets of Greek columns and Roman arches to give the cathedral the architectural political correctness you see in this painting. (The *Pietà* statue on the right edge of the painting is still in Notre-Dame today.)

David was the new republic's official painter and propagandist, in charge of costumes, flags, and so on for all public ceremonies and spectacles. (Find his self-portrait in the *Coronation*, way up in the second balcony, far right, with the curly gray hair.) His "neoclassical" style influenced French fashion. Take a look at his *Madame Juliet Récamier* portrait nearby, showing a modern Parisian woman in ancient garb and Pompeii hairstyle reclining on a Roman couch. Nearby paintings such as *The Death of Socrates* and the *Oath of the Horatii (Le Serment des Horaces)* are fine examples of neoclassicism, with Greek subjects, patriotic sentiment, and a clean, simple style.

Ingres—*La Grande Odalisque*

Take *Venus de Milo*, turn her around, lay her down, and stick a hash pipe next to her and you have the *Grande Odalisque*. OK, maybe you'd have to add a vertebra or two.

Using clean, polished, sculptural lines, Ingres (ang-gruh, with a soft "gruh") exaggerates the S-curve of a standing Greek nude. As in the *Venus de Milo*, rough folds of cloth set off her smooth

skin. The face, too, has a touch of *Venus'* idealized features (or like Raphael's kindergarten teacher), taking nature and improving on it. Contrast the cool colors of this statuelike nude with Titian's golden girls. Ingres preserves *Venus'* backside for posterior—I mean, posterity.

• *Cross back through the Salle Denon and into a room gushing with...*

ROMANTICISM (1800–1850)

Géricault—*The Raft of the Medusa* (*Le Radeau de la Méduse*)

Not every artist was content to copy the simple, unemotional style of the Golden Age Greeks. Like the ancient Hellenists, they wanted to express motion and emotion. In the artistic war between hearts and minds, the heart style was known as Romanticism. It was the complete flip side of neoclassicism, though they both flourished in the early 1800s.

What better setting for an emotional work than a shipwreck? This painting was based on the actual sinking of the ship *Medusa* off the coast of Africa. The survivors barely did, floating in open seas on a raft, suffering hardship and hunger, even resort-ing to cannibalism—all the exotic elements for a painter deter-mined to shock the public and arouse their emotions.

That painter was young Géricault (zher-ee-ko). He'd honed his craft sketching dead bodies in the morgue and the twisted faces of lunatics in asylums. Here he paints a tangle of bodies and lunatics sprawled over each other. The scene writhes with agitated, ominous motion—the ripple of muscles, churning clouds, and choppy seas. On the right is a deathly green corpse sprawled over-board. In the face of the man at left cradling a dead body, we see the despair of spending weeks stranded in the middle of nowhere.

But wait. There's a stir in the crowd. Someone has spotted something. The bodies rise up in a pyramid of hope culminating in a waving flag. They wave frantically trying to catch the atten-tion of the tiny ship on the horizon, their last desperate hope... which did finally save them. Géricault uses rippling movement and powerful colors to catch us up in the excitement. If art controls your heartbeat, this is a masterpiece.

Delacroix—*Liberty Leading the People* (*La Liberté Guidant le Peuple*)

France is the symbol of modern democracy. They weren't the first (America was), nor are they the best working example of it, but they've had to work harder to achieve it than any other country. No sooner would they throw one king or dictator out than they'd get another. They're now working on their fifth republic.

In this painting, the year is 1830. The Parisians have taken to the streets once again to fight royalist oppressors. There's a hard-bitten proletarian with a sword (far left), an intellectual with a top hat and a sawed-off shotgun, and even a little boy brandishing pistols.

Leading them on through the smoke and over the dead and dying is the figure of Liberty, a strong woman waving the French flag. Does this symbol of victory look familiar? It's the *Winged Victory*, wingless and topless.

To stir our emotions, Delacroix uses only three major colors—the red, white, and blue of the French flag.

This symbol of freedom is a fitting tribute to the Louvre, the first museum ever opened to the common rabble of humanity. The good things in life don't belong only to a small wealthy part of society, but to everyone. The motto of France is "Liberté, Egalité, Fraternité"—liberty, equality, and the brotherhood of all.
• *Exit the room at the far end (past the café) and go downstairs, where you'll bump into the bum of a large, twisting male nude looking like he's just waking up after a thousand-year nap.*

Michelangelo Buonarotti—*Slaves, c. 1513*

These two statues by earth's greatest sculptor are a fitting end to this museum—works that bridge the ancient and modern worlds. Michelangelo, like his fellow Renaissance artists, learned from the Greeks. The perfect anatomy, twisting poses, and idealized faces look like they could have been done 2,000 years earlier.

The so-called *Dying Slave* (also called the Sleeping Slave, who looks like he should be stretched out on a sofa) twists listlessly against his T-shirt-like bonds, revealing his smooth skin. Compare the polished detail of the rippling, bulging left arm with the sketchy details of the face and neck. With Michelangelo, the body does the talking. This is probably the most sensual nude ever done by the master of the male body.

The *Rebellious Slave* fights against his bondage. His shoulders turn one way while his head and leg turn the other, straining to get free. He even seems to be trying to free himself from the rock he's made of. Michelangelo said that his purpose was to carve away the marble to reveal the figures God put inside. This *Slave* shows the agony of that process and the ecstasy of the result.
• Finished? I am. *Où est la sortie?*

ORSAY
TOUR

The Musée d'Orsay (mew-zay dor-say) houses French art of
the 1800s (specifically, art from 1848–1914), picking up where
the Louvre leaves off. For us, that means Impressionism, the
art of sun-dappled fields, bright colors, and crowded Parisian
cafés. The Orsay houses the best general collection of Manet,
Monet, Renoir, Degas, van Gogh, Cézanne, and Gauguin anywhere. If you like Impressionism, visit this museum. If you
don't like Impressionism, visit this museum. I personally find
it a more enjoyable and rewarding place than the Louvre. Sure,
ya gotta see *Mona* and *Venus de Milo*, but after you get your
gottas out of the way, enjoy the Orsay.

Orientation

Cost: 40F, 30F on Sun and for ages 18 to 25 and over 60,
free for youth under 18 and for anyone first Sun of month;
covered by museum pass. Tickets are good all day. Museum-
pass holders can enter to the left of the main entrance.

Hours: Tue–Sat 10:00–18:00, Thu until 21:45, Sun 9:00–18:00,
closed Mon. June 20–Sept 20 the museum opens at 9:00. Last
entrance 45 minutes before closing. Galleries start closing
30 minutes early. Note: The Orsay is crowded on Tue, when
the Louvre is closed.

Getting There: Directly at the RER-C stop called Musée d'Orsay.
The nearest Métro stop is Solferino, three blocks south of the
Orsay. From the Louvre, it's a 15-minute walk across the river
and downstream (west) to the Orsay.

Information: The booth near the entrance gives free floor plans
in English (tel. 01 40 49 48 48).

Photography: Photography without a flash is allowed.

Cuisine Art: The elegant second-floor restaurant has a buffet salad bar. A simple fourth-floor café is sandwiched between the Impressionists.

Length of Our Tour: Two hours.

Orsay Tours: English-language tours usually run daily except Sunday at 11:30. The 90-minute tours cost 36F and are available on audioguide (30F). I recommend the free, self-guided tour described below.

Starring: Manet, Monet, Renoir, Degas, van Gogh, Cézanne, and Gauguin.

Gare d'Orsay: The Old Train Station

• *Pick up the free English map at the info desk, buy your ticket, and check bags to the right. Belly up to the stone balustrade overlooking the main floor and orient yourself.*

Trains used to run right under our feet down the center of the gallery. This former train station, or *gare*, barely escaped the wrecking ball in the 1970s when the French realized it'd be a great place to house their enormous collections of 19th-century art scattered throughout the city.

The main floor has early 19th-century art (as usual, Conservative on the right, Realism on the left). Upstairs (not visible from here) is the core of the collection—the Impressionist rooms. Finally, we'll end the tour with "the other Orsay" on the mezzanine level you see to the left. Clear as Seine water? *Bon.*

THE ORSAY'S 19TH "CENTURY" (1848–1914)

Einstein and Geronimo. Abraham Lincoln and Karl Marx. The train, the bicycle, the horse and buggy, the automobile, and the balloon. Freud and Dickens. Darwin's *Origin of Species* and the Church's Immaculate Conception. Louis Pasteur and Billy the Kid. V. I. Lenin and Ty Cobb.

The 19th century was a mix of old and new side by side. Europe was entering the modern Industrial Age, with cities, factories, rapid transit, instant communication, and global networks. At the same time it clung to the past with traditional, rural—almost medieval—attitudes and morals.

According to the Orsay, the "19th century" began in 1848 with the socialist and democratic revolutions (Marx's *Communist Manifesto*). It ended in 1914 with the pull of an assassin's trigger, igniting World War I and ushering in the modern world.

—— ORSAY GROUND FLOOR—OVERVIEW ——

The museum shows art that is also both old and new, conservative and revolutionary. We'll start with the Conservatives and early rebels on the ground floor, then head upstairs to see how a few visionary young artists bucked the system and revolutionized the art world, paving the way for the 20th century.

• *Walk down the steps to the main floor, a gallery filled with statues.*

Conservative Art

No, this isn't ancient Greece. These statues are from the same century as the Theory of Relativity. It's the Conservative art of the French schools that was so popular throughout the 19th century. It was popular because it's beautiful. The balanced poses, the perfect anatomy and sweet faces, the curving lines, the gleaming white stone—all this is very beautiful. (I'll be bad-mouthing it later, but for now appreciate the exquisite craftsmanship of this "perfect" art.)

• *Take your first right into the small Room 1, marked "Ingres." Look for a nude woman with a pitcher of water.*

Ingres—*The Source (La Source)*

Let's start where the Louvre left off. Ingres (ang-gruh, with a soft "gruh"), whose works help cap the Louvre collection, championed a neoclassical style. *The Source* is virtually a Greek statue on canvas. Like *Venus de Milo*, she's a balance of opposite motions—her hips tilt one way, her breasts the other; one arm goes up, the other down; the fluid curve of her body is matched by the water falling from the pitcher.

Ingres worked on this over the course of 35 years and considered it his "image of perfection." Famous in its day, *The Source* influenced many artists whose classical statues and paintings are in the Orsay gallery.

In this and the next few rooms you'll see more of these visions of idealized beauty—nude women in languid poses, Greek myths, and so on. The "Romantics," like Delacroix, added bright colors, movement, and emotion to the classical coolness of Ingres.

• *Walk uphill (quickly, this is background stuff) to the last room, with a pastel blue-green painting.*

Cabanel—*Birth of Venus (Naissance de Venus)*

This goddess is a perfect fantasy, an orgasm of beauty. The Love Queen stretches back seductively, recently birthed from the ephemeral foam of the wave. This is art of a pre-Freudian society,

when sex was dirty and mysterious and had to be exalted into a more pure and divine form. The sex drive was channeled into an acute sense of beauty. French folk would literally swoon in ecstasy before these works of art.

Get a feel for the ideal beauty and refined emotion of these Greek-style works. You'll find a statue with a pose similar to Venus' back out in the gallery. Go ahead, swoon. If it feels good, enjoy it.

• *Now, take a mental cold shower, grab a bench in the main gallery of statues, and read on.*

Academy and Salon

Who liked this stuff? The art world was dominated by two conservative institutions: the Academy (the state art school) and the Salon, where works were exhibited to the buying public.

Now let's literally cross over to the "wrong side of the tracks," to the art of the early rebels.
• *Head back toward the entrance and turn right into Room 4, marked "Daumier" (opposite the Ingres room).*

REALISM—EARLY REBELS
Daumier—36 Caricature Busts (Ventre Legislatif)
This is a liberal's look at the stuffy bourgeois establishment that controlled the Academy and the Salon. In these 36 bustlets, Daumier, trained as a political cartoonist, exaggerates their most distinct characteristic to capture

with vicious precision the pompos-ity and self-righteousness of these self-appointed arbiters of taste. The labels next to the busts give the name of the person being cari-catured, his title or job (most were members of the French parlia-ment), and an insulting nickname (like "gross, fat, and satisfied" and Monsieur "Platehead"). Give a few nicknames yourself. Can you find Reagan, Clinton, Yeltsin, Thatcher, and Gingrich?

These people hated what you're about to see. Their prudish faces tightened as their fantasy world was shattered by the Realists.
• *Go uphill four steps and through a few romantic and pastoral rooms to the final room, #6.*

Millet—*The Gleaners (Les Glaneuses)*
Millet (mee-yay) shows us three gleaners, the poor women who pick up the meager leavings after a field has already been harvested by the wealthy. Millet grew up on a humble farm. He didn't attend the Academy and hated the uppity Paris art scene. Instead of idealized gods, goddesses, nymphs, and winged babies, he painted simple rural scenes. He was strongly affected by the Revo-lution of 1848, with its affirmation of the working class. Here he

captures the innate dignity of these stocky, tanned women who work quietly in a large field for their small reward.

This is "Realism" in two senses. It's painted "real"-istically, unlike the prettified pastels of Cabanel's *Birth of Venus*. And it's

REALISM—THE REBELS

ESCALATOR
UP TO IMPRESSIONISM

MANET

CONSERVATIVE ART

DCH

1 - INGRES: The Source
2 - CABANEL: Birth of Venus
3 - DAUMIER: 36 Caricature Busts
4 - MILLET: The Gleaners
5 - COURBERT: The Painter's Studio
6 - COUTURE: The Romans of Fall
7 - MANET: Olympia
8 - Opera Exhibit

the "real" world—not the fantasy world of Greek myth, but the harsh life of the working poor.

• *Swoon briefly back out into the main gallery and hang a U-turn left, climbing the steps to a large alcove with two huge canvases. On the left...*

Courbet—*The Painter's Studio (L'Atelier du Peintre)*

In an age when "Realist painter" was equated with "bomb-throwing Socialist," it took great courage to buck the system. Rejected by the so-called experts, Courbet (coorbay) held his own one-man exhibit. He built a shed in the middle of Paris, defiantly hung his art out, and basically "mooned" the shocked public.

Here we see Courbet himself in his studio, working diligently on a Realistic landscape, oblivious to the confusion around him. Looking on are ordinary citizens (not Greek heroes), a nude model (not a goddess but a woman), and a little boy with an adoring look on his face. Perhaps it's Courbet's inner child admiring the artist who sticks to his guns, whether it's popular or not.

• *Return to the main gallery. Back across the tracks, the huge canvas you see is . . .*

Couture—*The Romans of the Fall (Les Romains de la Décadence)*

We see a *fin de siècle* (end-of-century) society that's stuffed with too much luxury, too much classical beauty, too much pleasure; it's wasted, burned-out, and in decay. The old, backward-looking order was about to be slapped in the face.

• *Continue up the gallery, then left into Room 14 ("Manet, avant 1870"). Find the reclining nude.*

Manet—*Olympia*

"This brunette is thoroughly ugly. Her face is stupid, her skin cadaverous. All this clash of colors is stupefying." So wrote a critic when Edouard Manet's nude hung in the Salon. The public hated it, attacking Manet (man-nay) in print and literally attacking the canvas.

Think back on Cabanel's painting, *The Birth of Venus*—an idealized, pastel, Vaseline-on-the-lens beauty. Cabenel's nude was soft-core pornography, the kind you see selling lingerie and perfume. The public lapped it up (and Napoleon III purchased it).

Manet's nude doesn't gloss over anything. The pose is classic, used by Titian, Goya, and countless others. But the sharp outlines and harsh contrasting colors are new and shocking. Her hand is a clamp, and her stare is shockingly defiant, with not a hint of the seductive, hey-sailor look of most nudes. This prostitute, ignoring the flowers sent by her last customer, looks out to us as if to say "next." Manet replaced soft-core porn with hard-core art.

Manet had an upper-class upbringing, some formal art training, and he had been accepted by the Salon. He could have cranked out pretty nudes and been a successful painter. Instead he surrounded himself with a group of young artists experimenting with new techniques. With his reputation and strong personality, he was their master, though he learned equally from them. Let the Impressionist revolution begin.

• *Continue to the end of the gallery. Before taking the covered escalator up to the often-crowded Impressionist rooms, take a break and read ahead. Or you could visit the exhibit near the escalator.*

Opera Exhibit

Expand to 100 times your size and hover over a scale model section of the city. There's the 19th-century Garnier Opera House with its green roof in a diamond-shaped block in the center.

You'll also see a cross-section model of the Opera House. You'd enter from the right end, buy your ticket in the foyer, then move into the entrance hall with its grand staircase, where you could see and be seen by *tout* Paris. At curtain time, you'd find your seat in the golden auditorium, topped by a glorious painted ceiling. (The current ceiling, done by Marc Chagall, is even more wonderful than the model.) Notice that the stage is as big as the seating area, with elaborate riggings to raise and lower scenery. Nearby, there are models of set designs from some famous productions. These days, Parisians enjoy their Verdi and Gounod at the new opera house at place Bastille.

IMPRESSIONISM

The camera threatened to make artists obsolete. A painter's original function was to record reality faithfully like a journalist. Now a machine could capture a better likeness faster than you could say Etch-a-Sketch.

But true art is more than just painting reality. It gives us reality from the artist's point of view, putting a personal stamp on the work. It records not only the scene—a camera can do that—but the artist's impressions of the scene. Impressions are often fleeting, so you have to work quickly.

The Impressionist painters rejected camera-like detail for a quick style more suited to capturing the passing moment. Feeling stifled by the rigid rules and stuffy atmosphere of the Academy, the Impressionists' motto was "out of the studio, into the open air." They grabbed their berets and scarves and took excursions to the country, setting up their easels on riverbanks and hillsides or sketching in cafés and dance halls. Gods, goddesses, nymphs, and fantasy scenes were out; common people and rural landscapes were in.

The quick style and simple subjects were ridiculed and called childish by the "experts." Rejected by the Salon, the Impressionists staged their own exhibition in 1874. They brashly took their name from an insult thrown at them by a critic who laughed at one of Monet's "Impression" of a sunrise. During the next decade, they

EARLY IMPRESSIONISM

exhibited their own work independently. The public, opposed at first, was slowly drawn in by the simplicity, the color, and the vibrancy of Impressionist art.

• *Ride the escalator to the top floor. Take your first left for a commanding view of the Orsay. The second left takes you between a bookshop and a giant "backwards" clock to the art.*

    The Impressionist collection is scattered somewhat randomly through the next 10 or so rooms. Shadows dance and the displays mingle. You'll find nearly all of these paintings, but exactly where they're hung is a lot like their brushwork . . . delightfully sloppy. (If you don't see a described painting, move on. It's either hung farther down or on holiday.) Now, let there be . . .

Impressionism—Manet, Degas, Monet, Renoir

Light! Color! Vibrations! You don't hang an Impressionist canvas—you tether it. Impressionism features light colors, easygoing open-air scenes, spontaneity, broad brush strokes, and the play of light.

The Impressionists made their canvases shimmer by a simple but revolutionary technique. If you mix, say, red, yellow, and blue together you'll get brown, right? But Impressionists didn't bother to mix them. They'd slap a thick brushstroke of yellow down, then a stroke of green next to it, then red next to that. Up close all you see are the three messy strokes, but as you back up . . . *voilà*! Brown! The colors blend in the eye at a distance. But while your eye is saying "bland brown," your subconscious is shouting, "Red! Yellow! Blue! Yes!"

There are no lines in nature. Yet someone in the classical tradition (Ingres, for example) would draw an outline of his subject, then fill it in with color. But the Impressionists built a figure with dabs of paint . . . a snowman of color.

Manet—*Luncheon on the Grass (Le Déjeuner sur l'Herbe)*

Manet really got a rise out of people with this one. Once again the public judged the painting on moral terms rather than artistic ones.

What are these scantily clad women doing with these fully clothed men, they wondered? Or rather, what will they be doing after the last baguette is eaten?

A new revolutionary movement is budding: Impressionism. Notice the messy brushwork of the trees and leaves in the background, and the play of light on the pond in back and filtering through the trees onto the hazy woman stooping behind. And the strong contrasting colors (white skin, black clothes, green grass). And the fact that this is a true out-of-doors painting, not a studio production. The first shot had been fired.

Whistler—*Whistler's Mother* (*Portrait de la Mére de l'Auteur*)

Why so famous? I don't know either. It shouldn't be, of course, but it is. Perhaps because it's by an American, and we see in his mother some of the monumental solidity of our own ancestral moms made tough by pioneering the American wilderness.

Or perhaps because it was so starkly different in its day. In a roomful of golden goddesses, it'd stand out like a fish in a tree. The experts hated it and didn't understand it. (If music is the fear of silence, is art the fear of reality?) The subtitle is "Arrangement in Gray and Black," and the whole point is the subtle variations on dark shades softened by the rosy tint of her cheeks, but the critics kept waiting for it to come out in Colorization.

Degas—*The Dance Class (La Classe de Danse)*

Clearly, Degas loved dance and the theater. (Also catch his statue, *Tiny Dancer, 14 Years Old*, in the glass case.) The play of

stage lights off his dancers, especially the halos of ballet skirts, is made to order for an Impressionist.

Edgar Degas (day-gah) was a rich kid from a family of bankers who got the best classical-style art training. Adoring Ingres' pure lines and cool colors, he painted in the Conservative style. His work was exhibited in the Salon. He gained success and a good reputation, and then...he met the Impressionists.

Degas blends classical lines with Impressionist color and spontaneity. His dancers have outlines, and he's got them in a classic 3-D setting—with the floor lines slanting to the upper right.

So why is Degas an Impressionist? First off, he's captured a candid, fleeting moment, a momentary "impression"—the dancers are tired and bored, at the tail end of a long rehearsal. Look at the girl on the left scratching her back restlessly and the cuddly little bundle of dog in the foreground. Degas loved the unposed "snapshot" effect, catching his models off guard.

Finally, he's got that Impressionistic "fury" of the brush. In *The Dance Class*, look at the bright green bow on the girl with her back to us. Not only are the outlines sketchy, but see how he slopped green paint onto her dress and didn't even say, "*Excusez-moi*."

Degas—*The Glass of Absinthe (Au Café, dit L'Absinthe)*
Degas hung out with low-life Impressionists discussing art, love, and life in the cheap cafés and bars in Montmartre (the original Bohemia-ville). He painted Impressionistic snapshots of everyday people. Here a weary lady of the evening

meets morning with a last lonely coffin-nail drink in the glaring light of a four-in-the-morning café. The pale-green drink forming the center of the composition is that toxic substance absinthe that fueled many artists and burned out many more.

Look across the room at some later works by Manet. The old dog was learning new tricks from his former disciples.
• *The next rooms feature works by two Impressionist masters at their peak, Monet and Renoir. You're looking at the quintessence of Impressionism.*

Monet—*La Gare St. Lazare*
Claude Monet (mo-nay) is the father of Impressionism. He learned from Manet (*a* before *o*) but quickly went beyond even Manet's shocking slabs of colors. Monet fully explored the possibilities of open-air painting and lighter, brighter colors.

He could even make this drab train station glow with reflected light. The sun diffuses through the skylight and mingles

with the steam from the engine. The yellow buildings in the background merge with the blue smoke in the foreground to illuminate an otherwise color-less scene.

Stand a good six feet from the canvas and look at the tall building with the slanted Mansard roof behind the station.

Looks fine? Now get close up. At six inches it's a confusing pile of color blobs. And the smoke is truly "thick." Light on!

Monet—*The Cathedral of Rouen*
(La Cathédrale de Rouen)
Monet went to Rouen, rented a room across from the cathedral, set up his easel... and waited. He wanted to catch "a series of differing impressions" of the cathedral facade at different times of day and year. He often had several canvases going at once. In all he did 30 canvases, and each is unique. The time-lapse series

shows the sun passing slowly across the sky, creating different colored light and shadows. These five are labeled: in the morning, in gray weather, morning sun, full view, full sunlight.

As Monet zeroes in on the play of colors and light, the physical subject—the cathedral—is dissolving. It has become only a rack upon which to hang the light and color. Later artists would boldly throw away the rack, leaving purely abstract modern art in its place.

Monet—Paintings from Monet's Garden at Giverny

One of Monet's favorite places to paint was the garden of his home in Giverny, west of Paris (and worth a visit if you like

Monet more than you hate crowds). You'll find several different views of it along with the painter's self-portrait. The *Blue Water Lilies* is similar to the large and famous water lily paintings in the nearby L'Orangerie Museum (closed for restoration—another reason to return to Paris) across the river in the Tuileries Gardens.

Renoir—*Dance at the Moulin de la Galette (Bal du Moulin de la Galette)*

On Sunday afternoons, working-class folk would dress up and head for the fields on Butte Montmartre (near Sacré-Coeur church) to dance, drink, and eat little cakes (*galettes*) till dark. Renoir

(ren-wah) liked to go there to paint the common Parisians living and loving in the afternoon sun. The sunlight filtering through the trees creates a kaleidoscope of colors, like a 19th-century mirrored ball throwing darts of light on the dancers.

This dappled light is the "impression" that Renoir came away with. He captures it with quick blobs of yellow. Look at the sun-dappled straw hat (right of center) and the glasses (lower right). Smell the powder on the ladies' faces. The painting glows with bright colors.

Even the shadows on the ground, which should be gray or black, are colored a warm blue. As if having a good time was required, even the shadows are caught up in the mood, dancing. Like a photographer who uses a slow shutter speed to show motion, Renoir paints a waltzing blur.

Renoir—*The City Dance/The Country Dance (La Danse à la Ville/La Danse à la Campagne)*

In contrast to Monet's haze of colors, Renoir clung to the more traditional technique of drawing a clear outline, then filling it in.

This two-panel "series" by Renoir shows us his exquisite draftsmanship, sense of beauty, and smoother brushwork. Like Degas, Renoir had classical training and exhibited at the Salon.

Renoir's work is lighthearted with light colors, almost pastels. He seems to be searching for an ideal, the pure beauty we saw on the ground floor. In later years he used more and more red tones as if trying for even more warmth.

• *On the divider in the center of the room, you'll find...*

Pissarro and Others

We've neglected many of the founders of the Impressionist style. Browse around and discover your own favorites. Pissarro is one of mine. His grainy landscapes are more subtle and subdued than the flashy Monet and Renoir, but, as someone said, "He did for the earth what Monet did for the water."

You may find the painting *Young Girl in the Garden (Jeune Fille en Jardin)* with a pastel style as pretty as Renoir's. It's by Mary Cassatt, an American who was attracted to the strong art magnet that was and still is Paris.

• *Take a break. Look at the Impressionist effect of the weather on the Paris skyline. Notice the skylight above you—these Impressionist rooms are appropriately lit by ever-changing natural light. Then carry on...*

POST-IMPRESSIONISM

Take a word, put "-ism" on the end, and you've become an intellectual. Commune-ism, sex-ism, cube-ism, computer-ism... Post-Impression-ism.

"Post-Impressionism" is an artificial and clumsy concept to describe those painters who used Impressionist techniques after Monet and Renoir. It might just as well be called something like

POST-IMPRESSIONISM

"Premodernism," because it bridged Impressionism with the
20th century... or you could call it bridge-ism.

• *The Orsay's Post-Impressionist collection (we'll see van Gogh, Cézanne,
Gauguin, Rousseau, Seurat, and Toulouse-Lautrec) flip-flops back and
forth between here and the end of this gallery. Be prepared to skip around.*

Van Gogh

Impressionists have been accused of being "light"-weights. The
colorful style lends itself to bright country scenes, gardens, sunlight
on the water, and happy crowds of simple people. It took a remarkable genius to add profound emotion to the Impressionist style.

Vincent van Gogh (van-go, or van-HOCK to the Dutch and
the snooty) was the son of a Dutch minister. He too felt a religious
calling, and he spread the gospel among the poorest of the poor—
peasants and miners. When he turned to painting, he channeled
this same spiritual intensity into his work. Like Michelangelo,
Beethoven, Rembrandt, Wayne Newton, and a select handful of
others, he put so much of himself into his work that art and life
became one. In this room you'll see both van Gogh's painting
style and his life unfold.

Van Gogh—*Peasant (Paysanne près de l'Atre)*

As a young man, van Gogh left his steady clerking job to work with poor working people in overcast Belgium and Holland. He painted these hardworking, dignified folks in a crude, dark style reflecting the oppressiveness of their lives...and the loneliness of his own as he roamed northern Europe in search of a calling.

Van Gogh—*Self-Portrait, Paris (Portraite de l'Artiste)*, 1887

Encouraged by his art-dealer brother, van Gogh moves to Paris and, *voilà!* The color! He meets Monet and hobnobs with Gauguin and

Toulouse-Lautrec. He rents a room in Montmartre, learning the Impressionist style. (See how he builds a bristling brown beard using thick strokes of reds and greens side by side.)

At first he paints like the others, but soon he develops his own style. By using thick, swirling brush strokes, he infuses life into even inanimate objects. Van Gogh's brush strokes curve and thrash around like a garden hose pumped with wine.

Van Gogh—*Midday (La Méridienne)*, 1890, based on a painting by Millet

The social life of Paris becomes too much for the solitary van Gogh. He moves to the south of France. At first, in the glow of the bright spring sunshine, he has a period of incredible creativity and happiness, overwhelmed by the bright colors—an Impressionist's dream. Here again we see his love of the common people taking a glowing siesta in the noon sun.

Van Gogh—*Van Gogh's Room at Arles (La Chambre de Van Gogh à Arles)*, 1889

But being alone in a strange country begins to wear on him. An ugly man, he finds it hard to get a date. The distorted perspective of this painting makes his tiny rented room look even more cramped. He invites his friend Gauguin to join him, but after two months together arguing passionately about art, nerves get raw. Van Gogh threatens Gauguin with a knife, driving him back to Paris. In crazed despair, van Gogh mutilates his own ear.

The people of Arles realize they have a madman on their hands and convince van Gogh to seek help. He enters a mental hospital.

Van Gogh—*The Church at Auvers-sur-Oise (L'Église d'Auvers-sur-Oise)*, 1890

Van Gogh's paintings done in the peace of the mental hospital are more meditative—fewer bright landscapes, more closed-in scenes

with deeper and almost surreal colors.

There's also a strong sense of mystery. What's behind this church? The sky is cobalt blue and the church's windows are also blue, like we're looking right through the church to an infinite sky. There's something mysterious lurking on the other side. You can't see it, but you feel its presence like the cold air from an approaching Métro train still hidden in the tunnel. There's a road that leads from us to the church, then splits to go behind. A choice must be made. Which way?

Van Gogh—*Self-Portrait, St. Remy*, 1889

Van Gogh wavered between happiness and madness. He despaired of ever being sane enough to continue painting.

This self-portrait shows a man engulfed in a confused but beautiful world. The background brush strokes swirl and rave, setting in motion the waves of the jacket. He's caught in the current, out of control. But in the midst of this rippling sea of mystery floats a still, detached island of a face with probing, questioning, wise eyes.

Do his troubled eyes know that only a few months later he would take a pistol and put a bullet through his chest?

Cézanne

Cézanne's art brought Impressionism into the 20th century. There's less color here, less swirling brushwork, less passion. It's cleaner, chunkier, more intellectual. Cézanne (say-zahn) can be difficult to appreciate after the warmth of Renoir, and he won't give you the fireworks of van Gogh. But he's worth the effort.

Cézanne—*Self-Portrait (Portrait de l'Artiste)*

Cézanne was virtually unknown and unappreciated in his lifetime. He worked alone, lived alone, and died alone, ignored by all but a few revolutionary young artists who understood his efforts.

And Cézanne couldn't draw. His brush was a blunt instrument. With it, he'd bludgeon reality into submission, drag it across a canvas, and leave it there to dry.

But Cézanne the mediocre painter was a great innovator. His works are not perfected, finished products but revolutionary works-in-progress—gutter balls with wonderful spin. His work spoke for itself—which is good because, as you can see here, he had no mouth.

Cézanne—*Landscape (Rochers près des Grottes au dessus de Château-Noir)*

Cézanne used chunks of color as blocks to build three-dimensional forms. The rocky brown cliffs here consist of cubes of green, tan, and blue that blend at a distance to create a solid 3-D structure. It only makes sense from a distance. Try this: Start at six inches and fade back. At some point the messy slabs become reality on the rocks.

Why is this revolutionary? Past artists created the illusion of 3-D with lines (like when we draw receding lines to turn a square into a cube). The Impressionists pioneered the technique of using blobs of color, not lines, to capture a subject. But most Impressionist art is flat and two-dimensional, a wall of color like Monet's *Cathedral of Rouen* series. Cézanne went 3-D with chunks.

These chunks are like little "cubes." No coincidence that his experiments in reducing forms to their geometric basics influenced the . . . cubists.

Cézanne—*The Card Players (Les Joueurs de Cartes)*

These aren't people. They're studies in color and pattern. The

subject matter—two guys playing cards—is less important than the pleasingly balanced pattern they make on the canvas, two sloping forms framing a cylinder (a bottle) in the center. Later, abstract artists would focus solely on the shapes and colors.

Again, notice how the

figures are built with chunks of color. The jacket of the player to the right consists of tans, greens, and browns. As one art scholar put it: "Cézanne confused intermingled forms and colors, achieving an extraordinarily luminous density in which lyricism is controlled by a rigorously constructed rhythm." Just what I said—chunks of color.

Cézanne—*A Modern Olympia (Une Moderne Olympia)*

Is this Cézanne himself paying homage to Manet? And dreaming up a new, more radical style of painting? We've come a long way since Manet's *Olympia*, which seems tame to us now.

• *Exit to the café and consider a well-deserved break. From the café, continue ahead, walking under the large green beam, following signs saying, "suite de la visite."*
   A hallway leads past WCs to . . .

Redon

Now flip out the lights and step into his mysterious world. If the Orsay's a zoo, this is the nocturnal house. Prowl around. This is wild, wild stuff. It's intense—imagine Richard Nixon on mushrooms playing sax.

• *At cockcrow, pass into the gallery lined with metal columns containing the primitive art of Rousseau and Gauguin. Start in the first alcove to the left.*

PRIMITIVISM

Henri Rousseau—*War (La Guerre ou La Chevauchée de la Discorde)*

Some artists, rejecting the harried, scientific, and rational world, remembered a time before "-isms," when works of art weren't scholarly "studies in form and color" but voodoo dolls full of mystery and magic power. They learned from the art of primitive

tribes in Africa and the South Seas, trying to recreate a primal Garden of Eden of peace and wholeness. In doing so, they created another "ism": Primitivism.

   One such artist was Rousseau, a man who painted

like a child. He was an amateur artist who palled around with all the great painters, but they never took his naive style of art seriously.

This looks like a child's drawing of a nightmare. The images are primitive—flat and simple, with unreal colors—but the effect is both beautiful and terrifying. War in the form of a woman with a sword flies on horseback across the battlefield, leaving destruction in her wake—broken bare trees, burning clouds in the background, and heaps of corpses picked at by the birds.

Gauguin—*The Beautiful Angel (La Belle Angele)*

A woman in peasant dress sits in a bubble like the halos in a medieval religious painting. Next to it is a pagan idol. This isn't a scene but an ordered collage of images with symbolic overtones. It's left to us to make the connection.

Paul Gauguin (go-gan) learned the bright clashing colors from the Impressionists but diverged from this path about the time van Gogh waved a knife in his face.

Gauguin simplifies. His figures are two-dimensional with thick dark outlines filled in with basic blocks of color. He turned his back on the entire Western tradition of realism begun in the Renaissance, which tried to recreate the 3-D world on a 2-D canvas. Instead he returns to an age where figures become symbols.

Gauguin—*Arearea (Pleasantries) (Joyeusetes)*

Gauguin got the travel bug early in childhood and grew up wanting to be a sailor. Instead he became a stockbroker. In his spare time he painted and was introduced to the Impressionist circle. At the age

of 35, he got fed up with it all, quit his job, abandoned his wife (see her stern portrait bust), and took refuge in his art. He traveled to the South Seas in search of the exotic, finally settling on Tahiti.

In Tahiti, Gauguin found his Garden of Eden. He simplified his life to the routine of eating, sleeping, and painting. He simplified his painting still more to flat images with heavy black outlines filled in with bright, pure colors. He painted the native girls in their naked innocence (so different from Cabanel's seductive *Venus*). But this simple style had a deep undercurrent of symbolic meaning.

Arearea shows native women and a dog. In the "distance" (there's no attempt at traditional 3-D here), a procession goes by with a large pagan idol. What's the connection between the idol and the foreground figures who are apparently unaware of it? Gauguin makes us dig deep down into our medulla oblongata to make a mystical connection between the beautiful women, the dog, and religion. In primitive societies, religion permeates life. Idols, dogs, and women are holy.

Seurat—*The Circus (Le Cirque)*

With pointillism, Impressionism is brought to its logical conclusion—little dabs of different colors placed side by side to blend in the viewer's eye. Using only red, yellow, blue, and green points of paint, Seurat (sur-rah) creates a mosaic of colors that shimmers at a distance, capturing the wonder of the dawn of electric lights.

Toulouse-Lautrec—*The Clownesse Cha-U-Kao*

Henri de Toulouse-Lautrec was the black sheep of a noble family. At age 15 he broke both legs, which left him a cripple. Shunned by his family, a freak to society, he felt more at home in the underworld of other outcasts—prostitutes, drunks, thieves, dancers, and actors. He painted the nightlife lowlife in the bars, cafés, dance halls, and brothels he frequented. Toulose-Lautrec died young of alcoholism.

The *Clownesse Cha-U-Kao* is one of his fellow freaks, a fat lady clown who made her living being laughed at. She slumps wearily after a performance, indifferent to the applause, and adjusts her dress to prepare for the curtain call.

Toulouse-Lautrec was a true "impression"-ist, catching his models in candid poses. He worked spontaneously, never correcting his mistakes, as you can see from the blotches on her dark skirt and the unintentional yellow sash hanging down. Can you see a bit of Degas here, in the subject matter, snapshot pose, and colors?

Toulouse-Lautrec—*Jane Avril Dancing*

Toulouse-Lautrec hung out at the Moulin Rouge dance hall in Montmartre. One of the most popular dancers was this slim, graceful, elegant, and melancholy woman who stood out above the rabble of the Moulin Rouge. Her legs keep dancing while her mind is far away. Toulouse-Lautrec the artistocrat might have identified with her noble face—sad and weary of the nightlife, but stuck in it.

• *You've seen the essential Orsay and are permitted to cut out (the exit is straight below you). But there's an "Other Orsay" I think you'll find entertaining.*

To reach the mezzanine ("niveau median"), cross to the other side of the gallery and go down three flights. At the foot of the escalator, the mezzanine (which overlooks the main floor) is to your right. But first, go left to the palatial room of mirrors and chandeliers, marked "Salle des Fêtes" or "Arts et Decors de la IIIème République" (Room 52).

THE "OTHER" ORSAY—MEZZANINE

The beauty of the Orsay is that it combines all the art of the 1800s (1848–1914), both modern and classical, in one building. The classical art, so popular in its own day, has been maligned and was forgotten in the 20th century. It's time for a reassessment. Is it as gaudy and gawdawful as we've been led to believe? From our end-of-century perspective, let's take a look at the opulent, fin de siècle, French high society and its luxurious art.

The Grand Ballroom (Arts et Decors de la IIIème République)

This was one of France's most luxurious nightspots when the Orsay hotel was here. You can easily imagine gowned debutantes and white-gloved dandies waltzing the night away to the music of a chamber orchestra.

Notice:

1) The interior decorating: raspberry marble-ripple ice-cream columns, pastel ceiling painting, gold work, mirrors, and leafy strands of chandeliers.

2) The statue *Bacchante Couchée* sprawled in the middle of the room. Familiar pose? If not, you flunk this tour.

3) The statue *Aurore*, with her canopy of hair, hide-and-seek face, and silver-dollar nipples.

4) The large painting *The Birth of Venus (La Naissance de Venus)* by William Bouguereau. Van Gogh once said: "If I painted

THE OTHER ORSAY

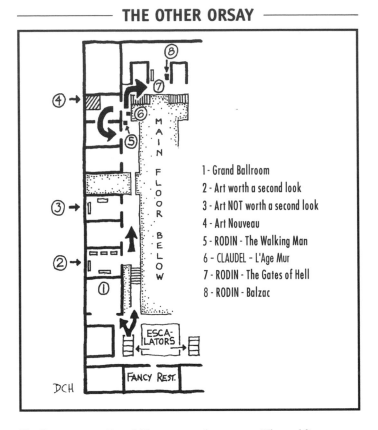

1 - Grand Ballroom
2 - Art worth a second look
3 - Art NOT worth a second look
4 - Art Nouveau
5 - RODIN - The Walking Man
6 - CLAUDEL - L'Age Mur
7 - RODIN - The Gates of Hell
8 - RODIN - Balzac

like Bouguereau, I could hope to make money. The public will never change—they love only sweet things."

5) *La Nature*, with the only see-through veil of marble I've ever seen through.

So here's the question: Is this stuff beautiful or merely gaudy? Divine or decadent?

• *Return to the mezzanine overlooking the main gallery. Head toward the far end. Enter the first room on the left (#55).*

Art Worth a Second Look

We've seen some great art; now let's see some not-so-great art—at least, that's what modern critics tell us. This is realistic art with a subconscious kick, art from a neurotic society before Freud articulated its demons.

• *Working clockwise, you'll see . . .*

Cain

The world's first murderer, with the murder weapon still in his belt, is exiled with his family. Archeologists had recently discovered a Neanderthal skull, so the artist shows them as a pre-historic hunter/gatherer tribe.

The Dream (Le Rêve)

Soldiers sleep, while visions of Gatling guns dance in their heads.

Payday (La Paye des Moissonneurs)

Peasants getting paid, painted by the man called "the grandson of Courbet and Millet." The subtitle of the work should be, "Is this all there is to life?"

The Excommunication of Robert Le Pieux

The bishops exit after performing the rite. The king and queen are stunned, the scepter dropped. The ritual candle has been snuffed out; it falls, fuming, echoing through the huge hall.... Again, is this art or only cheap theatrics?
• *Return to the mezzanine. Skip the next room, then go left into Room 59, labeled "Symbolisme."*

Art Not Worth a Second Look

The Orsay's director said: "Certainly we have bad paintings. But we have only the greatest bad paintings." And here they are.

Serenity

An idyll in the woods. Three nymphs with harps waft off to the right. These people are stoned on something.

The School of Plato (L'École de Platon)

Subtitled "The Athens YMCA." A Christlike Plato surrounded by adoring, half-naked nubile youths gives new meaning to the term

"Platonic relationship."
Will the pendulum shift so that one day art like *The School of Plato* becomes the new, radical avant-garde style?
• *Return to the mezzanine and continue to the far end. Enter the last room on the left (#65) and head for the far corner.*

ART NOUVEAU

The Industrial Age brought factories, row houses, machines, train stations, geometrical precision—and ugliness. At the turn of the century, some artists reacted against the unrelieved geometry of harsh, pragmatic, iron-and-steel Eiffel Tower art with a "new art"—Art Nouveau. Hmm. I think I had a driver's-ed teacher by that name.

Charpentier—*Dining Room of Adrien Benard (Boiserie de la Salle à Mangé de la Propriété Benard)*

Like nature, which also abhors a straight line, Art Nouveau artists used the curves of flowers and vines as their pattern. They were convinced that "practical" didn't have to mean "ugly" as well. They turned everyday household objects into art.

This wood-paneled dining room, with its organic shapes, is one of the finest examples of the Art Nouveau style (called Jugendstil in Germanic countries). Another is the curvy wrought-iron work of some of Paris' early Métro entrances (some survive), built by the same man who commissioned this dining room for his home.

• *Browse through the Art Nouveau rooms to the left. You'll spill out back onto the mezzanine. Grab a seat in front of the Rodin statue of a man missing everything but his legs.*

Auguste Rodin

Rodin completes the tour—from classical sculpture to Impressionist painting to an artist who brought them both together. Rodin combined classical solidity with Impressionist surfaces to become the greatest sculptor since Michelangelo.

Rodin—*The Walking Man (L'Homme Qui Marche)*

This muscular, forcefully striding man could be a symbol of the Renaissance Man with his classical power. With no mouth or hands, he speaks with his body. But Rodin also learned a thing or two from the comparatively lightweight Impressionist painters. Get close and look at the statue's surface. This rough "unfinished" look reflects light like the rough Impressionist brushwork, making the statue come alive, never quite at rest in the viewer's eye.

• *Near the far end of the mezzanine you'll see a small bronze couple* (L'Âge Mur) *by Camille Claudel, a student of Rodin's.*

Claudel—*The Ages of Life (L'Âge Mur)*

Camille Claudel, Rodin's student and mistress, may have portrayed their doomed love affair here. A young girl desperately reaches out to an older man, who is led away reluctantly by an older woman. The center of the composition is the empty space left when their hands separate. In real life, Rodin refused to leave his wife, and Camille (see her head sticking up from a block of marble) ended up in an insane asylum.

Rodin—*The Gates of Hell (Porte de l'Enfer)*

Rodin worked for decades on these doors depicting Dante's Hell, and they contain some of his greatest hits, small statues that he later executed in full size. Find *The Thinker* squatting above the doorway, contemplating Man's fate. And in the lower left is the same kneeling man eating his children (*Ugolin*) you'll see in full size nearby. Rodin paid models to run, squat, leap, and spin around his studio however they wanted. When he saw an interesting pose he'd yell "freeze" (or "statue maker") and get out his sketch pad.

Rodin—*Balzac*

The great French novelist is given a heroic, monumental ugliness. Wrapped in a long cloak, he thrusts his head out at a defiant angle, showing the strong individualism and egoism of the 19th-century Romantic movement. Balzac is proud and snooty—but

his body forms a question mark, and underneath the twisted features we can see a touch of personal pain and self doubt. This is hardly camera-eye realism—Balzac wasn't that grotesque—but it captures a personality that strikes us even if we don't know the man.

From this perch, look over the main floor at all the classical statues between you and the big clock and realize how far we've come— not in years but in style changes. Many of the statues below—beautiful, smooth, balanced, and idealized—were done at the same time as Rodin's powerful, haunting works. Rodin is a good place to end the tour. With a stable base of 19th-century stone, he launched art into the 20th century.

POMPIDOU CENTER TOUR

paris

The Pompidou Center contains possibly Europe's best museum of 20th-century art. After the super-serious Louvre and Orsay, finish things off with an artistic kick in the pants. You won't find classical beauty here, no dreamy Madonnas-and-Children—just a stimulating, offbeat, and, if you like, instructive walk through nearly every art style of the wild and crazy last century.

Orientation

Cost: 30F, covered by museum pass, 18 to 25 and over 65 pay 20F, under 18 and "job seekers" enter free. First Sun of the month is free. Buy tickets on ground floor. Other temporary exhibits require separate admission (or an all-day pass). Audio-guides for the museum cost 25F.

Hours: Wed–Mon 10:00–22:00, closed Tue and May 1.

Getting There: Metro: Rambuteau or Hôtel de Ville. The wild, color-coded exterior makes it about as hard to locate as the Eiffel Tower. To use the escalator to reach the museum (fourth floor), you need a ticket for the museum or a museum pass.

Information: Tel. 01 44 78 12 33, www.centrepompidou.fr. Parisians call the complex the "Centre Beaubourg" (sahn-truh boh-boor), but official publications call it the "Centre Pompidou."

Cloakroom: Ground floor.

Cuisine Art: View restaurant on sixth floor, café on mezzanine level, library cafeteria on second floor. Great café neighborhood.

Length of Our Tour: One hour.

Starring: Matisse, Picasso, Chagall, Dalí, Warhol, contemporary art.

MODERN ART COLLECTION

The "Musée National d'Art Moderne: Collection Permanente" (what we'll see) is on the fourth floor, reached by the escalator to the left as you enter. But there's plenty more art scattered all over the building, some free, some requiring a separate ticket. Ask at the information booth or just wander.

The "permanent" collection...isn't. It changes so often that this chapter is intentionally general—to give you an overview.

• *Buy your ticket on the ground floor, then ride up the escalator (or run up the down-escalator to get in the proper mood) to the fourth floor. When you see the view, your opinion of the Pompidou's exterior should improve a good 15 percent. Enter on the fourth floor and show your ticket. Take the interior stairs to the fifth floor, which covers roughly 1900 to 1970. (The fourth floor brings us up to today.)*

The Exterior

That slight tremor you may feel comes from Italy, where Michelangelo has been spinning in his grave ever since 1977 when the Pompidou Center first revolted Paris. Still, it's an appropriate modern temple for the controversial art it houses.

The building is "exoskeletal" (like Notre-Dame or a crab), with its functional parts—the pipes, heating ducts, and escalator—on the outside, and the meaty art inside. It's the epitome of modern architecture where "form follows function."

MODERN ART FROM 1900 TO 1970 (FIFTH FLOOR)

A.D. 1900: A new century dawns. War is a thing of the past. Science will wipe out poverty and disease. Rational Man is poised at a new era of peace and prosperity...

Right. This cozy Victorian dream was soon shattered by two world wars and rapid technological change. Nietzsche murdered God. Darwin stripped off man's robe of culture and found a naked ape. Freud washed ashore on the beach of a vast new continent inside each of us. Einstein made every truth merely "relative." Even the fundamental building blocks of the universe, atoms, were behaving erratically.

The 20th century—accelerated by technology and fragmented by war—was exciting and chaotic, and the art reflects the turbulence of that century of change.

Henri Matisse (1869–1954)

Matisse's colorful "wallpaper" works are not realistic. A man is a few black lines and blocks of paint. The colors are unnaturally bright. There's no illusion of distance and 3-D that was so important to Renaissance Italians. The "distant" landscape is as bright as things close up, and the slanted lines meant to suggest depth are crudely done.

Traditionally, the canvas was like a window that you looked "through" to see a slice of the real world stretching off into the distance. Now, a camera could do that better. With Matisse, you look "at" the canvas, like wallpaper. *Voilà*! What was a crudely drawn scene now becomes a sophisticated and decorative pattern of colors and shapes.

Though fully "modern," Matisse built on 19th-century art—the bright colors of van Gogh, the primitive figures of Gauguin, the colorful designs of Japanese prints, and the Impressionist patches of paint that only blend together at a distance.

Primitive Masks and Statues

Matisse was one of the Fauves ("wild beasts") who, inspired by African and Oceanic masks and voodoo dolls, tried to inject a bit of the jungle into bored French society. The result? Modern art that looked primitive: long mask-like faces with almond eyes; bright, clashing colors; simple figures; and "flat," two-dimensional scenes.

Cubism: Reality Shattered (1907–1912)

I throw a rock at a glass statue, shatter it, pick up the pieces, and glue them onto a canvas. I'm a Cubist.

Pablo Picasso (1881–1973) and Georges Braque (1882–1963)

Born in Spain, Picasso moved to Paris as a young man, settling into a studio (the Bateau-Lavoir) on Montmartre. He worked with next-door neighbor Georges Braque in poverty so dire they often didn't know where their next bottle of wine was coming from. They corrected each other's paintings (it's hard to tell whose is whose without the titles) and shared ideas, meals, and girlfriends while inventing a whole new way to look at the world.

They show the world through a kaleidoscope of brown and grey. The subjects are somewhat recognizable (with the help of the titles), but they're broken into geometric shards (let's call them "cubes," though there are many different shapes) then pieced back together.

Cubism gives us several different angles of the subject at

once—say, a woman seen from the front and side angles simultaneously, resulting in two eyes on the same side of the nose. This involves showing three dimensions, plus Einstein's new fourth dimension, the Time it takes to walk around the subject to see other angles. Newfangled motion pictures could capture this moving, 4-D world, but how to do it on a 2-D canvas? The Cubist "solution" is a kind of Mercator projection, where the round world is sliced up like an orange peel and laid as flat as possible.

Notice how the "cubes" often overlap. A single cube might contain both an arm (in the foreground) and the window behind (in the background), both painted the same color. The foreground and background are woven together, so that the subject dissolves into a pattern.

Pablo Picasso (1881–1973): Synthetic Cubism (1912–1915) and Beyond

If the Cubists were as smart as Einstein, why couldn't they draw a picture to save their lives? Picasso was one modern artist who could draw exceptionally well (see his partly finished "Harlequin"). But he constantly explored and adapted his style to new trends, becoming the most famous painter of the century. Scattered throughout the museum are works from the many periods of Picasso's life.

Picasso soon began to use more colorful "cubes" (1912–1915). Eventually, he used curved shapes to build the subject, rather than the straight-line shards of early Cubism.

Picasso married and had children. Works from this period (the 1920s) are more realistic, with full-bodied (and big-nosed) women and children. He tries to capture the solidity, serenity, and volume of classical statues.

As his relationships with women deteriorated, he vented his sexual demons by twisting the female body into grotesque balloon-animal shapes (1925–1931).

All through his life, Picasso was exploring new materials. He made collages, tried his hand at making "statues" out of wood, wire, or whatever, and even made statues out of everyday household objects. These "multimedia" works, so revolutionary at the time, have become stock-in-trade today.

Fernand Leger (1881–1955)

Fernand Leger's style has been called "Tubism"—breaking the world down into cylinder shapes rather than cubes. (He supposedly got his inspiration during World War I from the gleaming barrel of a cannon.) Leger captures the feel of the encroaching Age of Machines, with all the world looking like an internal combustion engine.

Marc Chagall (1887–1985)

Marc Chagall, at age 22, arrived in Paris with the wide-eyed
wonder of a country boy. Lovers are weightless with bliss. Animals
smile and wink at us. Musicians, poets, peasants, and dreamers
ignore gravity, tumbling in slow-motion circles high above the
rooftops. The colors are deep, dark, and

earthy—a pool of mystery with figures
bleeding through below the surface.
(Chagall claimed his early poverty forced
him to paint over used canvases, inspiring
the overlapping images.)

Chagall's very personal style fuses
many influences. He was raised in a small
Russian village, which explains his "naive"
outlook and fiddler-on-the-roof motifs.
His simple figures are like Russian Ortho-
dox icons. And his Jewish roots produce
Old Testament themes. Stylistically, he's
thoroughly modern—Cubist shards, bright
Fauve colors, and Primitive simplification.
This otherworldly style was a natural for
religious works, and his murals and stained glass, with both Jewish
and Christian motifs, decorate buildings around the world—
including the ceiling of Paris' Garnier Opéra (Metro: Opéra).

Georges Rouault (1871–1958)

Young Georges Rouault was apprenticed to a stained-glass
window maker. Enough said?

The paintings have the same thick, glowing colors, heavy
black outlines, simple subjects, and (mostly) religious themes.
The style is modern, but the mood is medieval, solemn, and
melancholic. Rouault captures the tragic spirit of those people—
clowns, prostitutes, and sons of God—who have been made
outcasts by society.

Abstract Art

Abstract art simplifies. A man becomes a stick figure. A squiggle
is a wave. A streak of red expresses anger. Arches make you want
a cheeseburger. These are universal symbols that everyone from a
caveman to a banker understands. Abstract artists capture the
essence of reality in a few lines and colors, even things a camera
can't—emotions, abstract concepts, musical rhythms, and spiritual
states of mind. With abstract art, you don't look "through" the
canvas to see the visual world, but "at" it to read the symbolism
of lines, shapes, and colors.

Vassily Kandinsky (1866–1944)

The bright colors, bent lines, and lack of symmetry tell us that Kandinsky's world was passionate and intense.

Notice the titles like "Improvisation" and "Composition." Kandinsky was inspired by music, an art form that's also "abstract" though it still packs a punch. Like a jazz musician improvising a new pattern of notes from a set scale, Kandinsky plays with new patterns of related colors, looking for just the right combination. Using lines and color, Kandinsky translates the unseen reality into a new medium... like lightning crackling over the radio. Go man, go.

Piet Mondrian (1872–1944)

Like blueprints for modernism, Mondrian's T-square style boils painting down to its basic building blocks (black lines, white canvas) and the three primary colors (red, yellow, and blue) arranged in orderly patterns.

(When you come right down to it, that's all painting ever has been. A schematic drawing of, say, the *Mona Lisa*, shows that it's less about a woman than about the triangles and rectangles she's composed of.)

Mondrian started out painting realistic landscapes of the orderly fields in his native Holland. Increasingly, he simplified it into horizontal and vertical patterns. For Mondrian, heavy into Eastern mysticism, "up vs. down" and "left vs. right" were the perfect metaphors for life's dualities: "good vs. evil," "body vs. spirit," "man vs. woman." The canvas is a bird's-eye view of Mondrian's personal landscape.

Constantin Brancusi (1876–1957)

Brancusi's curved, shiny statues reduce things to their essence. A bird is a single stylized wing, the one feature that sets it apart from other animals. He rounds off to the closest geometrical form, so a woman's head is a perfect oval on a cubic pedestal.

Humans love symmetry (maybe because our own bodies are roughly symmetrical), finding geometric shapes restful, even worthy of meditation. Brancusi follows the instinct for order that has driven art from earliest times, from circular Stonehenge to Egyptian pyramids to Greek columns to Roman arches to Renaissance symmetry to the American Indian medicine "wheel."

Paul Klee (1879–1940)
Paul Klee's small and playful canvases are deceptively simple, containing shapes so basic they could be read like universal symbols. Klee thought a wavy line, for example, would always suggest motion, and a stick-figure would always mean a human (like the psychologist Carl Jung's universal dream symbols, part of our "collective unconscious").

Klee saw these universals in the art of children, who express themselves without censoring or cluttering things up with learning. His art has a childlike playfulness and simple figures, painted in an uninhibited frame of mind.

Klee also turned to nature. The same forces that cause the wave to draw a line of foam on the beach can cause a meditative artist to draw a squiggly line of paint on a canvas. The result is a universal shape. The true artist doesn't just paint Nature, he becomes Nature.

Design: Chairs by Rietveld and Alvar Aalto
Hey, if you can't handle modern art, sit on it! (Actually, don't.) The applied arts—chairs, tables, lamps, and vases—are as much a part of the art world as the fine ones. (Some say the first art object was the pot.) As machines became as talented as humans, artists embraced new technology and mass production to bring beauty to the masses.

Robert and Sonia Delaunay
This husband-and-wife team's colorful, fragmented canvases (including a psychedelic Eiffel Tower) prove that the modern style does not have to be ugly or puzzling.

World War I: The Death of Values
Ankle-deep in mud, a soldier shivers in a trench, waiting to be ordered "over the top." He'll have to run through barbed wire, over fallen comrades, and into a hail of machine-gun fire, only to capture a few hundred yards of meaningless territory that will be lost the next day. This soldier was not thinking about art.

World War I left 9 million dead. (During the war, France often lost more men in a single day than America lost in all of Vietnam.) The war also killed the optimism and faith in mankind that had guided Europe since the Renaissance. Now, rationality just meant scheming, technology meant machines of death, and morality meant giving your life for an empty cause.

Expressionism: Kirchner, Beckmann, Grosz, Soutine, Dix, and Kokoschka
Cynicism and decadence settled over post-War Europe. Artists "expressed" their disgust by showing a distorted reality that

emphasized the ugly. Using the lurid colors and simplified figures of the Fauves, they slapped paint on in thick brushstrokes, depicting a hypocritical, hard-edged, dog-eat-dog world that had lost its bearings. The people have a haunted look in their eyes, the fixed stare of corpses and of those who have to bury them.

Dada: Duchamp's Urinal (1917)

When they could grieve no longer, they turned to its giddy twin, laughter. The war made all old values a joke, including artistic ones. The Dada movement, choosing a purposely childish name, made art that was intentionally outrageous: a moustache on the *Mona Lisa*, a shovel hung on a wall, or a modern version of a Renaissance "fountain"—a urinal (by either Marcel Duchamp or I. P. Freeley, 1917). It was a dig at all the pompous prewar artistic theories based on the noble intellect of Rational Women and Men. While the experts ranted on, Dadaists sat in the back of the class and made cultural fart noises.

Hey, I love this stuff. My mind says it's sophomoric, but my heart belongs to Dada.

Surrealism: Dalí, Ernst, and Magritte (1920–1940)

Greek statues with sunglasses, a man as a spinning top, shoes becoming feet, and black ants as musical notes—Surrealism. The world was moving fast, and Surrealists caught the jumble of images. The artist scatters seemingly unrelated things on the canvas, leaving us to trace the connections in a kind of connect-the-dots without numbers. If it comes together, the synergy of unrelated things can be pretty startling. But even if the juxtaposed images don't ultimately connect, the artist has made you think, rerouting your thoughts through new neural paths. Like with Dada and so much other modern art, if you don't "get" it… you got it.

Complicating the modern world was Freud's discovery of the "unconscious" mind that thinks dirty thoughts while we sleep. Many a Surrealist canvas is an uncensored, stream-of-consciousness "landscape" of these deep urges, revealed in the bizarre images of dreams.

In dreams, sometimes one object can be two things at once. "I dreamt that you walked in with a cat…no, wait, maybe you were the cat…no…" Surrealists paint opposites like these and let them speak for themselves.

Salvador Dalí (1904–1989)

Salvador Dalí could draw exceptionally well. He painted "unreal" scenes with photographic realism, making us believe they could

really happen. Seeing familiar objects in an unfamiliar setting—like a grand piano adorned with disembodied heads of Lenin—creates an air of mystery, the feeling that anything can happen. That's both exciting and unsettling. Dalí's images— crucifixes, political and religious figures, and naked bodies—pack an emotional punch. Take one mixed bag of reality, jumble in a blender, and serve on a canvas— Surrealism.

Abstract Surrealists: Miró, Calder, and Arp

Abstract artists described their subconscious urges using color and shapes alone—Rorschach inkblots in reverse.

The thin-line scrawl of Joan Miró's work is like the doodling of a three-year-old. You'll recognize crudely drawn birds, stars, animals, and strange cell-like creatures with whiskers ("Biological Cubism"). Miró was trying to express the most basic of human emotions using the most basic of techniques.

Alexander Calder's mobiles hang like Mirós in the sky, waiting for a gust of wind to bring them to life.

And talk about a primal image! Jean Arp builds human beings out of amoeba-like shapes.

Decorative Art: Bonnard, Balthus, and Later Picasso and Braque

Most 20th-century paintings are a mix of the real world ("representation") and the colorful patterns of "abstract" art. Artists purposely distort camera-eye reality to make the resulting canvas more decorative. So, Picasso flattens a woman into a pattern of colored shapes, Bonnard makes a man a shimmer of golden paint, and Balthus turns a boudoir scene into colorful wallpaper.

Patterns and Textures: Jean Dubuffet, Lucio Fontana, and Karel Appel

Increasingly, you'll have to focus your eyes to look "at" the canvases, not "through" them.

Enjoy the lines and colors, but also a new element, texture. Some works have very thick paint piled on, where you can see the brush stroke clearly. Some have substances besides paint applied to the canvas, like Dubuffet's brown, earthy rectangles of real dirt and organic wastes. Fontana punctures the canvas so the fabric itself (and the hole) becomes the subject. Artists show their skill by mastering new materials. The canvas is a tray, serving up a delightful array of different substances with interesting colors, patterns, shapes, and textures.

Alberto Giacometti (1901–1966)
Giacometti's skinny statues have the emaciated, haunted, and faceless look of concentration camp survivors. Their simplicity is "Primitive," but these aren't stately, sturdy, Easter Island heads. Man is weak in the face of technology and the winds of history.

Abstract Expressionism: Pollock, Newman, Rothko, and Rauschenberg
America emerged from World War II as the globe's superpower. With Europe in ruins, New York replaced Paris as the art capital. The trend was toward bigger canvases, abstract designs, and experimentation with new materials and techniques. It was called "Abstract Expressionism"—expressing emotions and ideas using color and form alone.

Jackson Pollock (1912–1956)
"Jack the Dripper" attacks convention with a can of paint, dripping and splashing a dense web onto the canvas. Picture Pollock in his studio, jiving to the hi-fi, bouncing off the walls, throwing paint in a moment of enlightenment. Of course, the artist loses some control this way—over the paint flying in mid-air and over himself in an ecstatic trance. Painting becomes a whole-body activity, a "dance" between the artist and his materials.

The act of creating is what's important, not the final product. The canvas is only a record of that moment of ecstasy.

Big, Empty Canvases: Rothko and Yves Klein
All those big, empty canvases with just a few lines or colors—what reality are they trying to show?

In the modern world, we find ourselves insignificant specks in a vast and indifferent universe. Every morning, each of us must confront that big, blank, Existentialist canvas and decide how we're going to make our mark on it. Like wow.

Another influence was the simplicity of Japanese landscape painting. A Zen master studies and meditates for years to achieve the state of mind where he can draw one pure line. These canvases, again, are only a record of that state of enlightenment. (What is the sound of one brush painting?)

On more familiar ground, postwar painters were following in the footsteps of artists such as Mondrian, Klee, and Kandinsky (whose work they must have considered "busy"). The geometrical forms here reflect the same search for order, but these artists painted to the 5/4 symmetry of "Take Five."

• *Descend to the fourth floor, which houses more current works.*

Pop Art: Andy Warhol (1930–1987)

America's postwar wealth made the consumer king. Pop art is created from the "pop"-ular objects of that throwaway society— a soup can, a car fender, mannequins, tacky plastic statues, movie icons, advertising posters. Take something out of Sears and hang it in a museum, and you have to think about it in a whole different way.

Is this art? Are these mass-produced objects beautiful? Or crap? If not art, why do we work so hard to acquire them? Pop art, like Dada, questions our society's values.

Andy Warhol (who coined "15 minutes of fame" and became a pop star) concentrated on another mass-produced phenomenon— celebrities. He took publicity photos of famous people and repeated them. The repetition—like the constant bombardment we get from repeated images on TV—cheapens even the most beautiful things.

THE CONTEMPORARY COLLECTION (FOURTH FLOOR)

The modern world is history. Picasso and his ilk are now gathering dust and boring art students everywhere. Enter the postmodern world as seen through the eyes of current artists.

You'll see very few traditional canvases or sculptures. Artists have traded paintbrushes for blowtorches, exploring new materials and new media. (Miró said he was out to "murder" painting.) Mixed-media work is the norm, combining painting, sculpture, photography, welding, film/slides/video, and lighting and sound systems.

Here are some of the trends at the turn of 20th-century odometer:

Op Art: "Op"-tical illusions play tricks with your eyes (like how a spiral starts to spin when you stare at it).

Found Art: Artists raid dumpsters, recycling junk into the building blocks for larger "assemblages."

Deconstruction: Modern artists critique (or "deconstruct") society by examining things so familiar we take them for granted. A familiar object loaded with meaning (a crucifix), removed from

its usual circumstances (a church), and put it in a new setting
(in a jar of urine, to cite one notorious art project) makes you
see it in a different way.

Video and Film: Clips of inane, ordinary events, repeated
ad nauseam.

Words: Plaques of inane slogans or ad copy, repeated
ad nauseam.

Conceptual Art: This is a catchall for art that's interesting
even on paper ("Let's stick a crucifix in urine....")

The Occasional Sculpture: This is usually an abstract,
unrecognizable form that emphasizes the material it's made from.

The Occasional Canvas: This comes as a familiar relief.

Natural Objects: A rock in an urban setting is inherently
interesting.

Installations: An entire room is given to an artist to prepare.
Like an art funhouse, you walk in without quite knowing what
to expect (I'm always thinking, "Is this safe?"). Using the latest
technology, the artist engages all your senses, controlling the
lights, sounds, and sometimes even smells.

Contraptions: Weird, useless, Rube-Goldberg machines
make fun of technology.

Interaction: Some exhibits require your participation,
whether it's pushing a button to get the contraption going or just
walking around the room or touching something. In some cases,
the viewer "does" art rather than just stares at it. If art is really
meant to change, it has to move you, literally.

Performance Art: A kind of mixed media of live performance. Many artists that in another day would have painted canvases
have turned to music, dance, theater, and performance art. This art
form is often interactive, dropping the illusion of a performance
and encouraging audience participation. When you finish with the
Pompidou Center, go outside for some of the street theater.

Playful Art: Children love the art being produced today.
If it doesn't put a smile on your face, well, then you must be a
jaded grump like me, who's seen the same repetitious s#%t passed
off as "daring" since Warhol stole it from Duchamp. I mean, it's
so 20th century.

CARNAVALET MUSEUM TOUR

At the Carnavalet Museum (Musée Carnavalet—Histoire de Paris), French history unfolds in a series of stills—like a Ken Burns documentary, except you have to walk. The Revolution is the highlight, but you get a good overview of everything from Louis XIV to Napoleon to the belle epoque.

Orientation
Cost: 35F, covered by museum pass.
Hours: Tue–Sun 10:00–17:40, closed Mon.
Getting There: It's in the heart of the Marais district at 23 rue de Sévigné (Mo: Saint-Paul).
Information: Get the free (necessary) map. Tel. 01 42 72 21 13.
Length of Our Tour: 90 minutes.
Starring: Francois I, Louis XIV, Louis XV, Louis XVI, Madame de Sévigné, the Bastille, Robespierre, the guillotine, Napoleon, Napoleon III, the Paris Commune, la belle epoque.

OVERVIEW
After the ground floor (prehistory to 1600), go up to the first floor (1600–1789), then down a long hall to an adjoining building and up to the second floor (1789–1850), finishing back down on the first floor (1850–1920). Some rooms are closed part of the day, especially during lunch—ask as you enter. The Revolution is the museum's heart and soul, so don't burn out before 1500.

GROUND FLOOR
Rooms 1–4: Prehistory to 1500
Bone tools, broken columns, and stained leotards provide faint traces of Paris's first 2,000 years: The Celtic Parisii tribe fishing

in the Seine (100 B.C.); Julius Caesar and the Romans (52 B.C.–A.D. 500); Clovis and his Germanic invaders (508); Charlemagne, who united the Franks (800); Hugh Capet, whose descendants ruled for 800 years (1000); and the English, who were finally driven out by Joan of Arc (1453), ending the Middle Ages and birthing modern France.

Rooms 7–10: 1500s—Renaissance and Reformation

In Room 7, a **model of Île de la Cité** shows the medieval city before France became a world power—crowded, narrow-laned, steeple-dotted, with houses piled even on top of bridges. There's Notre-Dame on the east end, and Sainte-Chapelle with its royal palace and gardens on the west. The only straight road in town was the old Roman road that splits the island north-south (and is still used today).

King Francois I (1494–1547, Room 7) brought Paris into the modern world. Handsome, athletic Francois—a writer of poems, leader of knights, and lover of women—embodied the optimism of the Italian Renaissance. "*Le grand roi Francois*" (it rhymes) centralized the government around his charismatic self and made a rebuilt Louvre his home. His absolute right to rule was affirmed every time he ordered something done—"For such is our pleasure!"

Renaissance open-mindedness brought religious debate, even leading to open warfare between Catholics and Protestants (called Huguenots in France). The Catholic **King Charles IX** and his mother, **Catherine de Medicis** (both depicted in room 8), plotted to assassinate several prominent Protestants, but it quickly snowballed into the slaughter of thousands of Parisian Huguenots on St. Bartholomew's Day, 1572. The **Catholic League** organized parades, Bible studies, and the occasional Protestant barbecue to keep the faithful in good spirits.

• *Head upstairs to the first floor. The rooms on this floor are not laid out in neat numerical or chronological order, so expect to do some backtracking and wandering.*

FIRST FLOOR

Rooms 13–20 *(Paris au XVII siècle)*: 1600s—Louis XIII and XIV Modernize Paris

Many of the grand monuments that made Paris a world capital—the pont Neuf, the expanded Louvre, place Royale, and the Invalides dome—were begun or completed by **Louis XIII** (Room 14, rearing on his horse, with angels trumpeting his works) and his more-glorious son, Louis XIV, the Sun King. They financed the arts (Le Brun, etc., in Room 15), shifting Europe's cultural axis from Italy to Paris.

Rooms 17 through 20, with their flowery walls, Greek-myth ceiling paintings, and powdered-wig portraits, give a tiny glimpse of the opulence of Louis XIV's greatest monument, the palace at Versailles. Versailles was the physical symbol of Louis' absolute power, ruling over the largest, most populous, and richest nation in Europe. Whenever the nobles got uppity, the larger-than-life Sun King wouldn't hesitate to put his foot down (Room 20).

• *Backtrack to Room 13 and follow signs to . . .*

Rooms 21–23 *(Madame de Sévigné et son temps)*: Madame de Sévigné (1596–1696)

Esteemed hostess and letter writer Madame de Sévigné spent the last 20 years of her life here at Hotel Carnavalet, a mansion she bought to accommodate herself and her daughter's family. (See **portraits** of Madame, her daughter, and her son-in-law, M. de Grignan.) Widowed at age 25 when her husband was killed in a duel, Marie de Sévigné took her two young children to Paris and quickly charmed high society (including a young Louis XIV) with her beauty and wit. She hosted parties for writers (see **Molière**, acting the role of Caesar), thinkers, and political radicals. Her

romantic affairs were legendary, the parties were gay, and all the *mots* were *bon*. Still, in private, Marie stared out the windows of these rooms, pining away for the great love of her life—her daughter—who left a hole in Marie's life when she started her own family and moved south to Provence. Madame wrote a letter to Mademoiselle almost every day for 20 years. Her subjects range from the everyday ("This morning, we had a good chicken soup and some good cabbages") to the poetic ("I have come here to say goodbye to the leaves. They are still on the trees, but, instead of green, they have taken on tones as varied as dawn, as varied as a magnificent, golden brocade") to playful gossip ("I am about to tell you the most astonishing thing, the most surprising, the most miraculous, the most unheard of, the most . . . "). Most of all, the letters reveal her almost obsessive longing for her daughter ("Come visit me, then come, my darling, for as long as you're away, there is a dragon feasting on my heart"). Today, the vast store of letters is a gold mine of historical information, as well as a pioneering work that turned conversational speech and ordinary feelings into high art.

• *Backtrack through Room 21 to Room 24*, La municipalité parisienne sous l'ancien régime. *From here, the first floor layout gets confusing. Be prepared to get out your map to find specific rooms. Otherwise, just wander around and get a feel for the luxury of France's kings and nobles before the Revolution.*

Rooms 24–48: Louis XV (ruled 1715–1774)

Louis XV (portrait in Room 25) ascended the throne of Europe's most powerful nation when his great-grandfather, the Sun King, died after reigning 72 years. Only five years old at the time, he was forever a figurehead while the government was run by his mentors—a Regency during his childhood, his schoolteacher in youth, one of his many mistresses (Madame de Pompadour) in middle age, and bureaucrats at the end. Louis was intelligent and educated, and he personally embraced the budding democratic ideals of the Enlightenment, but he spent his time at Versailles, gaming and consorting with Europe's most cultured and beautiful people. Meanwhile, France's money was spent on costly wars with Austria and England (including the American "French and Indian War"). Louis, basking in the lap of luxury and the glow of the Enlightenment, looked to the horizon and uttered his prophetic phrase: "*Après moi—le deluge!*" ("After me—the flood!")

Rooms 49–64: Louis XVI (ruled 1774–1793), France's Last King

As you stroll through the first-floor rooms, you'll see luxurious wallpaper, tables, chairs, parquet floors, clocks, gaming tables, statues, paintings and even a doghouse costing more than a peasant hut (Room 53). Look for subtle differences in decoration and furnishings:

Louis XIV Style: Baroque. Gilded rooms, ceilings decorated with curved ornamental frames (cartouches) holding paintings of Greek myths. Heavy tables and chairs with thick, curved legs, animal feet, and bronze corner protectors.

Louis XV: Rococo. Pastel colors, lighter decoration, exotic landscapes. Chairs of highly polished, rare woods, with delicate curved legs and padded seats and backs. Chinese decor and objects (Ming vase).

Louis XVI: Neoclassical. Influenced by recently excavated Pompeii. Simpler, straighter, with classical motifs. Chairs with straight legs tapering to a point.

Imagine these rooms during the *ancien régime* (the traditional chessboard society with king on top, pawns on bottom, and the bishops that walk diagonally), lit by chandeliers glimmering off mirrors, the sound of a string quartet, exotic foods from newly colonized lands, billiards in one room and high-stakes card games in another, a Molière comedy downstairs, dangerous talk by radicals like Voltaire and Rousseau in Room 48, and dangerous liaisons among social butterflies dressed in high heels, make-up, wigs, and perfume... and that's just the men.

• *From Room 45, walk down a long blood-red corridor to another building, then upstairs to the second floor and* La Révolution francaise.

SECOND FLOOR

The Revolution: 1789–1799

No period of history is as charged with the full range of human emotions as the French Revolution. Bloodshed, martyrdom, daring speeches, lasting bonds of friendship, tolerance, murdering priests, emancipating women, feeding the starving, back-stabbing former friends—all done in the looming shadow of the guillotine. From the highest ideals to the pettiest jealousies, the bottled-up passions of ordinary men and women were suddenly uncorked, and what bubbled out wasn't always Dom Perignon. For the first time, common people with their everyday concerns were driving the engine of history... Or were they only foam bubbles swept along in the shifting tides of vast socioeconomic trends?

Room 101: The Estates General

It's 1789, France is bankrupt from wars and corruption, and the people want change. The large **allegorical painting by Dubois** shows King Louis XVI in the boat of France, navigating stormy seas. Lady Truth is trying to light the way, but the winged demon of tyranny keeps nagging at the king. Above shines the fleur-de-lis, whose petals are the three social groups that made France strong: clergy, king-and-people, and nobles.

In May, the king called these three groups together at Versailles to solve the financial crisis. But in a bold and unheard-of move, the Third Estate (the people), tired of being outvoted by the archaic system, split and formed their own National Assembly. Amid the chaos of speeches, debate, and deal making, they raise their hands, bravely pledging to stick together until a new constitution is written (see *The Oath of the Jeu-de-Paume*, on wall opposite allegorical painting). **Louis XVI** (see his pink-faced portrait to the left), who seemed to vacillate between democratic change and royalist repression, ordered the Assembly to dissolve (they refused), sent 25,000 Swiss mercenary soldiers to Paris, and fired his most popular, liberal minister.

Room 102: The Bastille (July 14, 1789)

The Bastille (see the **model**) was a medieval fortress turned prison. With its eight towers and 100-foot-high walls it dominated the

Parisian skyline, a symbol of oppression. On the hot, muggy morning of July 14, Paris' citizens waited on edge for a rumored attack by the king's Swiss guards. A crowd formed and marched on the Invalides armory (see series of **paintings**, left to right) and seized 30,000 rifles... but no gunpowder.

Word spread it was stored across town at the Bastille. The mob grew bigger and angrier as it went. By noon they stood at the foot of the walls of the Bastille, demanding gunpowder. The fort's governor stalled, but two citizens managed to scale the wall and cut the chains. The drawbridge crashed down, and the mob poured through. Terrified guards opened fire, killing dozens and wounding hundreds. At the battle's peak, French soldiers in red and blue appeared on the horizon... but whose side were they on? A loud cheer went up as they pointed their cannons at the Bastille, and soon the governor had no choice but to surrender. The mob trashed the Bastille, opened the dark dungeons, and brought seven prisoners into the light of day. They dragged the governor to City Hall (Hôtel de Ville) where he was literally torn apart by the hysterical crowd. His head was stuck on a stick and carried through the city. The Revolution had begun.

Today the events of July 14 are celebrated with equally colorful festivities every Bastille Day. The Bastille itself was soon dismantled stone by stone (nothing remains but the open space of place Bastille), but the memory became a rallying cry throughout the Revolution: "*Vive le quatorze Juillet!*" ("Long live July 14th!")

Room 103 *(La Fête de la Federation)*: The Celebration (1789)

Imagine the jubilation! To finally be able to shout out loud things formerly whispered in fear.

The large painting of *La Fête de la Federation* shows the joy and exuberance of the newly freed people, celebrating the first Bastille Day (July 14, 1790). Liberty! Equality! Fraternity! Members of every social class (even including, it appears, three women) hugged, kissed and mingled on the Champ de Mars, where the Eiffel Tower stands today. An artificial mound was built for heroes of the Revolution to ascend while a choir sang. Women, dressed up to symbolize Truth, Freedom, Justice, and other capital-letter virtues, were worshiped in a new kind of secular religion. Public demonstrations like these must have infuriated the king, queen, bishops, and nobles who were now quarantined in their palaces, fuming impotently.

The ***Declaration of the Rights of Man and the Citizen*** (see 2 different versions) made freedom the law. The preamble makes clear that "Le Peuple Francais" (the French people)—not the king—were the ultimate authority. "Men are born free and equal," it states, possessing "freedom of the individual, freedom of conscience, freedom of speech."

Room 104 *(de la Monarchie a la République)*:
Louis XVI Quietly Responds (1789–1792)

Louis XVI (1754–1793, see the bust)—studious, shy, aloof, and easily dominated—was stunned by the ferocious summer of 1789. The Bastille's violence spread to the countryside, where uppity peasants tenderized their masters with pitchforks. The Assembly was changing France with lightning speed, abolishing Church privileges, nationalizing nobles' land, and declaring the king irrelevant. Louis accepted his role as a rubber-stamp monarch, hoping the furor would pass, trying to appear idealistic and optimistic. But looming on the horizon was... *Le docteur Joseph-Ignace Guillotin* (1738–1814, see painting).

The progressive Assembly abolished brutal medieval-style torture and executions. In their place, Dr. Guillotin proposed a kinder-gentler execution device that would make France a model of compassion. The guillotine—also known as "the national razor," or, simply, "The Machine"—could nearly instantly make someone "a head shorter at the top." (In 1977 it claimed its last victim; now capital punishment is abolished.)

Room 105 *(La famille royale)*:
Royalty Loses Its Head (1793)

Louis' wife, **Queen Marie-Antoinette** (several portraits), became the focus of the citizens' disgust. She spent extravagantly, plunging France into debt. More decisive than her husband, she steered him toward repressive measures to snuff out the Revolution. And worst of all, she was foreign-born, known simply as "The Austrian," and Austria was soon making war on the French, trying to preserve the monarchy. When Marie was informed that the Parisians had no bread to eat, a rumor spread that she sneered, "Let them eat cake!"

Enraged and hungry, 6,000 Parisian women (backed by armed men) marched through the rain to Versailles to demand lower bread prices. On the night of October 5, 1789, a small band infiltrated the palace, burst into the Queen's room, killed her bodyguards, and chased her down the hall. The royal family was kidnapped and taken to Paris, where—though still monarchs—they were virtual prisoners in the Tuileries Palace (which once stood where, today, the Louvre meets the Tuileries Gardens).

Two years later, the royal family became actual prisoners (see the reconstructed and rather cushy **Prison du Temple** in Room 106) after trying to escape to Austria to begin a counter-revolution. One of their servants pretended to be a German baroness, while Louis dressed up

as her servant (the irony must have been killing him). When a citizen recognized Louis from his portrait on a franc note, they were captured, thrown into prison, and soon put on trial as traitors to France. The National Convention (the Assembly's successor) declared the monarchy abolished.

On January 21, 1793 (see **painting** in Room 105), King Louis XVI—excuse me, "Citizen Capet"—was led to the place de la Concorde, laid face down on a slab, and—shoop!—a thousand years of monarchy dating back before Charlemagne was decapitated.

A few months later, Marie-Antoinette was tearfully torn (see **painting**) from her eight-year-old son (Louis XVII) and moved to a prison in the Conciergerie. On October 16, 1793 (see **painting**), she too met her fate on place de la Concorde. Genteel to the end, she apologized to the executioner for stepping on his foot. The blade fell, the blood gushed, and her head was shown to the crowd on a stick—an exclamation point for the new rallying cry: *Vive la Nation!* (Ten-year-old Louis XVII died in prison shortly after his parents were beheaded. Rumors spread that the boy-king had escaped, fueled by Elvis-type sightings and impersonators. But recent DNA evidence confirms that the *dauphin*—heir to the throne— did indeed die in prison in 1795.)

Room 108 *(La Convention–La Terreur)*: The Reign of Terror (1793–1794)

Here are **portraits** of key players in the Revolutionary spectacle. Some were moderate reformers, some radical priest-killers. They all lived in fear that, with Europe ganging up on the Revolution, any backward step could tip the delicate balance of power back to the *ancien régime*. Enemies of the Revolution were everywhere— even in their own ranks.

By the summer of 1793, the left-of-center Jacobin party took control of France's fledgling democracy. Pug-faced but silver-tongued **Georges Danton** drove the Revolution with his personal charisma and bold speeches: "To conquer the enemies of the fatherland, we need daring, more daring, daring now, always daring." He led the "Committee of Public Safety" to root out and execute those enemies, even guillotining moderates opposed to the Jacobins.

More radical still, **Jean-Paul Marat** (the "Friend of the People") dressed and burped like a man-of-the-street, but he wrote eloquently against all forms of authority. Wildly popular with the commoners, he was seen by others as a loose cannon. A beautiful 25-year-old noblewoman named **Charlotte Corday** decided it was her mission in life to save France by silencing him. On July 11, 1793, she entered his home under the pretext of giving him names of counter-revolutionaries. Marat, seated in a bathtub to nurse a skin condition, wrote the names down and said, "Good. I'll have them all guillotined." Corday stood up, whipped a knife out from under her dress, and stabbed him fatally through the heart. Corday was guillotined and Marat was hailed a martyr to the cause.

Marat's death was further "proof" that counter-revolutionaries were everywhere. For the next year (summer of 1793 to summer of 1794, see **paintings of guillotine scenes**), the Jacobin government arrested, briefly tried, then guillotined anyone suspected of being "enemies of the Revolution"—nobles, priests, the rich, as well as many true Revolutionaries who simply belonged to the wrong political party. More than 2,500 Parisians were beheaded, 18,000 were executed by other means, and tens of thousands died in similar violence around the country. The violence begun at the **Bastille** in July 1789 would climax in July 1794.

Master of the Reign of Terror was **Maximilien Robespierre** (the portrait opposite Danton's), a 35-year-old lawyer who promoted the Revolution with a religious fervor. By July 1794, the guillotine was slicing 30 necks a day. In Paris's main squares, grim executions alternated with politically correct public spectacles honoring "Liberty," "Truth," and the heroes of France. As the death toll rose, so did public cynicism. Finally, Robespierre even sentenced to death his old friend Danton when he spoke out against the bloodshed. As Danton knelt under the blade, he joked— "My turn." The people had had enough.

Room 109 *(Thermidor—Le Directoire)*: Terror Ends (July 1794)

Engravings show Robespierre's meteoric fall from power. Food shortages, inflation, and Robespierre's own self-righteousness made him an easy target. On July 27, 1794, as Robespierre prepared to name the daily list of victims, his fellow committee members started yelling "Tyrant!" and shouted him down. Robespierre, stunned by the sudden fall from grace, tried to commit suicide by shooting himself in the mouth.

The next day, he walked the walk he'd ordered thousands to

French National Anthem: "La Marseillaise"
The genteel French have a gory past.

Allons enfants de la Patrie, (Let's go, children of
    the fatherland,)
Le jour de gloire est arrivé. (The day of glory has arrived.)
Contre nous de la tyrannie (The blood-covered
    flagpole of tyranny)
L'étendard sanglant est levé. (Is raised against us.)
Entendez-vous dans nos campagnes (Do you hear what's
    happening in our countryside?)
Mugir les féroces soldats? (The ferocious soldiers are howling)
Qui viennent jusque dans nos bras (They're coming nearly
    into our grasp)
Egorger nos fils et nos compagnes. (They're slitting the throats
    of our sons and our women.)
Aux armes citoyens, (Grab your weapons, citizens,)
Formez vos bataillons, (Form your battalions,)
Marchons, marchons, (March on, march on,)
Qu'un sang impur (So that their impure blood)
Abreuve nos sillons. (Will fill our trenches.)

take. Hands tied behind his back, he was carried through the streets on a two-wheeled cart, while citizens jeered and spat on him. At the guillotine, the broken-down demagogue had no last words, thanks to his wounded jaw. When the executioner yanked off the bandage, Robespierre let out a horrible cry, the blade fell, and the Reign of Terror came to an end.

From 1795 to 1799 France caught its breath, ruled by the Directory, a government so intentionally weak and decentralized (2 houses of parliament and 5 executives with no funding) that it could never create another Robespierre.

Room 110 *(La Guerre)*: France vs. Europe
The blade that dropped on Louis XVI rattled royal teacups throughout Europe. Even as early as 1792, France had to defend its young democracy against Austria and Prussia. Surprisingly, France's new army—ordinary citizens from a universal draft, led by daring young citizen-officers, singing a stirring, bloodthirsty new song, "La Marseillaise"—quickly defeated the apathetic mercenaries they faced. France vowed to liberate all Europe from tyranny. Europe feared that, by "exporting Revolution," France would export democracy . . . plus senseless violence and chaos.

The 29-year-old General **Napoleon Bonaparte** (see the bust) rose quickly through the ranks, proving himself by fighting royalists in Italy, Egypt, and on the streets of Paris. In 1799 he returned to Paris a conquering hero. Backed by an adoring public, he dissolved the Directory, established order, and gave himself the Roman-style title of "first consul."

Room 111 *(Vandalisme et Conservation)*: The Revolution vs. Religion

Three-fourths of France's churches were destroyed or vandalized during the Revolution, a backlash against the wealthy and politically repressive Catholic Church. In Notre-Dame, Christ was mothballed and a woman dressed as "Dame Reason" was worshiped on the altar.

Room 113: Souvenirs of Revolution

After Napoleon's dictatorship of 1799, "*Liberté, Egalité, Fraternité*" was just a slogan, remembered fondly on commemorative **plates and knickknacks**. The Revolution was over.

• *The visit continues downstairs—or down the elevator—on the ground floor.*

Room 115 *(Le Premier Empire)*: Napoleon Conquers Europe (1799–1815)

Here's **Napoleon** (see portrait, also breastplate and death mask in glass case) at the peak of power, master of western Europe. Dressed in his general's uniform, he's checking the maps to see who's left to conquer. Behind him is a throne with his imperial seal. This Corsican-born commoner, educated in Paris' military schools, became a young Revolutionary and daring general, rising to prominence as a champion of democracy. Once in power, he preached revolution but in fact became a dictator and crowned himself emperor (1804).

During the Empire, bishops such as **Talleyrand** and wealthy socialites such as **Juliette Recamier** could bring their fine clothes out of mothballs without fear of the guillotine. Paris was rebuilt (Room 117) with neoclassical monuments like the Arc de Triomphe to make it the "New Rome."

In 1812 Napoleon foolishly invaded Russia, starting a downward spiral that ended in defeat by allied Europe at the Battle of Waterloo in Belgium (1815). Napoleon was exiled and died (1822) on the island of St. Helena off the coast of Africa.

Room 118 *(La Restauration)*: The Monarchy Restored (1815–1830)

After 25 years in exile, **Louis XVIII**—younger brother of headless Louis XVI—returned to Paris with the backing of Europe's royalty and reclaimed the crown as a constitutional monarch (see painted crowd scene of *3 mai 1814*).

The next king, retro-looking **Charles X**, in glorious coronation robes, revived the fashion and oppression of the *ancien régime*, plotting to dissolve the people's Assembly. But the French people were not about to turn the clock back.

Room 119 *(Juillet 1830)*: Revolution of 1830

Parisians again blocked off the narrow streets with barricades to fight the king's soldiers. They **stormed the Louvre** (biggest painting), the king's palace, and slaughtered the mercenary Swiss Guards. After "Three Glorious Days" of fighting, order was restored by Louis-Philippe (see **model**), an unassuming nobleman who appeared on the balcony of Hôtel de Ville and was cheered by royalists, the middle class, and peasants alike.

Room 120 *(La Monarchie de Juillet)*: Constitutional Monarchy (1830–1848)

King Louis-Philippe (see black bust)—a former lieutenant turned banker with a few drops of royal blood—was a true constitutional monarch, harmlessly presiding over an era of middle-class progress fueled by the industrial revolution. Still, liberal reforms came too slowly—new factories brought division between wealthy employers and poor workers, and only 200,000 out of 30,000,000 French citizens (1:150) could vote.

Room 121 *(La Deuxième République)*: Revolution of 1848

In February 1848—a time of Europe-wide depression and socialist strikes—Parisians took to the streets again (**battle scenes**), battling at Bastille, Palais-Royal, Pantheon, and Concorde, and toppling the king. Even prosperous accountants and shoe salesmen caught the spirit of revolution. After five decades of dictators (Napoleon), retread Bourbons (the Restoration), and self-proclaimed monarchs (Louis-Philippe), France was back in the hands of the people—the Second Republic.

Room 122 *(Le Romantisme)*: Romanticism

Freedom of expression, the uniqueness of each person, the glories of the human spirit and the natural world—these values from the 1789 Revolution were continued by artists of the 1800s known as

Romantics. Working clockwise, you'll see **caricature busts** of many famous Frenchmen and visitors to the center of European culture, Paris: Victor Hugo (author of *Les Miserables* and *Hunchback*), Johann Strauss, Sr. (inventor of the scandalous waltz craze), Paganini (touring violinist who played like a man possessed), Chopin (Polish pianist who charmed Parisian society), Adolphe Sax (-ophone), Giuseppe Verdi (composer of stirring operas—*Aida*, etc.), and Rossini (Lone Ranger theme). There are also **paintings** of Romantic painter Delacroix and of glamorous pianist Franz Liszt and his mistress Marie d'Agoult—the ultimate Romantic. She left her husband and children to follow the dynamic Liszt on a journey of self-discovery in Italy and Switzerland—"the years of pilgrimage."
• *Journey upstairs and to the left toward* "Paris: Du Second Empire à nos jours"—*From the Second Empire to Today.*

Room 128 *(Le Second Empire)*: Napoleon III and the Second Empire (1852–1870)

Louis-Napoleon Bonaparte (in the big painting, with red pants and sash, waxed moustache, and goatee) was the nephew of the famous Emperor Napoleon I. He used his famous name to be elected president by a landslide in 1848, then combined democracy with monarchy to be voted "Emperor Napoleon III." He suppressed opposition but promoted liberal reforms and economic and colonial expansion.

Here he hands an order to **Baron Georges Haussmann** (mutton-chop sideburns) to modernize Paris. Haussmann cut the wide, straight boulevards of today to move goods, open up the crowded city... and prevent barricades for future revolutions. Parks, railroad stations, and the Garnier Opéra House made Paris the model for world capitals. (Room 129 shows building projects.)

The **boat-like cradle** (Room 128) is a copy of the famous cradle of Napoleon II (1811–1832, known to history as the "King of Rome"), the only son of Napoleon I, who died at 19 of tuberculosis before ever ruling anything.

Napoleon III pursued popular wars (the **model** in Room 129 celebrates Crimean War vets, 1855) and unpopular ones (backing Austrian Emperor Maximilian in Mexico). In the summer of 1870, he personally led a jubilant French Army to crush upstart Prussia—"On to Berlin!" Uh-oh.

Room 130 *(Le siège de Paris)*: The Franco-Prussian War (1870–1871)

Within weeks, the overconfident French were surrounded, Napoleon III himself was captured, and he surrendered. Paris was stunned. (See **painting of crowd** hearing the news on the legislature steps.) The Germans quickly put a stranglehold on Paris, and a long, especially cold winter settled in.

Some would not give up. Without an emperor, they proclaimed yet another democratic republic (France's third in a century) and sent minister Leon Gambetta in a newfangled balloon (**painting**) over the Germans' heads to rally the countryside to come save Paris. The Parisians themselves held out bravely (**painting** of Tuileries as army camp), but German efficiency and modern technology simply overwhelmed the French.

Room 131 *(La Commune)*: The Paris Commune (Spring 1871)

The Republic finally agreed to a humiliating surrender. Paris's liberals—enraged at the capitulation after such a brave winter and fearing a return of monarchy—rejected the surrender and proclaimed their own government, the Paris Commune. **Portraits** honor the proud idealists who barricaded themselves inside Paris' neighborhoods, refusing to bow to the German emperor.

Then, in one "bloody week" in May (**battle scenes**), French troops backing the Republic stormed through Paris, leaving 15,000 dead, 5,000 jailed, and 8,000 deported. The Commune was snuffed out, but the memory was treasured by generations of liberals in popular **souvenirs**—a jar of bread from the hungry winter, a carrier pigeon's feather, a box reading "*Vive la Commune!*"

The church of Sacre-Coeur (**painting**) was built after the war as a form of national penance.

Rooms 132–142 *(La Belle Epoque)*: The Beautiful Age (1871–1914)

The Third Republic restored peace to a prosperous middle-class society. The **Eiffel Tower** (Room 132) marked the 1889 centennial of the Revolution, and the **Statue of Liberty** (Room 133) honored America's revolution.

Paris was a capital of world culture, a city of **Impressionist painters** (Room 135); of the actress **Sarah Bernhardt** (Room 136), called the world's first international star ("a force of nature, a fiery soul, a marvelous intelligence, a magnificent creature of the highest order," raved one of the smitten); of **Georges Bizet** (Room 136), composer of *Carmen*; of balls, carriages, cafés, and parks (**paintings**, Rooms 137–140); and the city of Art Nouveau, the curvy decorative style of the *très chic* **Café de Paris** (Room 141) and the jewelry of **Boutique Fouquet** (Room 142).

Room 145: World War I (1914–1918)

Three costly wars with Germany—Franco-Prussian, World War I, and World War II—drained France. Although **Marshall Foch** (big painting) is hailed as the man who coordinated the Allied armies to defeat Germany in World War I, France was hardly a winner. More than 1.5 million Frenchmen died, a generation was lost, and the country would be a pushover when Hitler invaded in 1940. France's long history as a global superpower was over.

Room 147 *(La vie litteraire XXe siècle)*: Remembrance of Things Past

By producing such literary greats as the writer **Marcel Proust** (reconstructed bedroom) and the dreamy writer/filmmaker **Jean Cocteau**, France has remained a cultural superpower.

RODIN
MUSEUM
TOUR

paris

Auguste Rodin (1840–1917) was a modern Michelangelo, sculpting human figures on an epic scale, revealing through the body their deepest thoughts and feelings. Like many of Michelangelo's unfinished works, Rodin's statues rise from the raw stone around them, driven by the life force. With missing limbs and scarred skin, these are prefab classics, making ugliness noble. Rodin's people are always moving restlessly. Even the famous *Thinker* is moving. While he's plopped down solidly, his mind is a million miles away. The museum presents a full range of Rodin's work, housed in a historic mansion where he once lived and worked. The gardens are picnic perfect (BYO), but there's also a pleasant, if pricey, café.

Orientation

Cost: 28F, 18F on Sun and for seniors and students, free for youth under 18 and for anyone first Sun of month; 5F for garden only; all covered by museum pass.

Hours: April–Sept Tue–Sun 9:30–17:45, garden closes at 18:45. Oct–March Tue–Sun 9:30–17:00, garden closes at 17:00. Closed Mon. Last entrance 30 minutes before closing.

Getting There: It's near Napoleon's Tomb (77 rue de Varennes, Mo: Varenne).

Information: Tel. 01 44 18 61 10, www.musee-rodin.fr.

Length of Our Tour: One hour.

Entrance Hall

Two bronze men stride forward, as bold as the often-controversial Rodin. *The Walking Man* (*L'Homme Qui Marche*) plants his back foot forcefully as though he's about to step, while his front foot already has stepped. Rodin, who himself had one foot in the past, one in the future, captures two poses at once. Just ahead, a white-marble couple

RODIN MUSEUM AND GARDENS

locks lips in *The Kiss*, one of many statues of lovers entwined. We don't need to see their faces to know what they feel.

• *Pick up a museum plan with room numbers and walk left, through the shop, and to the far corner to start a circular tour of the ground floor.*

Room 1: Rodin's early works match the style of the time—pretty portrait busts and classical themes. Born of working-class roots, Rodin taught himself art by sketching statues at the Louvre and then sculpting copies.

The Man with the Broken Nose (*L'homme au nez casse*)—a deliberately ugly work—was 23-year-old Rodin's first break from the norm. He meticulously sculpted this deformed man (one of the few models the struggling sculptor could afford), but then the clay statue froze in his unheated studio, and the back of the head fell off. Rodin loved it! The Salon hated it. Rodin persevered.

See the painting of Rodin's future wife, Rose Beuret (*Portrait de Madame Rodin*), who suffered with him through obscurity and celebrity.

Room 2: To feed his new family, Rodin cranked out small works with his boss's name on them—portraits, ornamental vases, nymphs, and knickknacks to decorate buildings. Still, the series of mother-and-childs (Rose and baby Auguste?) allowed him to experiment on a small scale with the intertwined twosomes he'd do later.

His job gave him enough money to visit Italy, where he was inspired by Michelangelo's boldness, monumental scale, restless figures, and "unfinished" look. Rapidly approaching middle age, Rodin was ready to rock.

Room 3: He moved to Brussels, where his first major work, *The Bronze Age* (*L'âge d'arain*), brought controversy and the fame that surrounds it. This nude youth, perhaps inspired by Michelangelo's *Dying Slave* in the Louvre, awakens to a new world. It was so life-like that Rodin was accused of not sculpting it himself but simply casting it directly from a live body. The boy's left hand looks like he should be leaning on a spear, but it's just that missing element that makes the pose more tenuous and interesting.

The art establishment still snubbed Rodin the outsider, and no wonder. Look at his ultra-intense take on the symbol of France (*La Défense*)—this Marseillaise screams "Off with their heads" at the top of her lungs. Rodin was a slave to his muses, and some inspired monsters.

Room 4: Like the hand of a sculptor, *The Hand of God* (*La main de Dieu*) shapes Adam and Eve from the mud of the earth to which they will return. Rodin himself worked in "mud," using his hands to model clay figures, which were then reproduced in marble or bronze, usually by his assistants. Spin this masterpiece on its turntable. Rodin wants you to see it from every angle. He first worked from the front view, then checked the back and side profiles, then filled in the in-between.

Other works in this room show embracing couples who seem to emerge from the stone just long enough to love. Rodin left many works "unfinished," reminding us that all creating is a hard process of dragging a form out of chaos.

Room 5: The two hands that form the arch of *The Cathedral* (*La Cathèdrale*) are actually two right hands (a man's and a woman's?).

In *The Kiss*, a passionate woman twines around a solid man for their first, spontaneous kiss. In their bodies, we can almost read the thoughts, words, and movements that led up to this meeting of lips. *The Kiss* was the first Rodin work the public loved. Rodin despised it, thinking it simple and sentimental.

Rodin worked with many materials— he chiseled marble (*The Kiss*), used clay (the smaller, red-brown *Kiss*—opposite the big kiss), cast bronze, worked plaster, painted, and sketched. He often created different versions of the same subject in a different medium.

Room 6: This room displays works by Camille Claudel, mostly in the style of her master. The 44-year-old Rodin took 18-year-old Camille as his pupil, muse, colleague, and lover. We can follow the arc of their relationship:

Rodin was inspired by young Camille's beauty and spirit and he often used her as a model. You'll see her head emerging from a block of marble.

As his student, "Mademoiselle C" learned from Rodin, doing portrait busts in his lumpy style. Her bronze bust of Rodin (by the door) shows the steely-eyed sculptor with strong front and side profiles, barely emerging from the materials he worked with.

Soon they were lovers. *The Waltz* (*La Valse*) captures the spinning exuberance the two must have felt as they embarked together on a new life. The couple twirls in a delicate balance.

But Rodin was devoted as well to his lifelong companion, Rose. *Maturity* (*L'Âge Mur*) shows the breakup. A young girl on her knees begs the man not to leave her, as he's led away reluctantly by an older woman. The center of the composition is the hole left when their hands drift apart.

Rodin did leave Camille. Overwhelmed by grief and jealousy, she went crazy and had to be institutionalized until she died. *The Wave* (*La Vague*), carved in onyx in a very un-Rodin style, shows fragile women huddled under a wave about to engulf them.

Rooms 7 and 8: What did Rodin think of women? Here are many different images from which you can draw conclusions.

Eve buries her head in shame, hiding her nakedness. But she can't hide the consequences of that first sin—she's pregnant.

Rodin became famous, wealthy, and respected, and society ladies all wanted him to do their portraits. In Room 8, you'll also see his last mistress (*La Duchesse de Choiseul*), who lived with him here in this mansion.

Room 9: This dimly lit room is filled with Rodin's sketches. The first flash of inspiration for a huge statue might be a single line sketched on notepaper. Rodin wanted nude models in his studio at all times—walking, dancing, and squatting—in case they struck some new and interesting pose. Rodin thought of sculpture as simply "drawing in all dimensions."

• *Upstairs you'll find a glass display case that tries hard to explain how . . .* Rodin made his bronze statues by pouring molten bronze into the narrow space between an original clay model and the mold around it. Once you had a mold, you could produce other copies, which is why there are famous Rodin bronzes all over the world.

As the display case clearly fails to make clear, the classic "lost wax" technique works like this:

1) The artist sculpts a clay model.

2) It is covered with materials that harden to make a shell that's hard on the outside, flexible inside. The shell is removed by cutting it into two halves that can be pieced back together—this is your mold that can be used over and over.

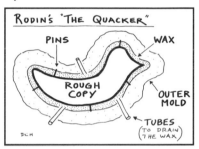

3) Cement is poured into the mold to make a durable, rough copy. The mold is removed.

4) The surface of the copy is sanded down slightly.

5) The mold is put back over it, using pins to keep quarter-inch space between the mold and the rough copy. Hot wax is poured into the space, it cools, and the mold is removed. The artist touches up the wax "skin" of the rough copy into its final form.

6) It is covered again with the mold and ventilation tubes.

7) The whole contraption is coated with heat-resistant materials.

8) The wax is heated—it melts and drains away (gets "lost"), leaving a quarter-inch of open space between the rough copy and the mold. Molten bronze is poured in to fill the space. As the bronze cools, it takes the shape of the mold.

9) The mold and the tubing are removed, the bronze is lifted off the rough copy, and you're left with a hollow bronze statue ready to be polished and varnished.

Rooms 10 and 11: For decades, Rodin wrestled with a massive project—a doorway encrusted with characters from Dante's *Inferno*. These *Gates of Hell* were never completed (see unfinished piece in the garden), but his studies created some of Rodin's masterpieces—including *The Thinker*, who was to be the centerpiece.

Rodin's figures struggle to come into existence. Rodin was fascinated with the theory of evolution—not Darwin's version of the survival of the fittest but the Frenchman Lamarck's. His figures survive not by the good fortune of random mutation (Darwin), but by their own striving (Lamarck). They are driven by the life force, a restless energy that animates and shapes dead matter (Lamarck and Bergson). Rodin must have felt that force even as a child when he first squeezed soft clay and saw a worm emerge.

In Room 11 you'll see studies of the female body in all its aspects—open, closed, wrinkled.

Room 12: A virtual unknown until his mid-30s, Rodin slowly began receiving major commissions for public monuments. *The Burghers of Calais* depicts the actual event in 1347, when, in order to save their people, the city fathers surrender the keys of the city—and their own lives—to the enemy. Rodin portrays them not in some glorious pose drenched in pomp and allegory but as a simple example of men sacrificing their lives together. As they head to the gallows, with ropes already around their necks, each shows a distinct emotion: from courage to despair. Compare the small plaster model in the glass case with the final, life-size bronze group out the window in the garden (near the street behind the ticket booth).

Room 15: Rodin's feverish attempts to capture a portrait of the novelist Balzac ranged from a pot-bellied Bacchus to a headless nude cradling an erection. In a moment of inspiration, Rodin threw a plaster-soaked robe over the nude and watched it dry into what would become the final, definitive version.

Room 17: Legendary lovers kiss, embrace, and intertwine in yin-yang bliss.

Room 14: Rodin's portrait busts of celebrities and some paintings by (yawn, are we through yet?) van Gogh, Monet, and Renoir. Rodin enjoyed discussions with Monet and other artists and incorporated their ideas in his work. Rodin is often considered an Impressionist because he captured spontaneous "impressions" of figures and created rough surfaces that catch reflected light.

Room 13: By the end of his life Rodin was more famous than his works. The museum's film clip shows Rodin making the marble chips fly. In fact, he rarely picked up a chisel, leaving that to assistants. Compare Rodin's small plaster "sketches" (in the glass case) with the final, large-scale marble versions executed by others.

The Gardens

Rodin lived and worked in this mansion, renting rooms alongside Matisse, the poet Rilke (Rodin's secretary), and the dancer Isadora Duncan. He loved placing his creations in the overgrown gardens. These are his greatest works, Rodin at his most expansive. The epic human figures are enhanced, not dwarfed, by nature.

• *Leaving the house, there are five more stops: two on the left and three on the right. Beyond these stops is a big breezy garden ornamented with statues, a cafeteria, and WC.*

The Thinker: Leaning slightly forward, tense and compact, every muscle working toward producing that one great thought, Man contemplates his fate. No constipation jokes, please.

This is not an intellectual but a linebacker who's realizing there's more to life than frat parties. It's the first man evolving beyond his animal nature to think the first thought. It's anyone who's ever worked hard to reinvent themselves or to make something new or better. Said Rodin: "It is a statue of myself."

There are 29 other authorized copies of this statue, arguably the most famous in the world.

• *To the left of* The Thinker *you'll find...*

Balzac: The iconoclastic novelist turns his nose up at the notion he should be honored with a statue. This final version also stands in the Musée d'Orsay and on a street median in Montparnasse. When the statue was unveiled, the crowd booed, a fitting tribute to both the defiant novelist and the bold man who sculpted him.

• *Along the street near the ticket booth are...*

The Burghers of Calais: The six city fathers trudge to their execution, and we can read in their faces and poses what their last thoughts are. They mill about, dazed, as each one deals with the decision he's made to sacrifice himself for his city.

• *Circling counterclockwise...*

The man carrying the key to the city tightens his lips in determination. The bearded man is weighed down with grief. Another buries his head in his hands. One turns, seeking reassurance from his friend, who turns away and gestures helplessly. The final key bearer (in back) has been stoic, but now he's raising his hand to his head.

Each is alone in his thoughts, but they're united by their mutual sacrifice, by the base they stand on, and by their weighty robes—gravity is already dragging them down to their graves.

Pity the poor bastards, then salute King Edward III, who, at the last second, pardoned them.

• *Follow* The Thinker's *gaze to the opposite side of the house. Standing before a tall white backdrop is a big dark door—the* Gates of Hell.

The Gates of Hell: These doors (never meant to actually open) were never finished for a museum that was never built. But the vision of Dante's trip into hell gave Rodin a chance to explore the dark side of human experience. "Abandon hope all ye who enter in," was hell's motto. The Three Shades at the top of the door point down—that's where we're going. Beneath The Shades, pondering the whole scene from above, is Dante as The Thinker. Below him, the figures emerge from the darkness just long enough to tell their sad tale of depravity. There's Paolo and Francesca (in the center of the right door), who were driven by the life force into an illicit love affair that brought them here. Ugolino (left door, just below center) crouches in prison over his kids. This poor soul was so driven by hunger that he ate the corpses of his own children. On all fours like an animal, he is the dark side of natural selection. Finally, find what some say is Rodin himself (at the very bottom, inside the right door jamb, where it just starts to jut out), crouching humbly.

You'll find some of these figures writ large in the garden. *The Thinker* is behind you, *The Shades* are 30 yards to the right, and *Ugolino* dines in the fountain at the far end.

It's appropriate that *The Gates*—Rodin's "cathedral"—remained unfinished. He was always a restless artist for whom the process of discovery was as important as the finished product.

• *To the right of the* Gates of Hell *is a glassed-in building, the . . .*

Gallery of Marbles: Unfinished, they show human features emerging from the rough stone. Imagine Rodin in his studio working to give them life.

Victor Hugo (at the far end of the Gallery), the great champion of Les Miz progress, leans back like Michelangelo's nude *Adam*, waiting for the spark of creation. He cups his ear, straining to hear the call from the blurry Muse above him. Once inspired, he can bring the idea to life with the strength of his powerful arms. Rodin must have often felt like this. It's been said that all of his work shows the struggle of mind over matter, of brute creatures emerging from the mud and evolving into a species of thinkers.

MARMOTTAN
TOUR

The Marmottan (or Musée Marmottan Monet) has the best collection of works by the master Impressionist, Claude Monet. In this mansion on the fringe of urban Paris, you can walk through Monet's life, from black-and-white sketches to colorful open-air paintings to the canvas that gave Impressionism its name. The museum's highlights (especially in 2001, with the Orangerie closed) are scenes of his garden at Giverny, including larger-than-life water lilies.

Orientation

Cost: 40F, 25F for students under 25, free for children under 8. The Marmottan is not covered by the museum pass.
Hours: Tue–Sun 10:00–17:30 (last entrance 17:00), closed Mon, May 1, and Dec 25.
Getting There: It's in northwest Paris at 2 rue Louis Boilly (Metro: La Muette and a 10-min walk, following signs; or RER-C: Boulainvilliers; or bus #32, #63, #22, #52, or PC).
Information: Tel. 01 44 96 50 33, www.marmottan.com.
Photography: Not allowed.
Length of Our Tour: One hour.
Starring: Claude Monet, including *Impression: Sunrise* (shown above), Rouen Cathedral, Gare St. Lazare, Houses of Parliament, scenes from Giverny, water lilies.

OVERVIEW

The museum traces Monet's life chronologically, but in a way that's as rough and fragmented as a Monet canvas. Keep the big picture.

First Floor (upstairs): Works from the first half of Monet's life, plus paintings by Impressionist colleagues (Renoir, Pissarro, Morisot, and more).

Ground floor: Bookstore and eclectic collection of non-Monet objects.

Basement: Works from the last half of his life, mostly of his gardens at Giverny (including water lilies).

FIRST FLOOR: FROM LE HAVRE TO LONDON (1857–1900)

Portraits of Monet and his wife Camille (by Renoir and others) and Memorabilia

Claude Monet (1840–1926) was the leading light of the Impressionist movement that revolutionized painting in the 1870s. Fiercely independent and dedicated to his craft, Monet gave courage to Renoir and others in the face of harsh criticism. The letters (in the glass case) from Monet asking for survival money from his friends show the price he paid for his bohemian principles.

Impression: Sunrise (1873)

Here's the painting—a simple, serene view of boats bobbing under an orange sun—that started the revolution. At the first public showing by Monet, Renoir, Degas, and others in Paris in 1874, critics howled at this work and ridiculed the title. "Wallpaper," one called it. The sloppy brushstrokes and ordinary subject looked like a study, not a finished work. The whole group and style got dubbed "Impression"-ist . . . a pretty accurate name.

The misty harbor scene obviously made an "impression" on Monet, who faithfully rendered the fleeting moment in quick strokes of paint. The waves are simple horizontal brushstrokes. The sun's reflection on the water is a few thick, bold strokes of orange tipped with white. They zigzag down the canvas, the way a reflection shifts on moving water.

• *Follow the arrow to the right, into "Debut d'exposition," passing through a big room of colorful canvases (which we'll return to later) into a smaller room in the corner.*

Growing up in Le Havre (1840–1860): Caricature Drawings (c. 1858)

Teenage Monet's first works—black-and-white, meticulously drawn, humorous sketches of small-town celebrities—are as different as can be from the colorful, messy oils that would make him famous. Still, they show his gift for quickly capturing an overall impression with a few simple strokes.

The son of a grocer, he defied his family, insisting he was an artist, and sketched the world around him—beaches, boats, and small-town life. A fellow artist encouraged him to don a scarf, set

up his easel outdoors, and paint the scene exactly as he saw it.
(Well, duhh! But "open-air" painting was unorthodox for artists
trained to study their subject thoroughly in the perfect lighting
of a controlled studio setting.)

The 1860s: Paris

At 19, he went to Paris but refused to enroll in the official art
schools. He teamed up with Auguste Renoir and Alfred Sisley,
leading them on open-air painting safaris to the countryside.
Inspired by the realism of Edouard Manet, they painted everyday
things—landscapes, seascapes, street scenes, ladies in parasols,
family picnics—in bright, basic colors.
• *Return to the big room with colorful canvases (spanning 1870–1890).*
To follow Monet chronologically, you'll have to browse around this room
and others on the first floor.

The 1870s: Pure Impressionism

In 1870 Monet married his girlfriend Camille (the dark-haired
woman in many of his paintings) and moved just outside Paris to
the resort town of Argenteuil. Playing host to Renoir, Manet, and
others, he perfected the Impressionist style—painting nature as a
mosaic of short brushstrokes of different colors placed side by side,
suggesting shimmering light.

First, he simplified. In *The Beach at Trouville* (1870), a lady's
dress is simply a few thick strokes of paint. Gradually (*Stroll Near
Argenteuil*, 1872), Monet broke things down into smaller dots of
different colors. If you back up from a Monet canvas, the colors
blend into one (for example, red plus green plus yellow equal a
brown boat). Still, they never fully resolve, creating the effect of
colorful, shimmering light. Monet limited his palette to a few
bright colors—cobalt blue, white, yellow, two shades of red,
and emerald green abound. But no black—even shadows are a
combination of bright colors.

Monet's constant quest was to faithfully reproduce nature in
colored blobs of paint. His eye was a camera lens set at a very slow
shutter speed to admit maximum light. Then he "developed"
the impression made on his retina with an oil-based, pigmented
solution. Even as the heartbroken Monet watched Camille die of
tuberculosis in 1879, he was (he admitted later) intrigued by the
changing colors in her dying face.

The 1880s: Travels

In search of new light and new scenes, Monet traveled throughout France and Europe. As you look at canvases of fields, trees,
seashores, churches, lakes, and farmhouses in all kinds of weather,

picture Monet at work—hiking to a remote spot; carrying an easel, several canvases, brushes (large-size), a palette, tubes of paint (an invention that made open-air painting practical), food and drink, a folding chair, and an umbrella; and wearing his trademark hat, a cigarette on his lip. He weathered the elements, occasionally putting himself in danger (clambering on cliffs) to get the shot.

The key was to work fast before the weather changed and the light shifted, completely changing the colors. Monet worked "wet-in-wet," applying new paint before the first layer dried, mixing colors on the canvas, and piling them up into a thick paste.

The 1890s: Series

Monet often painted the same subject several times under different light (such as one of Paris' train stations, the *Gare St. Lazare*, 1870s). In the 1890s he conceived of a series of paintings to be shown as a group, giving a time-lapse view of a single subject.

He rented a room overlooking the *Cathedral of Rouen* and worked on up to 14 different canvases at a time, shuffling the right one onto the easel as the sun moved across the sky. The cathedral is made of brown stone, but at sunset it becomes gold and pink with blue shadows, softened by thick smudges of paint. The true subject is not the cathedral, but the full spectrum of light that bounces off it.

These series—of the cathedral, of haystacks, poplars, and mornings on the Seine—were very popular. Monet, poverty-stricken until his mid-40s, was slowly becoming famous, first in America, then London, and finally in France.

The 1900s: London

Turning a hotel room into a studio, Monet—working on nearly a hundred different canvases simultaneously—painted the changing light on the River Thames. The *London Houses of Parliament*, reflected in the Thames, stretch and bend with the tide. *Charing Cross Bridge* is only a few smudgy lines enveloped in fog.

London's fog epitomized Monet's favorite subject—the atmosphere that distorts distant objects. That filtering haze gives even different-colored objects a similar tone, resulting in a more harmonious picture. When the light was just right and the atmosphere glowed, the moment of "instantaneity" had arrived, and Monet worked like a madman.

In truth, many of Monet's canvases were begun quickly in the open air then painstakingly perfected later in the studio. He composed his scenes with great care—clear horizon lines give a strong horizon-tal, while diagonal lines (of trees or shore-lines) create solid triangles. And he wasn't above airbrushing

out details that might spoil the composition—like Cleopatra's Needle near Charing Cross.
• *Find portraits of Monet's family in the small octagonal room.*

Monet's Two Families

Camille died in 1879, leaving Monet to raise 12-year-old Jean and babe-in-arms Michel. (Michel would grow up to inherit the family home and many of the paintings that ended up here.) But Monet was also involved with Alice Hoschede, who had recently been abandoned by her husband. Alice moved in with her six kids, took care of the dying Camille, and the two families made a Brady-Bunch merger. Baby Michel became bosom buddies with Alice's baby Jean-Pierre, and teenage Jean Monet and stepsister Blanche fell in love and later married.

In 1883 the brood settled into a farmhouse in Giverny (80 kilometers west of Paris). Monet would spend the next 40 years here, traveling less with each passing year. Financially stable and domestically blissful, he turned Giverny into a garden paradise—painting nature without the long commute.
• *Before leaving the first floor, check out the fine collection of paintings by Monet's Impressionist colleagues: Renoir, Gauguin, Pissarro, Morisot, and others.*

BASEMENT: PAINTINGS OF GIVERNY (1883–1926)

These large, colorful canvases immerse you in Monet's garden at Giverny. He did his own landscaping: flower beds of lilies, iris, and clematis, arbors of climbing roses forming a tunnel-like "Grand Alley," and a Japanese garden with an arched footbridge, willows, bamboo, and a pond filled with water lilies.

In the last half of his life, Monet's world shrank—from the broad vistas of the world traveler to the tranquility of his home, family, and garden. But his artistic vision expanded as he painted smaller details on bigger canvases and helped invent modern, abstract art.
• *Working roughly clockwise around the room . . .*

Path with Rose Trellises

The arched trellises form a natural tunnel effect that leads your eye down the path "into" the canvas. But the canvas is fully saturated with color, with distant objects as bright as close ones. Monet's mosaic of brushstrokes form a colorful design that's beautiful even if you just look "at" the canvas like wallpaper. He wanted his paintings to be realistic (3-dimensional), but with a pleasant (2-dimensional) pattern.

The Japanese Bridge (several versions)

In 1890 Monet started work on a Japanese garden, inspired by tranquil scenes from the Japanese prints he collected. He diverted a river to form a pond, planted willows and bamboo on the shores, filled the pond with water lilies, then crossed it with this wooden footbridge. As years passed (compare early and later canvases), the bridge became overgrown with wisteria. He painted it at different times of day and year, exploring different color schemes.

Monet uses the bridge as the symmetrical center of simple, pleasing designs. The water is drawn with horizontal brushstrokes that get shorter as you move up the canvas ("farther away"), creating the illusion of distance. The horizontal water contrasts with the vertical-stroke willows, while the bridge "bridges" the sides of the square canvas, lacing the scene together.

In 1908 Monet—the greatest "vision"-ary, literally, of his generation—began to go blind. Cataracts distorted his perception of depth and color, and sent him into a tailspin of despair. The (angry?) red paintings date from this time.

Water Lilies (several versions)

As his vision slowly failed, he concentrated on painting close-ups of the surface of the pond and its water lilies (scientific name *Nympheas*), using red, white, yellow, lavender, and various combos. Some lilies are just a few broad strokes on a bare canvas (a study), while others are piles of paint formed with overlapping colors.

But the true subject is not the lilies but the changing reflections on the surface of the pond—of the blue sky, white clouds, and green trees that line the shore. Pan slowly around the room and watch the pond turn from predawn to bright sunlight to twilight. Monet, assisted by his favorite daughter, Blanche (a painter and a widow when Jean died young), worked on several canvases at once, moving with the sun from one to the next.

Early lily paintings (c. 1900) show the shoreline as a reference point. But increasingly, Monet cropped the scene ever closer until there was no shoreline, no horizon, no sense of what's up or down. Lilies float among clouds. Stepping back from the canvas, the lilies just hang there on the museum wall, suspended in space. The surface of the pond and the surface of the canvas are one. Modern, abstract art—a colored design on a flat surface—is just around the corner.

Big Weeping Willow

Get close—Monet did—and analyze the trunk. Rough "brown" bark is made of thick strokes (an inch wide and 4 inches long) of pink, purple, orange, and green. Impressionism lives. But to get these colors to resolve in your eye, you'd have to back up all the way to Giverny.

Later Water Lilies (1915–1926)

Like Beethoven going deaf, blind Monet wrote his final symphonies on a monumental scale. He planned a series of huge canvases (6 feet tall) of water lilies to hang in special rooms at the Orangerie (closed in 2001). He built a special studio with skylights and wheeled easels, and worked on them obsessively. A successful eye operation in 1923 gave him new energy. Here at the Marmottan are smaller-scale studies for that series.

Some lilies are patches of thick paint circled by a squiggly "caricature" of a lily pad. Monet simplifies in a way that Matisse and Picasso would envy. But getting close, you see that the lily is made of many brushstrokes, and also that each brushstroke is itself a mix of different colored paints.

Monet is thought of as a "light"-weight, but he deals with the fundamentals of life, especially in his later work: green lilies floating among lavender clouds reflected in the blue water. Staring into Monet's pond, we see the intermingling of the four classical elements, earth (foliage), air (the sky), fire (sunlight), and water—the primordial soup where life begins.

When Monet died in 1926, he was famous. Starting with meticulous line drawings, he evolved to open-air realist to Impressionist color-analyst to serial painter to master of reflections. As the subjects of his work became fuzzier, the colors and patterns predominated. Monet builds a bridge between Impressionism and modern abstract art.

NAPOLEON'S TOMB & LES INVALIDES TOUR

If you've ever considered being absolute dictator of a united Europe, come here first. Hitler did, before going out and making the same mistakes as his mentor. (Hint: Don't invade Russia.)

Napoleon's tomb can be seen where it rests beneath the golden dome of Les Invalides church. Also in the church, a one-time veterans' hospital built by Louis XIV, are various military museums. The best is the new World War II wing (see tour, below).

Orientaton

Cost: 38F, 28F for students and ages 12 to 17, free for under 12, covered by museum pass.

Hours: Daily 10:00–17:45, closes off-season at 16:45 (Napoleon's Tomb open June 15–Sept 15 until 18:45). Closed Jan 1, May 1, Nov 1, and Dec 25.

Getting There: The tomb is at Hôtel Les Invalides at 129 rue de Grenelle (near Rodin Museum, Mo: La Tour Maubourg, Varennes, or Invalides).

Information: Tel. 01 44 42 37 67 or 01 44 42 38 77, www.invalides.org.

Length of Our Tour: Women—90 minutes, men—two hours, Republican men—all day.

• *Start at Napoleon's tomb, underneath the golden dome. It's at the back end (farthest from the Seine) of this vast complex of churches and museums.*

NAPOLEON'S TOMB

Enter the church, gaze up the dome, then lean over the railing and bow to the emperor lying inside the red porphyry, scrolled tomb. If the lid were opened, you'd find an oak coffin inside, which holds another ebony coffin, housing two lead ones, then mahogany, then tinplate . . . until finally you'd find Napoleon himself staring up, with his head closest to the door. When his body was exhumed from the original grave and transported here, even after 19 years in the ground it was still perfectly preserved.

Born of humble Italian heritage on the French-owned isle of Corsica, Napoleon Bonaparte (1769–1821) went to school at Paris' École Militaire (Military School), then rose quickly through the ranks amid the chaos of the Revolution. The charismatic "Little Corporal" won fans by fighting for democracy at home and abroad. In 1799 he assumed power and, within five short years, conquered most of Europe. The great champion of the Revolution had become a dictator, declaring himself emperor of a new Rome.

Napoleon's red tomb on its green base stands 15 feet high in the center of a marble floor. It's exalted by the dome above (where dead Frenchmen cavort with saints and angels), forming a golden halo over Napoleon.

Napoleon is surrounded by family. After conquering Europe, he installed his big brother Joseph as king of Spain (turn around to see Joseph's tomb in the alcove to the left of the door); his little brother Jerome became king of Westphalia (to right of door); and his baby boy, Napoleon Junior (downstairs), sat in diapers on the throne of Rome.

In other alcoves, you'll find more dead war heroes (including World War I's Marshall Foch) and many painted saints, making this the French Valhalla in the Versailles of churches.

The Crypt

• *The stairs behind the altar (with the corkscrew columns) take you down to crypt level for a closer look at the tomb.*

Wandering clockwise, read the names of Napoleon's battles inlaid on the floor. Rivoli marks the battle where the rookie 26-year-old general took a ragtag band of "citizens" and thrashed the professional Austrian troops in Italy. He returned to Paris a celebrity. In Egypt (Pyramids), he fought Turks and tribesmen to a standstill, but the exotic expedition caught the public eye, and he returned home a legend.

Austerlitz made him Europe's top dog. At the head of the million-man Grand Army, he made a three-month blitz attack through Germany and Austria. As a general he was daring, relying on a mobile force of independent armies. His personal charisma on the battlefield was said to be worth 10,000 additional men.

Pause in the battles to gaze at the grand statue of Napoleon the emperor in the alcove at the head of the tomb—royal sceptre and orb of Earth in his hands. By 1805, all of Europe was at his feet. He held an elaborate ceremony in Notre-Dame, where he proclaimed his wife, Josephine, as Empress, and himself—the 36-year-old son of humble immigrants—as Emperor. The laurel wreath, the robes, and the Roman eagles proclaim him the equal of the Caesars. The floor at the statue's feet marks the grave of his son, Napoleon II (Roi de Rome).

Around the crypt are relief panels showing Napoleon's constructive side. Dressed in toga and laurel leaves, he dispenses justice, charity, and pork-barrel projects to an awed populace.

• *In the first panel to the right of the statue...*

He establishes an Imperial University to educate naked boys throughout "*tout l'empire*." The roll of great scholars links modern France with those of the past: Plutarch, Homer, Plato, and Aristotle.

Hail Napoleon. Then, at his peak, came his fatal mistake.

• *Continue around the tomb to the Battle of Moscow (Moscowa)...*

Napoleon invaded Russia with 600,000 men and returned to Paris with 100,000 frostbitten survivors. Two years later, the Russians marched into Paris, and Napoleon's days were numbered. After a brief exile on the isle of Elba, he skipped parole, sailed to France, bared his breast, and said, "Strike me down or follow me!" For 100 days they followed him, finally into Belgium, where the British finished him off at the Battle of Waterloo (conspicuously absent on the floor decor). Exiled again by a war tribunal, he spent his last days in a crude shack on the small South Atlantic island of St. Helena.

LES INVALIDES AND THE ARMY MUSEUM (MUSÉE DE L'ARMEE)

Your tomb ticket also admits you to several military museums scattered around the complex (listed in free English map/guide in ticket hall). Most of it consists of dummies in uniforms and endless glass cases full of muskets, without historical context, but the new wing on World War II is worthwhile.

Exiting the church with Napoleon's tomb, make a U-turn right and march past the ticket hall and café. Halfway down the long hallway, on the right, you'll see the three bare stone slabs beside weeping willows that originally marked Napoleon's grave on the island of St. Helena. There was no

——— LES INVALIDES ———

epitaph, since the French and British wrangled over what to call the hero/tyrant. The stones read simply, "Here lies…"

Continuing on, you'll spill out into the large Courtyard of Honor, where Napoleon honored his troops and de Gaulle once kissed Churchill. The Army Museum flanks both sides of the courtyard.

ARMY MUSEUM: EAST WING

This traces uniforms and weapons through French history, from Louis XIV to World War I. This is interesting for Napoleo-philes.

• *Enter under golden letters and go up to the second floor.*

As you circle this floor, you'll follow the history and art of French warfare from about 1700 to 1850: Pre-Revolution, Revolution, Napoleon, Restoration.

The "First Republic: 1793–1804" section has early Napoleonic exhibits. In the Salle Boulogne are the emperor's hat and sword. The tent (behind screen) shows his bivouac equipment—a bed with mosquito netting, a director's chair, and a table that you can imagine his generals hunched over, making battle plans.

In the rooms covering "Napoleon and The Empire 1804–1814" (first room: Salle Austerlitz), you'll find the famous portrait by Ingres of Napoleon at his peak of power, stretching his right arm to supernatural lengths. Then comes Napoleon's beloved horse, Le Vizir, who weathered many a campaign and grew old with him in exile (stuffed in a glass case, third room: Salle Eylau).

Later, in Salle Montmirail, there's a portrait of a dejected Napoleon after his first abdication in 1814. A glass case is dedicated to Napoleon's son, the "Roi de Rome." His little soldier boots are there and an engraving shows the child king in a royal carriage. When he grew up (miniature portrait in the center), he looked a lot like his dad, a fact that kept French Royalists wary until his death. Junior's mother (engraving to the left) was Maria-Louise, whom Napoleon married after divorcing barren Josephine.

Napoleon's big white dog (in a glass case after you turn the corner into the long blue Corridor de Tarascon) suffered the same fate as his horse. On the wall to the left of the dog hang proclamations of thanks and good-byes Napoleon sent to his soldiers and the French people, announcing the surrender at Waterloo. Directly behind the dog, a shining breastplate shows the effectiveness of British artillery in the Battle of Waterloo. In about the middle of the long blue room, you'll find Napoleon's death mask and a reconstruction of his final home on St. Helena. Picture a lonely man suffering from ulcers sitting here in his nightcap and slippers, playing chess, not war.

After the Salle Restauration (the mid-1800s, when France brought back the royalty), the last display before the exit is an American flag in a glass case, honoring General La Fayette of France, who helped George Washington take Yorktown. It has the only English-language description in the entire place.

ARMY MUSEUM: WEST WING

Across the courtyard is a twin museum in the West Wing. The ground floor covers military implements from stone axes to Axis powers. Near the entry, two huge, interesting rooms of armor and medieval weaponry have good English descriptions.

Upstairs on the second floor you'll find the World War I wing. Photos and films spice up the uniforms and guns.

The Musée des Plans Reliefs (top floor of West Wing) has 18th-century models of fortified cities (see flier at the door).

The Musée de l'Ordre de la Liberation (free, no English descriptions, located in another building back near Napoleon's gravestones) tells the story of the Resistance in World War II. The French refer to World War II as "The War of '39–40," but this proud collection makes it clear that the French were busy during the Nazi occupation.

ARMY MUSEUM: WORLD WAR II WING

World War II was the most destructive of earth's struggles. In this new exhibit, the war unfolds in photos, displays, and newsreels, with special emphasis on the French contribution. You may never have realized that it was Charles de Gaulle who won the war for us.

The wing is located in the southwest corner of the main courtyard; go upstairs, following signs to "General de Gaulle: Deuxième Guerre Mondiale, 39/45." The museum has two other names as well: "General de Gaulle, Seconde Guerre Mondiale" and "France Libre, France Combattante."

The free museum map (in French) is helpful for locating the displays we'll see.

Climb to the top floor and work back down, from Germany's quick domination (third floor) to the Allies turning the tide (second floor) to the final surrender (first floor).

Third Floor: Axis Aggression

Treaty of Versailles to 1939 ("Du Traité de Versailles à 1939"): In 1918, the "war to end all wars" ground to a halt, leaving 10 million dead, a defeated Germany, and a devastated (if victorious) France. For the next two decades, Adolf Hitler would feed off German resentment for the Treaty of Versailles that had humiliated and ruined Germany.

The Defeat of 1940 ("La Defaite de 1940"): On September 1, 1939, Hitler invaded Poland, starting World War II. France and Britain mobilized, but Germany did nothing for six months. Then, in the spring of 1940, came the Blitzkrieg ("lightning war"), and Germany's better-trained and better-equipped soldiers and tanks swept west through Belgium. France was immediately overwhelmed and British troops barely escaped across the Channel from Dunkirk. Within a month, Nazis were goose-stepping down the Champs-Élysées, and Hitler—faithfully following *Rick Steves' Paris*—was on his way to Napoleon's tomb.

The Appeal of 18 June, 1940: Just like that, virtually all of Europe was dominated by fascists. During those darkest days, as France fell and Nazism spread across the Continent, one Frenchman—an obscure military man named Charles de Gaulle—refused to admit defeat. He escaped to London and made inspiring speeches over the radio, slowly convincing a small audience of French expatriates that victory was still possible.

Charles de Gaulle (1890–1970): This 20th-century John of Arc had an unshakable belief in his mission to save France. He was born into a literate, upper-class family, raised in military academies, and became a WWI hero and POW. After the war he helped administer the occupied Rhineland. When World War II broke out he was only a minor officer (the title of "Brigadier General" was hastily acquired during the invasion). With limited political experience, he was virtually unknown to the French public. But he rallied France, became the focus of French patriotism, and later guided the country in the postwar years.

The Vichy Government ("La France après l'Armistice," "L'Empire colonial: un enjeu"): After the surrender, Germany ruled northern France (including Paris) but allowed the French to administer the south and the colonies (North Africa). This puppet government, centered in the city of Vichy, was right-wing and traditional, bowing to Hitler's demands as he looted France's raw materials and manpower for the war machine. (The movie *Casablanca*, set in Vichy-controlled Morocco, has French officials following Nazi orders while French citizens defiantly sing "The Marseillaise.")

The Battle of Britain—June 1940–May 1941 ("La Bataille d'Angleterre," "Du Refus de la Defaite a l'Esprit de Résistance"): Facing a "New Dark Age" in Europe, British Prime Minister Winston Churchill pledged, "We will fight on the beaches... We will fight in the hills. We will never surrender."

In June 1940, Germany mobilized to invade Britain across the Channel. From June to September they paved the way, sending bombers—up to 1,500 planes a day—to destroy military and industrial sites. When Britain wouldn't budge, Hitler concentrated on London and civilian targets—this was "The Blitz" of the winter of 1940, which killed 30,000 and left London in ruins. But Britain hung on, armed with newfangled radar, speedy Spitfires, and an iron will.

They also had the Germans' secret "Enigma" code. The

"Enigma" machine (in display case), with its set of revolving drums, allowed German commanders to scramble orders into a complex code to safely broadcast to their troops. The British captured a machine, broke the code (a project called "Ultra"), then monitored German airwaves. For the rest of the war, they had advance knowledge of many top-secret plans. (Occasionally, Britain even let Germany's plans succeed—sacrificing their own people—to avoid suspicion.)

By spring of 1941, Hitler had given up any hope of invading the Isle of Britain. Churchill said of his people: "This was their finest hour."

Germany Invades Russia—June 1941 ("L'Allemagne Envahit l'Union Sovietique"): Perhaps hoping to one-up Napoleon, Hitler sent his state-of-the-art tanks speeding toward Moscow (betraying his former ally, Josef Stalin). By winter, the advance stalled at the gates of Moscow, bogged down by bad weather and Soviet stubbornness. The Third Reich had reached its peak. From now on, Hitler would have to fight a two-front war. The French Renault tank (displayed) was downright puny compared to the big, fast, high-caliber German Panzers. This war was often a battle of factories, to see who could produce the latest technology fastest and in greatest number.

The United States Enters the War ("Les États-Unis Entrent dans la Guerre"): "On December seventh, nineteen forty-one, a day that will live in infamy" (as F.D.R. put it), Japanese planes made a sneak attack on the U.S. base at Pearl Harbor, Hawaii, destroying the pride of the Pacific fleet in two hours. The United States quickly declared war on Japan and her ally, Germany. In two short years, America had gone from isolationist observer to supplier of Britain's arms to full-blown war ally against fascism. The United States now faced two wars—in Europe against Hitler, and against Japan's imperialist conquest of China, Southeast Asia, and the South Pacific.

America's first victory came in Hawaii when Japan tried a sneak attack on the U.S. base at Midway Island (June 3, 1942). This time—thanks to cracking Japan's "Enigma" code—America had the U.S.S. *Enterprise* (see model) and two of her buddies lying in wait. In five minutes, three of Japan's carriers (with valuable planes) were fatally wounded, their major attack force was sunk, and Japan and the United States were dead even and settling in for a long war of attrition.

Though slow to start, America eventually had an army 16 million strong, 80,000 planes, the latest technology,

$250 million a day, unlimited raw materials, and a population fighting for freedom to a boogie-woogie beat.

• *Continue downstairs to the second floor.*

Second Floor: The Tide Turns

In 1942 the Continent was black with fascism and Japan was secure on a distant island. The Allies had to chip away on the fringes.

Battle of the Atlantic ("La Bataille de l'Atlantique"):

German U-boats (short for "Unterseeboot," see model) and battleships such as the *Bismarck* patrolled Europe's perimeter, keeping America from aiding Britain. (Until long-range transport planes were invented near war's end, virtually all military transport was by ship.) The Allies traveled in convoys with air cover, used sonar and radar, and dropped depth charges, but for years they endured the loss of up to 60 ships per month.

Guadalcanal, El Alamein, Stalingrad—The War Turns:

Three crucial battles in autumn, 1942, put the first chink in the fascist armor. Off the east coast of Australia, 10,000 marines took an airstrip on Guadalcanal while 30,000 Japanese held the rest of the tiny, isolated island. For the next six months, the two armies were marooned together, duking it out in thick jungles and malaria-infested swamps while their countries struggled to reinforce or rescue them. By February 1943, America had won and gained a crucial launch pad for bombing raids.

A world away, German tanks under General Erwin Rommel rolled across the vast deserts of North Africa. In October 1942, a well-equipped, well-planned offensive by British General Bernard Montgomery attacked at El Alamein, Libya. "Monty" drove the "Desert Fox" east into Tunisia for the first real Allied victory against the Nazi Wehrmacht war machine.

Then came Stalingrad. In August 1942, Germany attacked the Soviet city, an industrial center and gateway to the Caucasus oil fields. By October, they'd battled their way into the city center and were fighting house-to-house, but their supplies were running low, the Soviets wouldn't give up, and winter was coming. The snow fell, their tanks had no fuel, and relief efforts failed. Hitler ordered them to fight on through the bitter cold. On the worst days, 50,000 men died. (America lost 58,000 in Vietnam.) Finally, on January 31, 1943, the Germans surrendered, against Hitler's orders. The six-month totals? Eight hundred thousand German and other Axis soldiers dead, 1.1 million Soviet dead. The Russian campaign put hard miles on the German war machine.

Also in 1942, the Allies began long-range bombing of German-held territory, including saturation bombing of civilians. It was global war and total war.

The Allies Land in North Africa ("Le Débarquement en Afrique du Nord," "La Campagne de Tunisie"):
Winston Churchill and U.S. President Franklin D. Roosevelt (see photo with de Gaulle), two of the century's most dynamic and strong-willed statesmen, decided to attack Hitler indirectly by invading Vichy-controlled Morocco and Algeria. On November 8, 1942, 100,000 Americans and British—under the joint command of an unknown, low-key problem solver named General Dwight ("Ike") Eisenhower—landed on three separate beaches (including Casablanca). More than 120,000 Vichy French soldiers, ordered by their superiors to defend the fascist cause, confronted the Allies and... gave up.

The Allies moved east, but bad weather, their own inexperience, and the powerful Afrika Korps under Rommel stopped them in Tunisia. But with flamboyant General George S. ("Old Blood-and-Guts") Patton punching from the west and "Monty" pushing from the south, they captured the port town of Tunis (May 7, 1943). The Allies now had a base from which to retake Europe.

The Red Army ("L'Armée Rouge Reprend l'Initiative"):
Monty, Patton, and Ike were certainly heroes, but the war was won on the Eastern Front by Soviet grunts who slowly bled Germany dry.

The French Resistance ("L'Unification de la Résistance," "La Lutte Clandestine"):
Inside occupied France, other ordinary heroes fought the Nazis—the "underground," or Resistance. Bakers hid radios in loaves of bread to secretly contact London. Barmaids passed along tips from tipsy Nazis. Communists in black berets cut telephone lines. Farmers hid downed airmen in haystacks. Housewives spread news from the front with their gossip. Printers countered Nazi propaganda with pamphlets.

Jean Moulin (see photo), de Gaulle's assistant, secretly parachuted into France and organized these scattered heroes into a unified effort. In May 1943, Moulin was elected chairman of the National Council of the Resistance. A month later, he was arrested by the Gestapo (Nazi secret police), imprisoned, tortured, and sent to Germany where he died in transit. Still, Free France now had a (secret) government again, rallied around de Gaulle and ready to take over when liberation came.

The Allies Land in Italy ("Premiers Débarquements Allies en Europe"): On July 10, 1943, the assault on Hitler's European fortress began. More than 150,000 Americans and British sailed from Tunis, landing on the south shore of Sicily. (See maps showing the campaigns.) Speedy Patton and methodical Monty began a "horse race" to take the city of Messina (the United States won the friendly competition by a few hours). They met little resistance from 300,000 Italian soldiers, and were actually cheered as liberators by the Sicilian people. Their real enemy was the 50,000 German troops sent by Hitler to bolster his ally, Benito Mussolini. By September, the island was captured. On the mainland, Mussolini was arrested by his own people, and Italy surrendered to the Allies. Hitler quickly poured troops into Italy (and reinstalled Mussolini) to hold off the Allied onslaught.

In early September, the Allies launched a two-pronged landing onto beaches of southern Italy. Finally, after four long years of war, free men set foot on the European continent.

The Italian Campaign ("La Campagne d'Italie"): Lieutenant General Mark Clark, leading the slow, bloody push north to liberate Rome, must have been reminded of the French trenches he'd fought in during World War I. Like that bloody war, the fighting in Italy was a war of attrition, fought on the ground by foot soldiers, costing many lives to gain just a few miles.

In January 1944, the Germans dug in between Rome and Naples at Monte Cassino, a rocky hill topped by the monastery of St. Benedict. Thousands died as the Allies tried inching up the hillside. In frustration, the Allies air-bombed the historic monastery, killing hundreds of monks ... but no Germans, who dug in deeper. Finally, after four months of vicious, sometimes hand-to-hand combat, the Allies—Americans, Brits, Free French, Poles, Italian partisans, Indians, etc.—stormed the monastery and the Germans' back was broken.

Meanwhile, 50,000 Allies had landed on Anzio (a beach near Rome), holding the narrow beachhead for months against massive German attacks. When reinforcements arrived, they broke out and joined the two-pronged assault on the capital. Rome fell without a single bomb threatening its historic treasures, on June 4, 1944.

D-Day—June 6, 1944, "Operation Overlord": Three million Allies and 6 million tons of materiel were massed in England in preparation for the biggest fleet-led invasion in history—across the Channel to France then eastward to Berlin. The Germans, hunkered down in Northern France, knew an invasion was imminent, but the Allies kept it top secret. On the night of June 5, 150,000 soldiers boarded ships and planes, not knowing where they were headed until they were underway. Each one carried a note from General Eisenhower: "The tide has turned. The free men of the world are marching together to victory."

At 6:30 a.m. on June 6, 1944, Americans spilled out of troop transports into the cold waters off a beach in Normandy code-named Omaha. The weather was bad, seas were rough, and the prep bombing had failed. The soldiers, many seeing their first action, were dazed and confused. Nazi machine guns pinned them against the sea. Slowly they crawled up the beach on their stomachs. A thousand died. They held on until the next wave of transports arrived.

All day long, Allied confusion did battle with German indecision—the Nazis never really counterattacked, thinking D-Day was just a ruse, not the main invasion. By day's end, the Allies had taken several beaches along the Normandy coast and began building artificial harbors, providing a tiny port-of-entry for the reconquest of Europe. The stage was set for a quick and easy end to the war. Right.

• *Go downstairs to . . .*

First Floor: The War Ends . . . Very Slowly (June 1944–Aug 1945)

Battle of Normandy ("La Bataille de Normandie"): For a month, the Allies (mostly Americans) secured Normandy, taking bigger ports (Cherbourg and Caen) and amassing troops and supplies for the assault on Germany. In July they broke out and sped eastward across France, Patton's tanks covering up to 40 miles a day. They had "Jerry" on the run.

Landing in Provence, August 1944 ("Le Debarquement de Provence"): On France's Mediterranean coast, American troops under General Alexander Patch landed near Cannes, took Marseilles, and headed north to meet up with Patton.

Liberation of Paris: As the Allies marched on Paris, Hitler ordered his officers to torch the city—they sanely disobeyed and prepared to surrender. On August 26, General Charles de Gaulle walked ramrod-straight down the Champs-Élysées, followed by Free French troops and U.S. GIs passing out chocolate and Camels. Two million Parisians went ape.

"Les Maquis": French Resistance guerrilla fighters helped reconquer France from behind the lines. The liberation of Paris was started by a Resistance attack on a German garrison.

On to Berlin—Offensive from the West ("Vers Berlin— Offensives a l'Ouest"): The quick advance through France, Belgium, and Luxembourg bogged down at the German border in autumn of 1944. Patton outstripped supply lines, a parachute invasion of Holland (Battle of Arnhem) was disastrous, and bad weather grounded planes and slowed tanks.

On December 16, the Allies met a deadly surprise. An enormous, well-equipped, energetic German army appeared from nowhere, punched a "bulge" deep into Allied lines, and demanded surrender. General Anthony McAuliffe sent a one-word response— "Nuts!"—and the tide turned. The Battle of the Bulge was Germany's last great offensive.

Germany retreated across the Rhine River, blowing up bridges behind them. The last bridge, at Remagen, was captured by the Allies just long enough to cross and establish themselves on German soil. Soon U.S. tanks were speeding down the autobahns and Patton could wire the good news back to Ike: "General, I have just pissed in the Rhine."

Offensive From The East: Soviet soldiers did the dirty work of taking fortified Berlin, launching a final offensive in January 1945, and surrounding the city in April. German citizens fled west to surrender to the more-benevolent Americans and Brits. Hitler, defiant to the end, hunkered in his underground bunker.

Germany Surrenders ("Capitulation de l'Allemagne"): On April 28, 1945, Mussolini and his girlfriend were killed and hung by their heels in Milan. Two days later, Adolf Hitler and his new bride, Eva Braun, avoided similar humiliation by committing suicide (pistol in mouth) and having their bodies burned beyond recognition. Germany formally surrendered on May 8, 1945.

Concentration Camps: Lest anyone mourn Hitler or doubt this war's purpose, gaze on photos from Germany's concentration camps. Some camps held political enemies and prisoners of war (including 2 million French), others were expressly built to extermi- nate peoples considered "genetically inferior" to the Aryan "master race"—namely, Jews, Gypsies, homosexuals, and the mentally ill.

War Of The Pacific ("Pacifique—Les Grandes Offensives Americaines"): Often treated as an afterthought, the final cam- paign against Japan was a massive American effort costing many lives but saving millions from Japanese domination.

Japan was an island bunker surrounded by a vast ring of fortified Pacific islands. America's strategy was to take one island at a time, "island hopping" until close enough for B-29 Super-fortress bombers to attack Japan itself. The war spread across thousands of miles. In a new form of warfare, ships carrying planes led the attack, preparing tiny islands for troops to land and build an airbase. While General Douglas MacArthur island-hopped south to retake the Philippines ("I have returned!"), others pushed north toward Japan.

In February 1945, marines landed on Iwo Jima, a city-size island-volcano close enough to Japan (800 miles) to launch air raids. Twenty thousand Japanese were dug in on the volcano-top, picking off the advancing Americans. On February 23, several U.S. soldiers raised the Stars and Stripes on the mountain (that famous photo), inspiring their mates to victory at a cost of nearly 7,000 men.

Japan Surrenders ("Capitulation du Japon"): On March 9, Tokyo was firebombed and 90,000 were killed. Japan was losing, but a land invasion would cost hundreds of thousands of lives. The "Japs" had a reputation for choosing death over the shame of surrender—they even sent bomb-laden "kamikaze" planes on suicide missions.

America unleashed its secret weapon, an atomic bomb (originally suggested by German-turned-American Albert Einstein). On August 6, a B-29 dropped one on the city of Hiroshima, instantly vaporizing four square miles and 100,000 people. Three days later a second bomb fell on Nagasaki. The next day, Emperor Hirohito unofficially surrendered. The long war was over, and U.S. sailors returned home to kiss their girlfriends in public places.

War Totals ("Le Bilan de la Guerre"): The death toll for World War II (Sept 1939–Aug 1945) totaled 40 million soldiers and civilians. The Soviet Union lost 20 million, China 13 million, France 600,000, and the United States 290,000.

World War II changed the world, with America emerging as the dominant political, military, and economic superpower. Europe was split in two. The western half recovered with American aid. The east remained under Soviet occupation. For 45 years, the United States and the Soviet Union would compete—without ever actually doing battle—in a "Cold War" of espionage, propaganda, and weapons production that stretched from Korea to Cuba, from Vietnam to the moon.

CLUNY MUSEUM TOUR

Musée National du Moyen Age

The "National Museum of the Middle Ages" doesn't sound quite so boring as I myself approach middle age. Aside from the solemn religious art, there is some lively stuff here.

Paris emerged on the world stage in the "Middle" Ages, the time between ancient Rome and the Renaissance. Europe was awakening from a thousand-year slumber. Trade was booming, people actually owned chairs, and the Renaissance was moving in like a warm front from Italy.

Orientation

Cost and Hours: 38F, 28F on Sun, covered by museum pass, Wed–Mon 9:15–17:45, closed Tue, tel. 01 53 73 78 00.
Getting There: It's at 6 place Paul-Painlevé, near the corner of boulevards St. Michel and St. Germain (Mo: Cluny/La Sorbonne, St. Michel, or Odéon).
Baggage Check: Required and free.
Length of Our Tour: One hour.

Room 2: The first art you see is not some grim, grey crucifixion but a colorful tapestry depicting grape-stomping peasants during the Vendange (the annual autumn harvest/celebration). A peasant man treads grapes in a vat while his wife collects the juice. A wealthy man gives orders. Above that, a peasant with a pimple turns a new-fangled mechanical press. On the right, you'll see the joy of picking—pawns, knights, and queens all working side by side.

Having survived their Y1K crisis, these people realize the world won't end, and they turn their attention to the beauty of the world around them.

Room 3: Colorful woven fabrics were brought back to France by crusaders, who went off to conquer barbarian infidels but returned with tales of enlightened peoples on the fringes of Europe.

Room 4: Six tapestries in wool and silk show the rich enjoying the simple, secular pleasures of their estate. The humans mingle harmoniously with the trees, flowers, and animals of the glorious physical world.

Reading clockwise: 1) A lady with a puppy spins wool while her husband relaxes with the morning paper. 2) Out in the garden, the sexes mingle unchaperoned by the Church. A lady takes a breath mint while a troubadour puts the moves on her servant. 3) A lady embroiders a pillow. 4) The family picks fruit from their plentiful orchards. 5) A lord goes hunting with his falcon, dog, and servant. 6) A naked woman takes a chilly bath, enjoying fruits, jewels, and music—the good things of a world becoming increasingly less sinful.

Room 6: Enter the Dark Ages, when life was harsh and violent, angels and demons made regular appearances, and the Church was your only refuge. Stained glass gave the poor a glimpse of the glories of heaven and served as a visual aid for teaching the illiterate masses. These panels (many from the cathedral of light, Sainte-Chapelle) give us a window into the magical, supernatural, miraculous—and often violent—medieval mind. What were these people thinking?

Reading clockwise around the room, lowest level: 1) The angel Gabriel blasts his horn on Resurrection morning, rousting the grateful dead from their coffins. Notice that Gabriel's royal purple robe is made up of several different pieces of glass—purples, whites, blues—held together with lead. 2) King Herod seems—shocked? pleased?—to see the head of John the Baptist presented to him on a plate by Salome, his dancing stepdaughter. 3) A red-faced, horned, horny demon (with his equally lascivious wolf and henchman) carries off a frightened girl in red to do unspeakable acts. 4) Blond, pious Joseph is sold into slavery to camel merchants by his plotting brothers.

Next wall: 5) Samson is about to pull down the temple . . . . 6) having had his eyes gouged out by Philistines. 7) Slaughter on the battlefield. Men with bloodstained hands and faces hack at each other with golden swords. 8) Aaron, disobeying God and Moses, worships a golden calf. 9) A king on a throne closes his eyes to all this wickedness.

Next wall (with some panels from the first Gothic church, St. Denis): 10) Two monks with prayer books gaze up as one of their brothers disappears into heaven. The Latin inscription, *"hec est via,"* means "This is the way". 11) Seated Jesus, in a royal purple robe, is consoled by two angels. 12) Theophilus ("Lover of God") has struck a Faustian deal with the devil and is now feeling buyer's remorse. 13) Sleeping St. Martin is visited by a heavenly vision. 14) Angels in Rock-and-Roll Heaven.

Last wall: Four apostles—John ("Ioanneus"), James, Peter ("Petrus," with key), and Paul.

Again, what were these people thinking? Bizarre stuff.

Room 8: These 21 stone heads (sculpted 1220–1230) of the kings of Judah from the Bible once decorated the front of Notre-Dame. Then, in 1793, an angry and misinformed mob of revolutionaries mistook the kings of Judah for the kings of France and abused and decapitated the statues. (Today's heads on the Notre-Dame statues are reconstructions.) Someone gathered up the heads and buried them in his backyard near the present-day Opéra. There they slept for two centuries, unknown and noseless, until 1977, when some diggers accidentally unearthed them and brought them to an astounded world. Their stoic expressions accept what fate, time, and liberals have done to them.

The statue of Adam that's here is also from Notre-Dame. He's scrawny and flaccid by Renaissance standards. And it will be another 200 years before naked Adam can step out from behind that bush.

Room 9: This echoing cavern was a Roman frigidarium. Pretty cool. The museum is located on the site of a Roman bathhouse, a reminder of the Romans' centuries of occupation. After hot baths and exercise in adjoining rooms, ordinary Romans would take a cold dip in the sunken pool (in the alcove), then relax cheek to cheek with notables such as Emperor Julian the Apostate (see his statue), who lived right next door. The 40-foot ceiling is the largest Roman vault in France, and it took the French another 1,000 years to improve on that crisscross-arch technology. The sheer size of this room, built in A.D. 200 when Rome was at its peak, gives an idea of the epic scale the Romans built on, inspiring Europeans to greatness during the less-civilized Middle Ages.

The four old square columns (Pilier des Nautes) are the oldest man-made objects you'll see from Paris. These pillars once supported a 20-foot-high altar to the king of the gods in the Temple of Jupiter, where Notre-Dame now stands. The carving on one says it was built in the time of the Emperor Tiberius, A.D. 14 through 37 ("TIB. CAESARE"), and was paid for by the Parisian boatmen's union (see them holding their canoe-shaped boats).

Room 10: Rome lived on after the Fall. The carved Byzantine ivories (first glass case) show how pagan gods, emperors, and griffins became Christian saints, gargoyles, and icons. Constantinople—the eastern half of the empire that survived the Fall—preserved Roman tastes and imagery, like the willowy, bare-breasted, dreamy-eyed *Ariadne* (*Ariane*), with the sneaky satyr peeking out. In painting, Byzantine gold-background icons inspired medieval altar pieces like others in the room.

Rome also lived on in the Romanesque grandeur of Christian churches like St. Germain-des-Prés (the 12-column capitals). The central capital shows Christ in robes on a throne ruling the world as a Roman emperor. These capitals were originally painted, much like the painted wooden statues across the room. Don't leave this room before eyeing the tusk of a narwhal (on the wall), which must have convinced superstitious folk to believe in unicorns.

• *Go upstairs to . . .*

"The Lady and the Unicorn" Tapestries

As Europeans emerged from the Dark Ages, they rediscovered the beauty of the world around them.

These six mysterious tapestries, designed by an unknown (but probably French) artist before 1500 and woven in Belgium out of wool and silk, are loaded with symbols, some serious, some playful. They have been interpreted many ways, but the series deals with each of the five senses.

• *Moving clockwise around the room . . .*

Taste: A blond lady takes candy from a servant's dish to feed it to her parakeet. A unicorn and a lion look on. At her feet, a monkey also tastes something, while the little white dog behind her wishes he had some. This was the Age of Discovery, when Columbus and Vasco da Gama spiced up Europe's bland gruel with new fruits, herbs, and spices.

The lion (symbol of knighthood?) and unicorn (symbol of "bourgeois nobility," purity, or fertility?) wave flags with the coat of arms of the family that bought the tapestries—three silver crescent moons in a band of blue.

Hearing: Wearing a stunning dress, the lady plays sweet music on an organ, soothing the savage beasts around her. The pattern and folds of the tablecloth are lovely. Humans and their fellow creatures live in harmony in a blue, enchanted garden filled with flowers, set in a red background.

Sight: The unicorn cuddles up and looks at himself in the lady's mirror, pleased with what he sees. The lion turns away and snickers. As the Renaissance dawns, vanity is a less-than-deadly sin.

Admire the great artistic skill in some of the detail work, such as the necklace and the patterns in her dress. This tapestry had quality control in all its stages—drawing the scene, enlarging and transferring it to a cartoon, and weaving it. Still, the design itself is crude by Renaissance 3-D standards. The fox and rabbits, supposedly in the distance, simply float overhead, as big as the animals at the lady's feet.

Smell: The lady picks flowers and weaves them into a sweet-smelling wreath. On a bench behind, the monkey apes her. The flowers, trees, and animals are exotic and varied. Each detail is exquisite alone; but stepping back, they blend together into pleasing patterns.

Touch: This is the most basic and dangerous of the senses. The lady "strokes the unicorn's horn," if you know what I mean, and the lion gets the double-entendre. Unicorns, a species extinct since the Age of Reason, were so wild that only the purest virgins could entice and tame them. Medieval Europeans were exploring the wonders of love and the pleasures of sex. The Renaissance is coming.

Tapestry #6: The most talked-about tapestry gets its name from the words on our lady's tent: *A Mon Seul Désir* ("To My Sole Desire"). What *is* her only desire?

Is it jewelry, as she grabs a necklace from the jewel box? Or is she putting the necklace away, renouncing material things in order to follow her only desire?

Our lady has tried all things sensual and is now prepared to follow the one true impulse. Is it God? Or love? Her friends the unicorn and lion open the tent doors. Flickering flames cover the tent. Perhaps she's going in to meet the object of her desire. An old, dark age is ending and a new Renaissance world dawns.

VERSAILLES
TOUR

If you've ever wondered why your American passport has French writing in it, you'll find the answer at Versailles (vehr-sigh). The powerful court of Louis XIV at Versailles set the standard of culture for all of Europe right up to modern times. Versailles was every king's dream palace. Today, if you're planning to visit just one palace in all of Europe, make it Versailles. And if you're with car, or simply prefer a smaller town base for Paris, see my "Sleeping in Versailles" recommendations on page 244.

Orientation

Hours: May–Sept Tue–Sun 9:00–18:30, Oct–April 9:00–17:30, closed Mon, last entry 30 minutes before closing. (Grand and Petit Trianon open at 10:00 year-round.) In summer, Versailles is especially crowded around 10:00 and 13:00, and all day Tue and Sun. Remember, the crowds gave Marie-Antoinette a pain in the neck too, so relax and let them eat cake. For fewer crowds, go early or late: Either arrive by 9:00 (when the palace opens, touring the palace first, then the gardens) or after 15:30 (you'll get a reduced entry ticket but you'll miss the last guided tours of the day, which generally depart at 15:00). If you arrive midday, see the gardens first and the palace later, at 15:00. The gardens and palace are great late. On my last visit, at 18:00 I was the only tourist in the Hall of Mirrors...even on a Tuesday.

Cost: 46F (covered with museum pass); 36F after 15:30, on Sunday, and for those over 60 or ages 18 to 25; under 18 free. Admission is payable at entrances A, C, and D. Tours cost extra (see below). The Grand Trianon is 25F and the Petit Trianon is 15F (both covered with museum pass); one ticket for both is 30F.

Fountain Spectacles: Classical music fills the king's backyard and the garden's fountains are in full squirt on Sat July–Sept and on

VERSAILLES

GRAND TRIANON

SUMMER HOUSE

GRAND CANAL →

PETIT TRIANON

TEMPLE OF LOVE

APOLLO BASIN

BIKE RENTAL

COLONNADE →

LE HAMEAU

GARDENS

❶ HOTEL LE CHEVAL ROUGE
❷ HOTEL IBIS
❸ HOTEL DU PALAIS
❹ HOTEL D'ANGLETERRE

LATONA BASIN

ORANGERIE →

CHÂTEAU

NEPTUNE BASIN

PLACE DU VIEUX MARCHÉ

AVE DE GAULLE

AVE DE L'EUROPE

VERSAILLES R.G. STN.

VERSAILLES TOWN

TO PARIS VIA R.E.R. TRAIN

DCH

WALKING TIMES
TRAIN STN TO CHÂTEAU = 10 MIN.
CHÂTEAU TO GRAND TRIANON = 30 MIN.
GRAND TRIANON TO LE HAMEAU = 20 MIN.
LE HAMEAU TO CHÂTEAU = 30 MIN.

Sun early April–early Oct (schedule for both days: 11:00–12:00, 15:30–17:00, and 17:20–17:30). On these "spray days," the gardens cost 30F (not covered by museum pass). Louis had his engineers literally reroute a river to fuel these fountains. Even by today's standards they are impressive. For more information, pick up the map of the fountain show ("Les Grandes Eaux Musicales") at any information booth.

Touring Versailles: Versailles' highlights are the State Apartments, the lavish King's Private Apartments, the Opera House, and the magnificent Hall of Mirrors. Most visitors are satisfied with a spin through the State Apartments (following my self-guided tour, below), the gardens, and the Trianons. Versailles aficionados should spend the time (and money) for the King's Private Apartments, which can be visited only with an audioguide or live guide (neither tour covered by museum pass).

Self-guided tour—For the basic self-guided tour, join the line at entrance A if you need to pay admission. Those with a museum pass are allowed in through entrance B-2 without a wait. Enter the palace and take a one-way walk through the State Apartments (follow my tour, below) from the "King's Wing," through the Hall of Mirrors, and out via the "Queen's Wing."

Audioguide tours—Two informative but dry audioguide tours are available (30F). One covers the State Apartments (includes Hall of Mirrors and queen's bedchamber; start at entrance A or, if you have a museum pass, entrance B-2). The other includes more of the King's Private Apartments (Louis XIV) and a sampling of nobles' chambers (entrance C).

Guided tours—You may select a one-hour guided tour of lesser-known nobles' apartments, like those of the well-coiffed Madame Pompadour (25F, several itineraries, join first English tour available). Or consider the 90-minute tour (37F) of the King's Private Apartments (Louis XV, Louis XVI, and Marie-Antoinette) and the chapel. This tour, which is the only way visitors can see the Opera House, can be long; the occasional dull guide stretches it to eternity. All guided tours end near the Hall of Mirrors, allowing direct entry to the hall and the State Apartments. Make reservations for a live tour upon arrival, at entrance D, as tours can sell out by 13:00. Guided tours begin at entrance F.

Location of entrances—As you approach the main palace, walk to the statue of Louis XIV on horseback. Look to the center of the courtyard beyond the statue. On the right are the State Apartments (including the Hall of Mirrors), to the left are the King's Private Apartments. From here you have five entrance options: 1) If you want to see the State Apartments but you don't have a museum pass, make a hard right at the statue, walk 50 yards, then turn left between the palace wing and the chapel and find entrance A (look for the line; keep your ticket to prove you've already paid for admission in case you decide to take a guided tour later). The cafeteria and WCs are next to this entry. 2) If you have a museum pass, walk straight past Louis about 75 yards to door B-2 on the right and enter here for the State Apartments (no lines). 3) For an audioguide tour of the State Apartments, use entrance A or B-2. 4) To tour Louis XIV's private apartments by audioguide, walk about 75 yards past the statue, veer left, and pass under the arch to entrance C. 5) Reserve live

VERSAILLES' ENTRANCES

QUEEN'S &
NOBLES
WING

KING'S
WING

HALL OF
MIRRORS

D

F

C

B-2

DCH

CAFE
& WC

EQUESTRIAN
STATUE

FROM
STATION

A

E N T R A N C E S

A = SELF-GUIDED TOURS ENTRANCE

B-2 = PASS HOLDERS ENTRANCE

C = ENTRANCE FOR AUDIOGUIDE TOURS OF
       PRIVATE APARTMENTS

D = BUY TICKETS FOR GUIDED TOURS HERE

F = GUIDED TOURS BEGIN HERE

••• = TOUR ROUTE

guided tours at entrance D, just past entrance C. Guided tours
begin across the courtyard from entrance D at entrance F
(see map of entrance points, shown above).

Getting There: Take the **RER-C train** (29F round-trip, 30
min one-way) to Versailles R.G. or "Rive Gauche" (not Versailles
C.H., which is farther from the palace). Trains, usually named
"Vick," leave about five times an hour for the palace. RER-C
trains leave from these RER/Métro stops: Invalides, Champ de
Mars, Musée d'Orsay, St. Michel, and Gare d'Austerlitz. Get off at
Versailles Rive Gauche (the end of the line), turn right out of the
station, and turn left at the first boulevard. It's a 10-minute walk
to the palace.

Your Eurailpass covers this inexpensive trip, but it uses up a
valuable "flexi" day. Instead of using your pass, consider seeing
Versailles on your way in or out of Paris. To get free passage,
show your railpass at an SCNF ticket window—for example, at
the Les Invalides or Musée d'Orsay RER stops—and get a
contremarque de passage. Keep this ticket to exit the system.

When returning from Versailles, look through the windows
past the turnstiles for the departure board. Any train leaving
Versailles goes as far as downtown Paris (they're marked "all
stations until d'Austerlitz").

Allow 225F each way for a **taxi** from Paris to Versailles.
To reach Versailles from Paris by **car**, get on the *peripherique* freeway that circles Paris and take the toll-free autoroute A-13 toward
Rouen. Follow signs into Versailles, then look for "château" signs
and park in the huge lot with reasonable rates in front of the
palace. The drive takes about 30 minutes one-way.

Information: A helpful tourist information office is just past the Sofitel Hôtel on your walk from the station to the palace (April–Oct daily 9:00–19:00, Nov–March daily 9:00–18:00, tel. 01 39 24 88 88). You'll also find information booths inside the château (doors A, B-2, and C). The useful brochure, "Versailles Orientation Guide," explains your sightseeing options.

Cuisine Art: The cafeteria is next to the general entrance, door A (described above). You'll find restaurants on the street to the right of equestrian statue, though the best places line the pleasant market square in the town center (turn right out of the train station, cross the avenue de Paris, and continue about 5 blocks to place du Marché). A handy McDonald's is immediately across from the train station (WC without crowds).

Length of Our Tour: Allow two hours for the palace and two for the gardens. Including two hours to cover your round-trip transit time, it's a six-hour day trip from Paris.

Starring: Louis XIV and the Old Regime.

KINGS AND QUEENS AND GUILLOTINES

• *Read this on the train ride out there. Relax, the palace is the last stop.*

Come the Revolution, when they line us up and make us stick out our hands, will you have enough calluses to keep them from shooting you? A grim thought, but Versailles raises questions like that. It's the symbol of the Old Regime, a time when society was divided into rulers and the ruled, when you were born to be rich or to be poor. To some it's the pinnacle of civilization, to others the sign of a civilization in decay. Either way it remains one of Europe's most impressive sights.

Versailles was the residence of the king and seat of France's government for a hundred years. Louis XIV (reigned 1643–1715) moved out of the Louvre in Paris, the previous royal residence, and built an elaborate palace in the forests and swamps of

Versailles, 12 miles west. The reasons for the move were partly personal—Louis loved the outdoors and disliked the sniping environs of stuffy Paris—and partly political.

Louis was creating the first modern, centralized state. At Versailles he consolidated Paris' scattered ministries so he could personally control policy. More important, he invited to Versailles all of France's nobles so he could control them. Living a life of almost

enforced idleness, the "domesticated" aristocracy couldn't inter-
fere with the way Louis ran things. With 18 million people
united under one king (England had only 5.5 million), a booming
economy, and a powerful military, France was Europe's number-
one power.

Versailles was also the cultural heartbeat of Europe. Every
king wanted a palace like Versailles. Everyone learned French.
French taste in clothes, hairstyles, table manners, theater, music,
art, and kissing spread across the Continent. That cultural
dominance continued to some extent right up to our century.

Louis XIV

At the center of all this was Europe's greatest king. He was a true
Renaissance man, a century after the Renaissance—athletic, good-
looking, a musician, dancer, horseman, statesman, art lover, lover.
For all his grandeur, he was one of history's most polite and
approachable kings, a good listener who could put even commoners at ease in his presence.

Louis called himself the Sun King because he gave life and
warmth to all that he touched. He was also thought of as Apollo,
the Greek god of the sun. Versailles became the personal temple
of this god on earth, decorated with statues and symbols of
Apollo, the sun, and Louis himself.

Louis was a hands-on king who personally ran affairs of state.
All decisions were made by him. Nobles, who in other countries
were the center of power, became virtual slaves dependent on
Louis' generosity. For 70 years he was the perfect embodiment
of the absolute monarch. He summed it up best himself with his
famous rhyme—"*L'état, c'est moi!*" ("The state, that's me!").

Only Two More Louis To Remember

Three kings lived in Versailles during its century of glory. Louis
XIV built it and established French dominance. Louis XV, his
great-grandson (Louis XIV reigned for 72 years), carried on the
tradition and policies but without the Sun King's flair. During
Louis XV's reign, France's power abroad was weakening and
there were rumblings of rebellion from within.

France's monarchy was crumbling, and the time was ripe for
a strong leader to reestablish the old feudal order. They didn't
get one. Instead, they got Louis XVI, a shy, meek bookworm,
the kind of guy who lost sleep over Revolutionary graffiti...
because it was misspelled. Louis XVI married a sweet girl from
the Austrian royal family, Marie-Antoinette, and together they
retreated into the idyllic gardens of Versailles while revolutionary
fires smoldered.

THE TOUR BEGINS

This tour covers the ceremonial center of the palace (the State, or Grand Apartments) and the extensive grounds. It begins outside the palace at the equestrian statue of Louis XIV.

The central palace, the part we'll tour, forms a U around the courtyard in front of you. The right half (King's Wing) is separated from the left half (Queen's Wing) by the Hall of Mirrors ahead of you. Then two long wings shoot out to the right and left (north and south) of this U. In this tour, we'll walk counterclockwise through the U-shaped part on the middle floor.

The Original Château

The part of the palace directly behind the horse statue, at the far end of the courtyard, is the original château. Louis XIV's dad used to come out to the forests of Versailles to escape the worries of kingship. Here he built this small hunting lodge. His son spent the happiest times of his boyhood at the lodge, hunting and riding. Louis XIV's three arched bedroom windows (beneath the clock) overlooked the courtyard. Naturally, it faced the rising sun. The palace and grounds are laid out on an east-west axis.

When he became king, Louis XIV spent more and more time here, away from the hubbub of Paris. He expanded the lodge, planted gardens, and entertained guests. The reputation spread about this "Enchanted Island," a kind of Disneyworld for dukes and duchesses. As visitors flocked here, Louis expanded around the original hunting château, attaching wings to create the present U-shape. Then, the long north and south wings were built. The total cost of the project has been estimated at half of France's entire GNP for one year.

Think how busy this courtyard must have been 300 years ago. There were as many as 5,000 nobles here at any one time, each with an entourage. They'd buzz from games to parties to amorous rendezvous in sedan-chair taxis. Servants ran about delivering secret messages and roast legs of lamb. Horse-drawn carriages arrived at the fancy gate with their finely dressed passengers, having driven up the broad boulevard that ran direct from Paris. (You can still see the horse stables lining the boulevard.) Incredible as it seems, both the grounds and most of the palace were public territory where even the lowliest peasant could come to gawk. Of course, this meant that

there were, then as now, hordes of tourists, pickpockets, and dark-skinned men selling wind-up children's toys.
• *Enter at Entrance A (or at B-2 if you have a museum pass) and buy your ticket. After showing your ticket, pass through the 21 rooms of the history museum, with paintings on the background of Versailles and its kings.*

Our tour starts upstairs, in the room that overlooks the lavish Royal Chapel. If you took the guided tour, you may spill out here, looking at the upper level of the Royal Chapel.

The State Apartments

Royal Chapel: In the vast pagan "temple" that is Versailles, built to glorify one man, Louis XIV, this Royal Chapel is a paltry tip of the hat to that "other" god, the Christian one. It's virtually the first, last, and only hint of Christianity you'll see in the entire complex. Versailles celebrates Man, not God, by raising Louis to almost godlike status, the personification of all good human qualities. In a way, Versailles is the last great flowering of Renaissance humanism and revival of the classical world.

Louis attended mass here every morning. While he sat on the upper level, the lowly nobles below would turn their backs to the altar and look up—worshiping Louis worshiping God. Important religious ceremonies took place here, including the marriage of young Louis XVI to Marie-Antoinette.
• *Take a seat in the next room, a large room with a fireplace and a colorful painting on the ceiling.*

Hercules Drawing Room: Pleasure ruled. The main suppers, balls, and receptions were held in this room. Picture elegant partygoers in fine silks, wigs, rouge, and lipstick (and that's just the men) dancing to the strains of Mozart played by a string quartet.

On the wall opposite the fireplace is an appropriate painting, showing Christ in the middle of a Venetian party. The work by Veronese, a gift from the Republic of Venice, was one of Louis' favorites, so they decorated the room around it.

The ceiling painting of Hercules being crowned a god gives the room its name. Hercules (with his club) rides up to heaven on a chariot, where the king of the gods is ready to give him his daughter in marriage. Louis XIV built the room for his own daughter's wedding reception.
• *The following rooms are listed in order. The names of the rooms generally come from the paintings on the ceilings. From here on it's a one-way tour—getting lost is not allowed. Follow the crowds into the small green room with a goddess in pink on the ceiling.*

The King's Wing

Cornucopia Room: If the party in the Hercules Room got too intense, you could always step in here for some refreshments. Silver trays were loaded up with liqueurs, coffee, juice, chocolates, and, on really special occasions, three-bean salad.

The ceiling painting shows the cornucopia of riches poured down on invited guests. Around the edges of the ceiling are painted versions of the king's actual dinnerware and treasures.

Louis himself might be here. He was a gracious host who enjoyed letting his hair down at night. If he took a liking to you, he might sneak you through those doors there (in the middle of the wall) and into his own private study, where he'd show off his collection of dishes, medals, jewels, or ... the *Mona Lisa*, which hung on his wall.

Venus Room: Love ruled at Versailles. In this room, couples would cavort beneath a canopy of golden garlands (on the ceiling) sent down to Earth by the goddess of love to ensnare mortals in love. Notice how a painted garland goes "out" the bottom of the central painting, becomes a gilded wood garland held by a satyr, and then turns back to a painting again. Baroque artists loved to mix their media to fool the eye. Another illusion is in the paintings at both ends of the room, which extend this grand room into mythical courtyards.

Don't let the statue of a confident Louis as a Roman emperor fool you. He started out as a poor little rich kid with a chip on his shoulder. His father had died before he was old enough to rule, and, during the regency period, the French Parliament treated little Louis and his mother like trash. They were virtual prisoners, humiliated in their home (the Louvre), surviving on bland meals, hand-me-down leotards, and pointed shoes. Once he attained power and wealth, there was one topic you never discussed in Louis' presence—poverty. Maybe Versailles was his way of saying, "Living well is the best revenge."

Diana Room: This was the billiards room. Men played on a table that stood in the center of the room, while ladies sat surrounding them on Persian-carpet cushions.

The famous bust of Louis by Bernini (now in the center) shows a handsome, dashing, 27-year-old playboy-king. His gaze is steady amid his windblown cloak and hair. Young Louis loved life. He hunted by day (notice Diana the Huntress on the ceiling) and partied by night.

Games were actually an important part of Louis' political strategy known as "the domestication of the nobility." By distracting the nobles with the pleasures of courtly life, he was free to run the government his way. Billiards, dancing, and concerts were popular, but the biggest distraction was gambling, usually a card game similar to blackjack. Louis lent money to the losers, making them even more indebted to him. The good life was an addiction, and Louis kept the medicine cabinet well stocked.

Mars Room: Decorated with a military flair, this was the room for Louis' Swiss bodyguards. On the ceiling there's Mars, the Greek god of war, in a chariot pulled by wolves. The bronze cupids in the corners are escalating from love arrows to heavier artillery. Notice the fat walls that hid thin servants who were to be at their master's constant call—but out of sight when not needed. Don't miss the view of the sculpted gardens out the window.

Mercury Room: Louis' life was a work of art, and Versailles was the display case. Everything he did was a public event designed to show his subjects how it should be done. This room served as Louis' official bedroom, where the Sun King would ritually rise each morning to warm his subjects.

The tapestry on the wall shows how this ceremony might have looked. From a canopied bed, Louis would rise, dress, and take a seat for morning prayer. Meanwhile, the nobles (on the left) stand behind a balustrade, in awe of his piety, nobility, and clean socks. When Louis went to bed at night, the nobles would fight over who got to hold the candle while he slipped into his royal jammies. Bedtime, wake-up, and meals were all public rituals.

The two chests that furnish the room, with their curved legs, gilding, and heavy animal feet, are done in the "Louis the XIVth" style. Later furniture found in other rooms is lighter, straighter, and less ornamented. The clock dates from Louis' time. When the cocks crowed at the top of the hour and the temple doors opened, guess who popped out?

Apollo Room: This was the grand throne room. Louis held court from a 10-foot silver-canopied throne on a raised platform placed in the center of the room. (Notice the 4 metal bolts in the ceiling that once supported the canopy.)

Everything in here reminds us that Louis was not just any ruler, but the Sun King who lights the whole world with his presence. The ceiling shows Apollo in his chariot, dragging the sun across the heavens every day. Notice the ceiling's beautifully gilded frame and Goldfinger maidens.

In the corners are the four corners of the world—all, of course, warmed by the sun. Counterclockwise from above the exit door are: 1) Europe, with a sword; 2) Asia, with a lion; 3) Africa, with an elephant; and 4) good old America, an Indian maiden with a crocodile.

The famous portrait by Rigaud over the fireplace gives a more human look at Louis. He's shown in a dancer's pose, displaying the legs that made him one of the all-time dancing fools of kingery. At night, they often held parties in this room, actually dancing around the throne.

Louis (who was 63 when this was painted) had more than 300 wigs like this one, and he changed them many times a day. This fashion "first" started when his hairline began to recede, then sprouted all over Europe, spreading even to the American colonies in the time of George Washington.

Louis may have been treated like a god, but he was not an overly arrogant man. His subjects adored him because he was a symbol of everything a man could be, the fullest expression of the Renaissance Man.

The War Room: Versailles was good propaganda. It showed the rest of the world how rich and powerful Louis was. One look at this eye-saturating view of the gardens sent visitors reeling.

But France's success also made other countries jealous and nervous. The semicircles on the ceiling show Germany (with the double eagle), Holland (with its ships), and Spain (with a red flag and roaring lion) ganging up on Louis. Two guesses who won. Of course, these mere mortals were no match for the Sun King. The stucco relief on the wall shows Louis on horseback triumphing over his fallen enemies.

But Louis' greatest triumph may be the next room, the one that everybody wrote home about.

The Hall of Mirrors: No one had ever seen anything like this hall when it was opened. Mirrors were still a great luxury at the time, and the number and size of these monsters were astounding. The hall is almost 250 feet long. There are 17 arched mirrors matched by 17 windows with that breathtaking view of the gardens. Lining the hall are 24 gilded candelabras, eight busts of Roman emperors, and eight classical-style statues (7 of them ancient). The ceiling decoration chronicles Louis' military accomplishments, topped off by Louis himself in the central panel (with cupids playing cards at his divine feet), doing what he did best—triumphing.

This was where the grandest festivities were held for the most important ambassadors and guests. The throne could be moved from the Apollo Room and set up at the far end of the hall. Imagine

this place filled with guests dressed in silks and powdered wigs, lit by the flames of thousands of candles. The mirrors are a reflection of an age when beautiful people loved to look at themselves. It was no longer a sin to be proud of good looks or fine clothes or to enjoy the good things in life: laughing, dancing, eating, drinking, flirting, and enjoying the view.

From the center of the hall, you can fully appreciate the epic scale of Versailles. The huge palace (by architect Le Vau), the fantasy interior (Le Brun), and the endless gardens (Le Notre) made Versailles *le* best.

In more recent times, the Hall of Mirrors is where the Treaty of Versailles was signed, ending World War I (and, some say, starting World War II).

• *Enter the small Peace Room and grab a bench.*

The Peace Room: "Louis Quatorze was addicted to wars…" but by the end of his life, he was tired of fighting. In this sequel to the War Room, peace is granted to Germany, Holland, and Spain as cupids play with the discarded cannons, armor, and swords.

The oval painting above the fireplace shows 19-year-old Louis bestowing an olive branch on Europe. Beside him is his wife, Marie Therese, cradling their two-year-old twin daughters. If being a

father at 17 seems a bit young, remember that Louis was married when he was four.

The Peace Room marks the beginning of the queen's half of the palace. On Sundays the queen held chamber-music concerts here for family and friends.

• *Enter the first room of the Queen's Wing, with its canopied bed.*

The Queen's Wing

The Queen's Bedchamber: This was the queen's official bedroom. It was here that she rendezvoused with her husband. Two queens died here. This is where 19 princes were born. The chandelier is where two of them were conceived. Just kidding.

True, Louis was not the most faithful husband. There was no attempt to hide the fact that the Sun King warmed more than one bed, for he was above the rules of mere mortals. Adultery became acceptable—even fashionable—in court circles. The secret-looking doors on either side of the bed were for Louis' late-night liaisons—they lead straight to his rooms.

Some of Louis' mistresses became more famous and powerful than his rather quiet queen, but he was faithful to the show of marriage and had genuine affection for his wife. Their private apartments were connected, and Louis made a point of sleeping with the queen as often as possible, regardless of whose tiara he tickled earlier in the evening.

This room looks like it did in the days of the last queen, Marie-Antoinette. That's her bust over the fireplace, and the double eagle of her native Austria in the corners. The big chest to the left of the bed held her jewels.

The queen's canopied bed is a reconstruction. The bed, chair, and wall coverings switched with the seasons. This was the cheery summer pattern.

Drawing Room of the Nobles: The queen's circle of friends met here, seated on the stools. Discussions ranged from politics to gossip, food to literature, fashion to philosophy. The Versailles kings considered themselves enlightened monarchs who promoted the arts and new ideas. Folks like Voltaire—a political radical—and the playwright Molière participated in the Versailles court. Ironically, these discussions planted the seeds of liberal thought that would grow into the Revolution.

Queen's Antechamber: This is where the Royal Family dined publicly while servants and nobles fluttered around them, admiring their table manners and laughing at the king's jokes like courtly Paul Shaeffers. A typical dinner consisted of four different soups, two whole birds stuffed with truffles, plus mutton, ham slices, fruit, pastry, compotes, and preserves.

The central portrait is of luxury-loving, "Let-them-eat-cake" Marie-Antoinette, who became a symbol of decadence to the peasants. The portrait at the far end is a public-relations attempt to soften her image, showing her with three of her nine children.

Queen's Guard Room: On October 6, 1789, a mob of revolutionaries—appalled by their queen's taste in wallpaper—stormed
the palace. They were fed up with the life of luxury led by the
ruling class in the countryside while they were starving in the
grimy streets of Paris.

The king and queen locked themselves in. Some of the
revolutionaries got access to this upper floor. They burst into
this room, where Marie-Antoinette had taken refuge, then killed
three of her bodyguards and dragged her and her husband off.
(Some claim that, as they carried her away, she sang "Louis,
Louis, oh-oh...we gotta go now.")

The enraged peasants then proceeded to ransack the place,
taking revenge for the years of poverty and oppression they'd
suffered. Marie-Antoinette and Louis XVI were later taken to
the place de la Concorde in Paris, where they knelt under the
guillotine and were made a foot shorter at the top.

Did the king and queen deserve it? Were the revolutionaries
destroying civilization or clearing the decks for a new and better
one? Was Versailles progress or decadence?

Coronation Room: No sooner did they throw out a king than
they got an emperor. The Revolution established democracy, but
it was shaky in a country that wasn't used to it. In the midst of the
confusion, the upstart general Napoleon Bonaparte took control
and soon held dictatorial powers. This room captures the glory of
the Napoleon years, when he conquered most of Europe. In the
huge canvas on the left-hand wall, we see him crowning himself
emperor of a new, revived "Roman" Empire. (This is a lesser-
quality copy of a version hanging in the Louvre.)

Catch the portrait of a dashing, young, charismatic Napoleon
by the window on the right. This shows him in 1796, when he was
just a general in command of the Revolution's army in Italy. Compare this with the portrait next to it from 10 years later—looking
less like a revolutionary and more like a Louis. Above the young
Napoleon is a portrait of Josephine, his wife and France's empress.
In David's *Distribution of Eagles* (opposite the *Coronation*), the victorious general (in imperial garb) passes out emblems of victory to
his loyal troops. In *The Battle of Aboukir* (opposite the window),
Napoleon looks rather bored as he slashes through a tangle of
dark-skinned warriors. His horse, though, has a look of "What are
we doing in this mob? Let's get out of here!" Let's.

• *Pass through a couple of rooms to the exit staircase on your left. The
long Battle Gallery ahead of you shows 130 yards of scenes from famous
French battles, arranged chronologically clockwise around the gallery.
The exit staircase puts you outside on the left (south) side of the palace.*

The Gardens— Controlling Nature

Louis was a divine-right ruler. One way he proved it was by controlling nature like a god. These lavish grounds, so elaborately planned out, pruned, and decorated, showed everyone that Louis was in total command.

• *Exiting the palace into the gardens, veer to the left toward the concrete railing about 75 yards away. You'll pass by horse carriages for hire and through flowers and cookie-cutter patterns of shrubs and green cones. Stand at the railing overlooking the courtyard below and the Louis-made lake in the distance.*

The Orangerie: The warmth from the Sun King was so great that he could even grow orange trees in chilly France. Louis had a thousand of these to amaze his visitors. In winter they were kept in the greenhouses (beneath your feet) that surround the courtyard. On sunny days they were wheeled out in their silver planters and scattered around the grounds.

• *From the stone railing, turn about-face and walk back toward the palace, veering left toward the two large pools of water. Sit on the top stair and look away from the palace.*

View down the Royal Drive: This, to me, is the most impressive spot in all of Versailles. In one direction, the palace. Stretching out in the other, the endless grounds. Versailles was laid out along an eight-mile axis that included the grounds, the palace, and the town of Versailles itself, one of the first instances of urban planning since Roman times and a model for future capitals like Washington, D.C., and Brasilia.

Looking down the Royal Drive (also known as "The Green Carpet"), you see the round Apollo fountain way in the distance. Just beyond that is the Grand Canal. The groves on either side of the Royal Drive were planted with trees from all over, laid out in an elaborate grid and dotted with statues and fountains. Of the original 1,500 fountains, 300 remain.

Looking back at the palace, you can see the Hall of Mirrors— it's the middle story, with the arched windows.

• *Stroll down the steps to get a good look at the frogs and lizards that fill the round Latona Basin.*

The Latona Basin: The theme of Versailles is Apollo, the god of the sun, associated with Louis. This round fountain tells the story of the birth of Apollo and his sister Diana. On top of the fountain are Apollo and Diana as little kids with their mother, Latona (they're facing toward the Apollo fountain). Latona, an unwed mother, was insulted by the local peasants. She called on the king of the gods, Zeus (the children's father), to avenge the insult. Zeus swooped down and turned all the peasants into the frogs and lizards that ring the fountain.

• *As you walk down past the basin toward the Royal Drive, you'll pass by "ancient" statues done by 17th-century French sculptors. The Colonnade is hidden in the woods on the left-hand side of the Royal Drive, about three-fourths of the way to the Apollo Basin.*

The Colonnade: Versailles had no prestigious ancient ruins, so they built their own. This prefab Roman ruin is a 100-foot circle of 64 marble columns supporting arches. Beneath the arches are small birdbath fountains. Nobles would picnic in the shade to the tunes of a string quartet, pretending they were the enlightened citizens of the ancient world.

The Apollo Basin: The fountains of Versailles were its most famous attraction, a marvel of both art and engineering. This one was the centerpiece, showing the Sun God—Louis—in his sunny chariot starting his journey across the sky. The horses are half submerged, giving the impression, when the fountains play, of the sun rising out of the mists of dawn. Most of the fountains were only turned on when the king walked by, but this one played constantly for the benefit of those watching from the palace.

All the fountains are gravity powered. They work on the same principle as when you block a hose with your finger to make it squirt. Underground streams feed into smaller pipes at the fountains that shoot the water high into the air.

Looking back at the palace from here, realize that the distance you just walked is only a fraction of this vast complex of buildings, gardens, and waterways. Be glad you don't have to mow the lawn.

The Grand Canal: Why visit Venice when you can just build your own? In an era before virtual reality, this was the next best thing to an actual trip. Couples in gondolas would pole along the waters accompanied by barges with orchestras playing *O Sole Mio*. The canal is actually cross-shaped, this being the long arm, a mile from end to end. Of course, this too is a man-made body of water with no function other than pleasing.

The Trianon Area—Retreat from Reality

Versailles began as an escape from the pressures of kingship. In a short time, the palace was as busy as Paris ever was. Louis needed an escape from his escape and built a smaller palace out in the tules. Later, his successors retreated still farther into the garden, building a fantasy world of simple pleasures from which to ignore the real world, which was crumbling all around them.

• *You can rent a bike or catch the TGV tram (5/hrly, 4 stops), but the walk is half the fun. It's about a 30-minute walk from here to the end of the tour, plus another 30 minutes to walk back to the palace.*

Grand Trianon: This was the king's private residence away from the main palace. Louis usually spent a couple nights a week here, but the two later Louis spent more and more time retreating.

The facade of this one-story building is a charming combination of pink, yellow, and white, a cheery contrast to the imposing Baroque facade of the main palace. Ahead you can see the gardens through the columns. The king's apartments were to the left of the columns.

The flower gardens were changed daily for the king's pleasure—for new color combinations and new "nasal cocktails."

Walk around the palace (to the right) if you'd like, for a view of the gardens and rear facade.

• *Facing the front, do an about-face. The Summer House is not down the driveway but about 200 yards away, along the smaller pathway at about 10 o'clock.*

The Summer House of the French Garden: This small white building with four rooms fanning out from the center was one more step away from the modern world. Here the queen spent summer evenings with family and a few friends, listening to music or playing parlor games. All avenues of *la douceur de vivre*—"the sweetness of living"—were explored. To the left are the buildings of the Menagerie, where cows, goats, chickens, and ducks were bred.

• *Continue frolicking along the path until you run into...*

Petit Trianon: Louis XV developed an interest in botany.

He wanted to spend more time near the French Gardens, but the Summer House just wasn't big enough. He built the Petit Trianon (the "small" Trianon), a masterpiece of neoclassical architecture.

This grey, cubical building has four distinct facades, each a perfect and harmonious combination of Greek-style columns, windows, and railings. Walk around it and find your favorite.

Louis XVI and his wife, Marie-Antoinette, made this their home base. Marie-Antoinette was a sweet girl from Vienna who never quite fit in with the fast, sophisticated crowd at Versailles. Here at the Petit Trianon she could get away and re-create the simple home life she remembered from her childhood. On the lawn outside she installed a merry-go-round.

• *Five minutes more will bring you to* ...

The Temple of Love: A circle of 12 marble Corinthian columns supporting a dome decorates a path where lovers would stroll. Underneath, there's a statue of Cupid making a bow (to shoot arrows of love) out of the club of Hercules. It's a delightful monument to a society whose rich could afford that ultimate luxury, romantic love. When the Revolution came, I bet they wished they'd kept the club.

• *And finally you'll reach* ...

Le Hameau—The Hamlet: Marie-Antoinette longed for the simple life of a peasant. Not the hard labor of real peasants— who sweated and starved around her—but the fairy-tale world of simple country pleasures. She built this complex of 12 buildings as her own private village.

This was an actual working farm with a dairy, a waterwheel mill, and domestic animals. The harvest was served at Marie's table. Marie didn't do much work herself, but she "supervised," dressed in a plain white muslin dress and a straw hat.

The Queen's House is the main building, actually two buildings connected by a wooden gallery. Like any typical peasant farmhouse, it had a billiard room, library, elegant dining hall, and two living rooms.

Nearby was the small theater. Here Marie and her friends acted out plays far from the rude intrusions of the real world ...

• *The real world and the main palace are a 30-minute walk to the southeast. Along the way, stop at the Neptune Basin near the palace, an impressive miniature lake with fountains, and indulge your own favorite fantasy.*

CHARTRES CATHEDRAL TOUR

Many children who watched the old church burn to the ground on June 10, 1194, grew up to build Chartres cathedral and attend the dedication mass in 1260. That's astonishing, considering that other Gothic cathedrals, such as Paris's Notre-Dame, took hundreds of years to build. Having been built so quickly, Chartres is arguably Europe's best example of pure Gothic, with a unity of architecture, statues, and stained glass that captures the spirit of the Age of Faith.

Orientation

Cost and Hours: Free. Daily 7:00–19:00.

Getting There: Chartres is a one-hour train trip from Paris' Gare Montparnasse (about 75F one-way, 10/day, last train on Sat departs Chartres about 19:00; figure on a round-trip total of 3 hrs from Paris to cathedral doorstep and back). Upon arrival in Chartres, confirm your return schedule. Leaving the train station and heading uphill, you'll soon see the medieval church rise above the modern city of Chartres.

Bring: Binoculars.

Information: The tourist office (daily 9:30–18:45, tel. 02 37 18 26 26) is located 100 meters in front of the church.

Cathedral Tours by Malcolm Miller: Fine one-hour tours Mon–Sat at 12:00 and 2:45 cost 40F and are led by either Malcolm Miller or his capable assistant. Tours begin at the gift shop inside the church. Private tours can be arranged (tel. 02 37 28 15 58, fax 02 37 28 33 03).

Length of Our Tour: One hour, but Chartres is an all-day excursion from Paris.

Accommodations: See end of chapter (on page 220).

— CHARTRES —

THE CHARTRES GENERATION—THE 1200s

• *Kill train time with this.*

From king to bishop to knight to pawn, French society was devoted to the Christian faith. It inspired knights to undertake the formidable Crusades, artists to re-create heaven in statues and stained glass, and architects to build sky-scraping cathedrals filled with the mystic light of heaven. They aimed for a golden age, blending faith and reason, though misguided faith often outstripped reason, resulting in very un-Christian intolerance and violence.

Timeline

1194—The old cathedral burns down.

c. 1200—The University of Paris is founded, using human reason to analyze Christian faith. Borrowing from the pagan Greek philosopher Aristotle, scholars described the Christian universe as a series of concentric rings spinning around the Earth in geometrical perfection.

1202—The pope calls on all true Christians to rescue the Holy Land from Moslem "infidels" (including Genghis Khan) in the Fourth Crusade (1202–1204). This crusade ends disastrously in the sacking of Constantinople, a Christian city.

1206—Chartres's cornerstone is laid. The style is *opus francigenum*

("French-style work")—what the people in Gothic times called Gothic. Chartres is just one of several great cathedrals under construction in Europe.

1207—Francis of Assisi, a rebellious Italian youth, undergoes a conversion to a life of Christian poverty and love. His open spirit inspires many followers, including France's King Louis IX (a generation later).

1209—France's King Phillip Augustus, centered in Paris, invades southern France, massacring fellow Christians (the Cathars or Albigensians) as heretics.

1212—Thousands of boys and girls idealistically join the Children's Crusade (1212) to save the Holy Land. Most die in transit or are sold into slavery.

1220—The external structure of Chartres cathedral is nearly finished. Work begins on the statues and stained glass.

1226—Eleven-year-old Louis IX is crowned as *rex et sacerdos*, "King and Priest," beginning a 45-year golden age combining church and state. His mother, Blanche of Castile (granddaughter of Eleanor of Aquitaine), is his life-long mentor.

1230—Most of Chartres' stained glass is completed.

1244—At age 30, Louis falls sick and sees a vision in a coma that changes his life. His personal trustworthiness helps unify the nation. He reforms the judicial system along Christian lines, helping the poor.

1245—The last Albigensian heretics are burned at Montsegur, in a crusade ordered by Louis and his mother Blanche.

1248—Louis personally leads the Seventh Crusade by walking barefoot from Paris to the port of departure. During the fighting, he is captured and ransomed. He later returns home a changed man. Humbled, he adopts the poverty of the Franciscan brotherhood. His devotion earns him the title of Saint Louis.

1260—Chartres cathedral is dedicated. The church is the physical embodiment of the Age of Faith, with architecture as mathematically perfect as God's Creation, sculpture serving as sermons in stone, and stained glass lit by the light of God.

Mary's Church ("Notre-Dame"="Our Lady" of Chartres)

The church is (at least) the fourth church on this spot dedicated to Mary, the mother of Jesus, who has been venerated here for some 1700 years. There's even speculation that the pagan Romans dedicated a temple to a mother-goddess. In earliest times, Mary was worshiped next to a natural spring with healing waters (not visible today). In the ninth century, the church acquired Mary's cloth birth tunic (which we'll see) as the focus of devotion. A crude wooden statue of Mary also attracted pilgrims (the statue was destroyed in 1793, but copies remain).

The Book of Chartres

Historian Malcolm Miller calls Chartres a picture book of statues, stained glass, and symbolic architecture, telling the entire Christian story—from Creation to Christ's birth (the north side of the church), from Christ and his followers up to the present (south entrance), to the end of time when Christ returns as judge (west entrance).

The Christian universe is a complex web of heaven and earth, angels and demons, and prophets and martyrs. Much of the medieval symbolism is obscure today. Expect to be overwhelmed by the thousands of things to see, but to appreciate the perfect unity of this Gothic masterpiece.

THE TOUR BEGINS
1. The Main Entrance (West Facade), c. 1150:

The two mismatched steeples, three doors, rose window, and various statues are the only survivors of the intense, lead-melting fire that incinerated the rest of the church in 1194. The church of today was rebuilt behind this facade in a single generation (1194–1260).

Towers: The right (south) tower with a stone steeple is original Romanesque. The left (north) tower lost its wooden steeple in the 1194 fire. In the 1500s it was topped by a steeple bigger than the tapered lower half was meant to hold.

The West Doors: Christ, the center of Christian history, sits above the **central door**, surrounded by symbolic animals.

The anorexic statues between the doors are pillars of the faith who foretold the coming of Christ. With solemn gestures and faces, they patiently endure the wait.

History's pivotal event is shown above the **right door**, where Mary (seated) produces baby Jesus from her loins. This Mary-and-baby sculpture is a 12th-century stone version of an older wooden statue (burned 1793). Centuries of pilgrims have visited

CHARTRES

① MAIN FACADE
② NAVE
③ LABYRINTH
④ VIEW OF 3 ROSE WINDOWS
⑤ BLUE VIRGIN WINDOW
⑥ CHOIR SCREEN SCULPTURES

NORTH PORCH

SOUTH PORCH

⑦ MARY'S BIRTH TUNIC
⑧ CHARLEMAGNE WINDOW
⑨ OUR LADY OF PILLAR CHAPEL
⑩ NOAH WINDOW
⑪ FLYING BUTTRESSES
⑫ SOUTH PORCH
⑬ NORTH PORCH

BOOK-SHOP

20 YARDS

WEST FAÇADE

MAIN ENTRANCE

DCH

Chartres to see Mary's statue, gaze at her birth tunic (which we'll see), and ponder the mystery of how God in Heaven became Man on Earth, passing through immaculate Mary like sunlight through stained glass.

• *Enter the church and wait for your pupils to enlarge.*

2. Nave: The church has a long, tall central nave, flanked by raised side aisles for crowd flow, so pilgrims could circle the church without disturbing worshipers. The 12 pillars lining the nave support pointed crisscross arches on the ceiling which lace together the heavy stone vaulting. The pillars are supported by flying buttresses on the outside of the church (which we'll see later). This skeleton structure was the miracle of Gothic, allowing tall buildings with ribbed walls and lots of stained-glass windows (like the big saints in the upper stories of the nave). The floor of the nave slopes in to the center, for easy drainage when hosing down dirty pilgrims who camped here.

3. The Labyrinth: The round maze inlaid in black stone on the floor of the nave is a spiritual journey. Pilgrims enter from the west rim by foot or on knees and wind inward, meditating.

Three hundred meters later they hope to meet God in the middle.
(Current world record for reaching enlightenment is 3:42.)
• *Walk up the nave to where the transept crosses. As you face the altar,
north is to the left.*

4. The Rose Windows—North, South, and West:
The three big, round "rose" (floral-shaped) windows over the
entrances open like flowers to receive sunlight at different times
of day. All three are predominantly blue and red, but each has
different "petals," and each tells a different part of the Christian
story in a kaleidoscope of fragmented images.

Having trouble making out the tiny, distant details? As
we've all read, stained glass was a way to teach Bible stories to
the illiterate medieval masses... who apparently owned state-
of-the-art binoculars. Yes, the windows tell stories, but obviously, their main purpose was to light a dark church in a colorful
and decorative way.

The **north rose window** charts history from the distant past
up to the birth of Jesus. On the outer rim, murky, ancient (barely
visible) prophets foretell Christ's coming. Then (circling inward),
there's a ring of red squares with kings who are Christ's direct
ancestors. Still closer, a circle of white doves and winged angels
zero in on the central event of history—Mary, the heart of the
flower, with her newborn baby Jesus.

This window was donated by King Louis IX (who built Paris's
Sainte-Chapelle) and his mom, Blanche of Castile. See their coats
of arms just below the rose—Louis's yellow fleur-de-lis on a blue
background and Blanche's yellow castles on a red background.

In the **south rose window**, the Old Testament prophecies are
fulfilled. Christ sits in the center (dressed in blue, with a red background), setting in motion the radiating rings of angels, beasts, and
apocalyptic elders who labor to bring history to its close. The five
lancet windows below show Old Testament prophets lifting New
Testament writers on their shoulders (in first window on left, see
white-robed Luke riding piggyback on dark-robed Jeremiah),
demonstrating how the ancients prepared the way for Christ. A
dark Christ rings in history's final Day of Judgment at the center
of the **west rose window**. Around him, winged angels blow their
trumpets and the dead rise, are judged, and are sent to hell or
raised to eternal bliss. The frilly edge of this glorious "rose" is
flecked with tiny clover-shaped dewdrops.

God = Light
You can try to examine the details, but a better way to experience
the mystery of Chartres is to just sit and stare at these enormous

panels as they float in the dark of empty space like holograms or space stations or the Queen of Heaven's crown jewels. Ponder the medieval concept that God is light.

To the Chartres generation, the church was a metaphor for how God brings his creation to life, like the way light animates stained glass. They were heavy into mysticism, feeling a oneness with all creation in a moment of enlightenment. The Gospel of John (as well as a writer known to historians as the Pseudo-Dionysius) was their favorite. Here are select verses from John 1:1-12 (loosely translated):

"In the beginning was The Word.
He (Jesus) was the light of the human race.
The light shines in the darkness, and the darkness
    cannot resist it.
It was the real light coming into the world, the light
    that en-light-ens everyone.
He was in the world, but the world did not recognize Him.
    But to those who did, He gave the power to become
    the children of God."

5. The Blue Virgin Window: Mary, dressed in blue on a rich red background, cradles purple Jesus, while the dove of the Spirit descends on her. This is some of the oldest stained glass (1150), a survivor of the 1194 fire, which was reinserted into this new window frame around 1230. The Blue Virgin was one of the most popular stops for pilgrims—especially pregnant ones—of the cult of the Virgin-about-to-give-birth. Devotees prayed, carried stones to repair the church, or donated to the church coffers—Mary rewarded them with peace of mind, easy births, and occasional miracles.

Below Mary, see **Christ being tempted** by a red-faced, horned, smirking devil.

Hail, maiden, what's your sign? Pick up chicks at the **Zodiac Window** (second window to the left). The 12 signs are in the right half of the window; read from the bottom up—Pisces, Aries, Gemini (in the cloverleaf), Taurus, Cockroach, Leo, Virgo, etc.

6. The Choir Screen—Life of Mary: In the center of the church sits the stone **choir** (the enclosed area behind the altar where church officials sat), ringed with **41 statue-groups** illustrating Mary's life (by various sculptors, 1520–1714). Although the Bible says little about the mother of Jesus, legend and lore fleshed out her life.

Scene #1 (south side) shows an angel telling her dad that Mary's on the way. In #4 Anne gives birth to Mary. In #6 Mary marries Joseph. In #10 she gives birth to Jesus in a manger. In

#12 the Three Kings arrive. In #s 15 through 27, scenes show her famous son's life. In #28 Jesus is crucified. In #34 the resurrected Jesus appears to his mother. In #38 Mary dies...in #39 she's raised by angels into heaven...and in #41 she's crowned Queen of Heaven by the Father, Son, and the Holy Ghost.

The **plain windows** surrounding the choir date from the 1770s, when the dark mystery of medieval stained glass was replaced by the open light of the French Enlightenment. The plain windows and the choir are some of the only "new" features. Most of the 1200s church has remained despite style changes, Revolutionary vandals, and war bombs.

7. Mary's Birth Tunic: Sitting in a glass case with a gold frame held by angels, this is the torn, 2,000-year-old cloth **tunic** supposedly worn by Mary when she gave birth to Jesus. Since the ninth century, this has been the main object of adoration for the cult of the Virgin, and stories abound of its magical powers.

In A.D. 911, with the city surrounded by Vikings, the bishop hoisted the tunic like a battle flag and waved it at the invaders. It scared the bejesus out them with visions of extended labor, and the town was saved.

When the fire of 1194 incinerated the old church, the tunic was feared lost. Lo and behold, several days later they found it miraculously unharmed in the crypt (beneath today's choir). The people were so stoked, they worked like madmen to erect this grand cathedral to display it in.

8. Charlemagne Window: The window tells the story of how the tunic ended up here. **Charlemagne** (bottom left semi-circle), the great king of the Franks (A.D. 800), sits on his throne between two advisers and plans a great adventure—a crusade to the Holy City of Jerusalem. Next (the semicircle just above), he attacks the Moslem infidels occupying Jerusalem. Charlemagne (heart-shaped shield) stabs a Saracen (round shield) in the neck, driving the Moslems out of the city.

On the way home, Charlemagne stops in the great Christian city of Constantinople (in the diamond directly to the right), where he's welcomed at the gate by the emperor. The emperor rewards him (semicircle directly to the right) with three chests of holy relics...including Mary's tunic. Charlemagne returns home (the circle above the diamond) to his palace in Aix, kneels, and places the relics before the altar. Charlemagne's grandson, Charles the Bald, gave the tunic to Chartres in 876.

The fashion-conscious will notice the clothes are from the 1220s, when the window was made.

9. Chapel of Our Lady on the Pillar: A 16th-century
statue of Mary and baby—draped in cloth, crowned and
sceptered—sits on a column in a wonderful carved-wood alcove.
This is today's pilgrimage center, built to keep visitors from clog-
ging up the altar area. Modern pilgrims adore the Virgin, place
flowers, light candles, and kiss the column. The cult lives.

10. The Noah Window: Read Chartres's windows from left
to right and bottom to top.

Bottom-left is a man making a wheel. He's one of the donors
of this window. His colleagues to the right are from the axe- and
barrel-maker guilds.

Then comes the story of **Noah** (read from the bottom up):
God tells Noah he'll destroy the earth (#1, bottom diamond).
Noah hefts an axe to build an ark, while his son hauls wood
(diamond #2). He loads horses (cloverleaf, above left), purple
elephants (cloverleaf, above right), and other animals. The psychedelic ark sets sail (diamond #3). Waves cover the earth, drowning
the wicked (two cloverleaves). The ark survives (diamond #4)
and Noah releases a dove. Finally, up near the top (diamond #7),
a rainbow arches overhead, God drapes himself over it, and Noah
and his family give thanks.
• *Exit the church (through the main entrance or the door in the south
transept) to view its south side.*

11. South Exterior—Flying Buttresses: Six flying but-
tresses on the south side (the arches that stick out from the upper
walls) push against six pillars lining the nave inside, helping to
hold up the heavy stone ceiling and sloped, lead-over-wood roof.
The ceiling and roof push down onto the pillars, of course, but
also outward (north and south) because of the miracle of Gothic,
the pointed arch. These flying buttresses push back, channeling
the stress outward to the six vertical buttresses, then down to the
ground. The result is a tall cathedral held up by slender pillars
buttressed from the outside, allowing the walls to be opened up
for stained glass.

The church is built from large blocks of limestone. Peasants
trod in hamster-wheel contraptions to raise these blocks into
place—a testament to their great faith.

12. South Porch: The three doorways of the south entrance
show the world from Christ to the present, as Christianity
triumphs over persecution.

Center Door—Christ and Apostles: Jesus stands between the
double doors, holding a book and raising his arm in blessing. He's a

simple, itinerant, bareheaded, barefoot rabbi, but underneath his feet he tramples symbols of evil, the dragon and lion (which is which?). Christ's face is among the most noble of all Gothic sculpture.

Christ is surrounded by his **Apostles**, who spread the good news to a hostile world. **Peter** (to the left as you face Jesus), with curly hair and beard, holds the key to the kingdom of heaven and the slender cross on which he was crucified upside down. **Paul** (to the right of Jesus) fingers the sword of his martyrdom, contemplating the inevitable loss of his head and the hair upon it. In fact, all the Apostles were killed or persecuted, and their faces are humble with sad eyes. But their message prevailed, and under their feet they crush the squirming emperors who once persecuted them.

The final triumph comes above the door in the **Last Judgment**. Christ sits in judgement, raising his hands, while Mary and John beg him to take it easy on poor mankind. Beneath Christ, the souls are judged—the righteous on our left, the wicked on the right, who are thrown into the fiery jaws of Hell. Farther to the right (above the statues of Paul and the Apostles), horny demons subject wicked women to an eternity of sexual harassment.

Left Door—Martyrs: Eight martyrs flank the left door. **St. Lawrence** (second from left) cradles the grill on which he was barbecued alive. His last brave words to the Romans: "You can turn me over—I'm done on this side." **St. George** (far right) wears the knightly uniform of the 1200s, when Chartres was built and King Louis IX was crusading. Beneath the martyrs are rather gruesome **scenes of torture** (e.g., George stretched on the wheel), many of which were used in the 1200s against heretics, Moslems, Jews, and Albigensians (the Cathar sect of southern France).

Right Door—Confessors: Among these eight pillars of the faith, find **Jerome** (third from the right), holding the Bible he translated into everyday Latin; and **Gregory** (second from the right), the pope who organized church hierarchy and wrote Gregorian chants.

• *Reach the north side by circling around the back end of the church (great views) or cutting through the church.*

13. The North Porch: In the Book of Chartres, the north porch is chapter one, from the Creation up to the coming of Christ.

Center Door: Baby Mary (headless), in the arms of **her mother Anne** (the statue between the double doors), marks the culmination of the Old Testament world.

History begins in the tiny details in the concentric arches over the doorway. **God creates Adam** (at the peak of the outer arch) by cradling his head in his lap like a child.

Melchizedek (farthest to the left of Mary and Anne), with cap and cup, is the Biblical model of the *rex et sacerdos* (king-priest), the title bestowed on King Louis IX.

Abraham (second from left) holds his son by the throat and raises a knife to slit him for sacrifice. Just then, he hears something and turns his head up to see God's angel who stops the bloodshed. The drama of this frozen moment anticipates Renaissance naturalism 200 years early.

John the Baptist (fourth to the right from Mary/Anne), the last Old Testament prophet who prepared the way for Jesus, holds a lamb, the symbol of Christ. John is skinny from his diet of locusts and honey. His body twists and flickers like a flame.

All these **prophets**, with their beards turning down the corners of their mouths, have the sad, wise look of having been around since the beginning of time, and seen it all—from Creation to Christ to Apocalypse. They are some of the last work done on the church, completing the church's sermon in stone and glass.

Imagine all this painted and covered with gold leaf in preparation for the dedication ceremonies in 1260, when the Chartres generation could finally stand back and watch as their great-grandchildren, carrying candles, entered the cathedral.

THE REST OF THE CHURCH

Malcolm Miller's tours and books: This fascinating English scholar illuminates a new detail of the church with each tour (see "Orientation," above). His tours are worthwhile even if you've taken this self-guided tour. For a detailed look at Chartres' windows, sculpture, and history, pick up Malcolm Miller's two guidebooks (sold at the church bookstore).

The crypt: The foundations (below the present church) can be visited only as part of a guided tour in French. You'll see remnants of the earlier churches, a modern copy of the old wooden Mary-and-baby statue, and hints of the old well and Roman wall (30-min tours start in La Crypte bookstore, located outside church near south porch).

Climb the north tower: Three hundred steps lead to a great view (25F, students-15F, children free, Mon–Sat 9:00–18:00 in summer, Sun 13:00–18:00, entrance inside church near bookstore).

TOWN OF CHARTRES

Explore Chartres' cobbled old center and discover the picnic-friendly park behind the cathedral. The helpful tourist office, next to the cathedral, has a map with a self-guided tour of Chartres.

Sleeping and Eating: Chartres makes a convenient first or last night for those flying to/from Orly, and a pleasant overnight from Paris. These two hotels face each other, 200 meters straight out of the train station, 300 meters below the cathedral: **Hôtel Jehan de Beauce**** is basic, but clean and quiet, with some tiny bathrooms (S-160F, D-180F, Ds-200F, Db-240–310F, Tb-315F, 19 avenue Jehan de Beauce, tel. 02 37 21 01 41, fax 02 37 21 59 10); **Hôtel Chatelet***** is comfortable, from its spacious lobby to its spotless, spacious, well-furnished rooms (Sb-370–470F, Db-430–510F, streetside rooms are cheaper, CC:VM, 6 avenue Jehan de Beauce, tel. 02 37 21 78 00, fax 02 37 36 23 01). For a good and inexpensive meal, try **Le Change** (45 rue des Changes, tel. 02 37 21 99 36).

MORE DAY TRIPS FROM PARIS

Grand Châteaus • Giverny • Disneyland Paris

GRAND CHÂTEAUS NEAR PARIS

The region around Paris (the Île de France) is dotted with sumptuous palaces. Paris' booming upper class made this the heartland of European château building in the 16th and 17th centuries. Most of these châteaus were lavish hunting lodges—getaways from the big city. The only things they defended were noble and royal egos.

Consider four very different châteaus:

- ▲▲▲ **Versailles**—for its history, grandeur, and accessibility (closed Mon)
- ▲▲▲ **Vaux-le-Vicomte**—for sheer beauty and intimacy (open daily)
- ▲▲ **Fontainebleau**—for its history and fine interior (closed Tue)
- ▲ **Chantilly**—for its beautiful setting and fine collection of paintings (closed Tue)

If you only have time for one château, choose between Vaux-le-Vicomte and Versailles (see tour on page 191). Except for Versailles, these châteaus are quiet on weekdays. Versailles and Chantilly are covered by the Paris museum pass.

Vaux-le-Vicomte

While Versailles is most travelers' first choice for its sheer historic weight, Vaux-le-Vicomte (voh-luh-vee-komt) offers a more intimate interior and a far better sense of 17th-century château life. Sitting in a huge forest with magnificent gardens and no urban sprawl in sight, Vaux-le-Vicomte gave me just a twinge of palace envy.

Vaux-le-Vicomte was the architectural inspiration of Versailles and set the standard for European châteaus to come. The proud owner, Nicolas Fouquet (Louis XIV's finance minister), threw a château-warming party. Louis was so jealous that he

DAY TRIPS FROM PARIS

arrested his host, took his architect (Le Vau), artist (Le Brun), and landscaper (Le Notre), and proceeded with the construction of the bigger and costlier (but not necessarily more splendid) palace of Versailles. Monsieur Fouquet is thought to be Alexandre Dumas' man in *The Man in the Iron Mask*, which was recently filmed here.

Vaux-le-Vicomte is expensive to get to (because of cab fare) but a joy to tour. While the gift shop's souvenir booklet has helpful information, your ticket includes an English audioguide tour and most rooms have English explanations. Outside the gift shop is a reasonable café (55F *plats du jour*, 30F salads, open 11:30–18:00 and, during candlelit visits, until midnight). Start your tour with the fine horse-carriages exhibit (*équipages*) in the old stables. Wax figures and an evocative soundtrack get you in the proper mood. Next, stroll like a wide-eyed peasant across the stone bridge (any fish down there?) and up the front steps into the château. Turn around to admire the symmetry and elegance of the stables; horses lived well here.

As you wander through Fouquet's dream home, you'll understand Louis' jealousy. Versailles was a rather simple hunting lodge

when this was built. The furniture in Vaux-le-Vicomte is not
original—Louis confiscated it
for Versailles. You'll see cozy
bedrooms upstairs and grand
living rooms downstairs (billiards room, library, card room,
and dining room; feel free to
fast-forward the 90-min audioguide tour). The kitchen and

wine cellar are in the basement. Climb the cupola for a great view.

Survey the garden from the back steps of the palace. This was
the landscaper Le Notre's first claim to fame. This garden was the
cutting edge of sculpted French gardens. He integrated ponds,
shrubbery, and trees in a style that would be copied in palaces all
over Europe. Take the 30-minute walk (one-way) to the Hercules
viewpoint atop the grassy hill way in the distance. Rentable golf
carts (Club Cars, 80F/45 min, 800F deposit) make the trip easier.
Picnics are not allowed.

Cost and Hours: 63F for gardens, château, and carriage
museum (includes audioguide tour); 30F for gardens and carriage
museum only. Open March–Oct daily 10:00–18:00, less in winter,
tel. 01 64 14 41 90. The impressive fountains run 15:00–18:00
the second and last Sat of each month (April–Oct).

Candlelit Visits: Two thousand candles and piped-in classical
music illuminate the palace on Thu and Sat nights (open 20:00–
24:00) May–October and holidays (except July 14—call to ask
about any upcoming holidays). These *visites aux chandelles* are worth
the 80F entry, but remember, it doesn't get really dark until 22:00
in late May, June, and early July, and the last train to Paris leaves
Melun at about 22:00.

Getting to Vaux-le-Vicomte: To reach Vaux-le-Vicomte by
a train-and-taxi combination, you can take the RER train to Melun
from Paris' Gare du Nord or Chatelet stations. Faster SNCF Banlieue trains leave from Paris' Gare de Lyon to Melun (47F one-way,
hrly, 35 min). From Melun's station, taxis make the 10-minute drive
to Vaux-le-Vicomte (85F weekdays, 105F eves and Sun, taxi phone
number posted above taxi stand). Ask a staff person at the château to
call a cab for your return or schedule a pick-up time with your driver. In either direction, split the fare with other travelers. There's a
bus from the station on weekends and holidays only (departs from
Melun station at 10:55 and returns from Vaux-le-Vicomte at 12:27
or 17:40). Melun's tourist office is at 17 rue Paul Doumier (Tue–Sat
10:00–12:00, 14:00–18:00, closed Sun–Mon, tel. 01 64 37 11 31).

By car from Paris, take the A-6 autoroute toward Lyon, then

follow signs to Melun. In Melun, follow signs to Meaux (N-36), then Vaux-le-Vicomte.

Adding Fontainebleau: Vaux-le-Vicomte and Fontainebleau can be combined into a full, though manageable, day trip by car or train from Paris (except on Tue, when Fontainebleau is closed). Fontainebleau is 12 minutes by train from Melun.

Sleeping near Vaux-le-Vicomte: The modern, ugly, but handy **Ibis Hôtel** is between Melun and the château, just off N-105 (Db-300F, less on weekends, tel. 01 60 68 42 45, fax 01 64 09 62 00). Also consider sleeping in nearby Fontainebleau (see below).

Château of Fontainebleau

Fontainebleau's history rivals Versailles'. Many French kings have called this glamorous hunting lodge home. Napoleon welcomed the pope here during his coronation celebration, and it was here that he abdicated his rule when exiled to Elba in 1814. General Patton set up headquarters at this château on his way to Berlin.

While Vaux-le-Vicomte and Versailles are French designed, Fontainebleau was built a century earlier by an Italian. The palace

you see today is largely the work of Renaissance King Francois I. Inspired by his travels through Renaissance Italy, he hired Italian artists to build his palace.

Orient with a quick visit to the château information room, with its huge model of the château (first door on your right in the grand courtyard). The palace entry is next door. Your ticket provides access to the Chinese rooms and the main rooms of the château. Napoleon buffs will enjoy the little museum of Napoleonic history, which requires an additional ticket and a guided tour in French (16F, mornings only). The 20F guidebooks give excellent room-by-room descriptions, though basic English explanations are posted throughout.

Start downstairs with the small but impressive Chinese collection of the Empress of Napoleon III, then climb to the main rooms of the palace. Highlights include the stunning Renaissance hall of Francois I, the opulent dance hall with piped-in music (*salle de bal*), Napoleon's throne room, and Diana's Gallery (library). The gardens, designed a century later by the landscaper Le Notre, are worth a stroll. Rent a rowboat for the *étang des carpes* (carp pond), or walk its path for a good view of the château complex.

Cost and Hours: 35F, Wed–Mon 9:30– 17:30, closed Tue, last entry 45 minutes before closing.

Getting to Fontainebleau: Catch a train from Paris' Gare de Lyon in the direction of Montereau (about 55F one-way, 40 min) to the Fontainebleau-Avon station, where a bus goes to the château (Cars Verts, 10F, 4/hrly; schedules posted in English). Taxis to the château cost about 40F; to Vaux-le-Vicomte costs about 200F.

Town of Fontainebleau: Turn right out of the château courtyard and keep right to reach the town center where cafés and restaurants abound. The helpful tourist office is two blocks up from the château behind the Hôtel Londres and has hiking maps, bike-rental information, and hotel listings (Mon–Fri 9:30–17:30, Sun 10:00–16:00, tel. 01 60 74 99 99). You can rent a bike at the station, the tourist office, or, best, at La Petite Reine (95F/day, 60F/half day, 32 rue des Sablons, tel. 01 64 74 57 57).

Sleeping and Eating in Fontainebleau: The **Hôtel Londres***** offers a helpful staff and very pleasant rooms, many with point-blank views of the château (Db-550–850F, family rooms-750–950F, 1 place du General de Gaulle, tel. 01 64 22 20 21, fax 01 60 72 39 16, www.hotellondres.com). Turn right out of the château entrance and keep right for about five blocks to reach these hotels: **Hôtel Legris et Parc***** is a quiet, dreamy getaway with a pleasant garden, pool, and an elegant restaurant (Db-460–570F, CC:VMA, 36 rue Paul Seramy, tel. 01 64 22 24 24, fax 01 64 22 22 05). **Hôtel a la Carpe d'Or**** is one block away, above the Bakardi bar (Db-300–350F, 7 rue d'Aven, tel. 01 64 22 28 64, fax 01 64 22 39 95). To eat well, try one of these central places: **Croquembouche** (*menus* from 130F, closed Wed, 43 rue de France) or **Chez Arrighi** (*menus* from 100F, closed Mon, 53 rue de France).

Château of Chantilly

Chantilly (shahn-tee-yee), 35 minutes north of Paris, floats serenely on a reflecting pond amid grand gardens. Unfortunately, the château interior is disappointing. Its best rooms can be seen only on a boring French-language guided tour, and the fine works of art in the picture galleries are poorly displayed. Still, Chantilly can be a pleasant experience if approached in the right way. Allow most of a day for Chantilly.

This extravagant hunting palace was destroyed during the Revolution. Today's château was largely rebuilt during the 19th century. It's divided into two parts: the painting gallery, with paintings by Raphael, Titian, Poussin, Delacroix, and others; and the private apartments, which require a French-language tour. The highlight of the otherwise dull apartments is the first stop, the prince's library, lined with more than 13,000 books and beautiful copies of pages from *Les Tres Riches Heures du Duc du Berry*, a much-admired 15th-century illuminated manuscript.

The gardens immediately behind the château are formal and austere. With your back to the château, follow the signs to the right to *le Hameau*. This little hamlet with a delightful garden café was the prototype for the more famous *Hameau* at Versailles. Just beyond is a small kiosk offering a tethered balloon ride (45F, great view) and boat trips along the canals (35F, tel. 03 44 57 35 35).

Cost and Hours: 42F (included with museum pass), 17F for gardens only, Wed–Mon 10:00–18:00, closed Tue, off-season 10:30–12:45, 14:00–17:00; tel. 01 44 57 08 00.

Live Horse Stables (Les Écuries Vivant): The Prince de Conde believed he'd be reincarnated as a horse, so he built this opulent horse château for his next go-round. You'd have to have similar beliefs to pay the 50F entry for this horse museum (albeit impressive and thorough). The museum features 40 live horses in their stables and a daily demonstration, generally at 15:30, more often in summer (April–Oct Wed–Mon 10:30–17:30, also open Tue in summer; Nov–March Wed–Fri 14:00–17:30, Sat–Sun 10:30–17:30, tel. 03 44 57 13 13).

Getting to Chantilly: Leave from Paris' Gare du Nord for Chantilly-Gouvieux. While the RER serves Chantilly, service is faster on the main lines at Grandes Lignes level. Ask at the information desk opposite track 18 for the next departure (about 45F one-way, nearly hrly, 35 min). Upon arrival in Chantilly, confirm your return times (fewer trips on weekends). The tourist office is a block in front of the station. To get to the château, it's a 40F taxi ride, a free bus ride on a rare city bus (ask at the station), or a 30-minute walk (follow signs, stay on path, turn right before BP gas station, cross grass field, "château" in distance is stables, the real château is beyond that).

The well-preserved medieval town of Senlis is a 30-minute bus ride (110F taxi) from the Chantilly station.

GIVERNY AND DISNEYLAND PARIS: FROM MONET'S HOUSE TO MICKEY MOUSE

Giverny

From 1883 to 1926, Monet spent 43 of his most creative years at Giverny (zhee-vayr nee), the Camp David of Impressionism.

Monet's gardens and home are, unfortunately, split by a busy road and very popular with tourists. Buy your ticket, walk through the gardens, and take the underpass into the artist's famous lily-pad land. The path leads over the Japanese Bridge, under weeping willows, and past countless scenes that leave artists aching for an easel. For Monet fans, it's strangely nostalgic. Back on the other side, continue your visit with a wander through his more robust and structured garden and his mildly interesting home. The jammed gift shop at the exit is the actual sky-lit studio where Monet painted his water-lily masterpieces. While lines may be long and tour groups may trample the flowers, true fans still find magic in those lily pads. Minimize crowds by arriving before 10:00 (get in line) or after 16:00 (35F, 25F for gardens only, April–Oct Tue–Sun 10:00–18:00, closed Mon and Nov–March, tel. 02 32 51 94 65).

Getting to Giverny: Take the Rouen-bound train from Paris' Gare St. Lazare station to Vernon (about 140F round-trip, long gaps in service, know schedule before you go). From the Vernon train station to Monet's garden (4 kilometers away), take the Vernon-Giverny bus (5/day, scheduled to meet most trains), hitch, taxi (70F for up to 3, 80F for 4), or rent a bike at the station (70F, crummy ride on a busy road). Get return bus times from the ticket office in Giverny or ask them to call a taxi if you don't see one waiting at the bus stop (tel. 02 32 51 70 17 or 06 07 34 36 68). Bus stops are in the parking lot across from the entry to Monet's home and just beyond the American Impressionist Art Museum. Big tour companies do a Giverny day trip from Paris for around $60. Ask at your hotel.

The new **American Impressionist Art Museum** (turn left when leaving Monet's place and walk 100 yards) is devoted to American artists who followed Claude to Giverny. Giverny had a great influence on American artists of Monet's day. This bright, modern gallery is well explained in English, has a good little Mary Cassatt section, and gives Americans a rare chance to see French people appreciating our artists (same price and hours as Monet's home).

Sleeping and Eating in Giverny: The adorable **Hôtel La Musardiere****, two blocks to the right out of Monet's home, makes an ideal Paris escape or stopover on your way farther into Normandy (Db-300–400F, Tb-380–480F, 132 rue Claude Monet, 27620 Giverny, tel. 02 32 21 03 18, fax 02 32 21 60 00). You'll find a café and sandwich stand near the entry to Monet's home, but the garden café at the overlooked American Impressionist Museum is better—peaceful (60F salads) and surrounded by gardens Monet would appreciate (picnics possible at the far end).

Disneyland Paris

Europe's Disneyland is a remake of California's, with most of the same rides and smiles. The main difference is that Mickey Mouse speaks French (and you can buy wine with your lunch). My kids went ducky. It's worth a day if Paris is handier than Florida or California. Crowds are a problem (tel. 01 64 74 30 00 for the latest). If possible, avoid Saturday, Sunday, Wednesday, school holidays, and July and August. After dinner, crowds are gone. Food is fun, but prepare for Paris prices (or smuggle in a picnic).

Disney brochures are in every Paris hotel. The RER (about 43F each way, hrly, direct from downtown Paris to Marne-la-Vallee in 30 min) drops you off right in the park. The last train back to Paris leaves shortly after midnight. (220F adults, 170F kids 3–11, 25F less in spring and fall. Daily 9:00–23:00 late June–early Sept and Sat–Sun off-season, shoulder season Mon–Fri 9:00–19:00, off-season 10:00–18:00, park and hotel reservations tel. 01 60 30 60 30, fax 01 60 30 60 65.)

To sleep reasonably near the park, try **Hôtel Sante Fe** (family rooms-780F, less off-season, ask about hotel-and-park deals, same tel. and fax as above).

SLEEPING IN PARIS

I've focused on three safe, handy, and colorful neighborhoods: rue Cler, Marais, and Contrescarpe. For each, I list good hotels, helpful hints, and restaurants (see chapter on Eating, page 246). Before reserving, read the descriptions of the three neighborhoods closely. Each offers different pros and cons, and your neighborhood is as important as your hotel to the success of your trip.

Reserve ahead for Paris, the sooner the better. Conventions clog Paris in September (worst), October, May, and June. In August, when Paris is quiet, some hotels offer lower rates to fill their rooms (if you're planning to visit Paris in the summer, the extra expense of an air-conditioned room can be money well spent). Most hotels accept telephone reservations, require prepayment with a credit-card number, and prefer a faxed follow-up to be sure everything is in order. For more information, see "Making Reservations" on page 12 in this book's Introduction.

French hotels are rated by stars (indicated in this book by an *). One star is simple, two has most of the comforts, and three is generally a two-star with a mini-bar and fancier lobby (though I've tried to find three-star hotels that merit the extra expense).

Old, characteristic, budget Parisian hotels have always been cramped. Retrofitted with elevators, toilets, and private showers (as most are today), they are even more cramped. Even three-star hotel rooms are small and often not worth the extra expense in Paris. Some hotels include the hotel tax (*taxe du séjour*, about 5F per person per day), though most will add this to your bill. Two- and three-star hotels are required to have an English-speaking staff. Nearly all hotels listed will have someone who speaks English.

Quad rooms usually have two double beds. Recommended hotels have an elevator unless otherwise noted. Because rooms with double beds and showers are cheaper than rooms with twin beds and baths, room prices vary within each hotel.

You can save as much as 100F by finding the increasingly rare room without a private shower, though some hotels charge for down-the-hall showers. Singles (except for the rare closet-type rooms that fit only 1 twin bed) are simply doubles used by one person. They rent for only a little less than a double. Continental breakfasts cost 25F to 35F, buffet breakfasts (baked goods, cereal, yogurt, and fruit) cost 50F to 60F. Café or picnic breakfasts are cheaper, but hotels usually give unlimited coffee.

Get advice from your hotel for safe parking (consider long-term parking at Orly Airport and taxi in). Meters are free in August. Garages are plentiful (90–140F/day, with special rates through some hotels). Self-serve Laundromats are common; ask your hotelier for the nearest one (*Où est un laverie automatique?*; ooh ay uh lah-vay-ree auto-mah-teek).

Sleep Code

S = Single, **D** = Double/Twin, **T** = Triple, **Q** = Quad, **b** = bathroom, **t** = toilet only, **s** = shower only, **CC** = Credit Card (**V** = Visa, **M** = MasterCard, **A** = Amex), ***** = French hotel rating system (0–4 stars). **Exchange rate:** 6.50F = about $1

Rue Cler Orientation

Rue Cler, a village-like pedestrian street, is safe, tidy, and makes me feel like I must have been a poodle in a previous life. How such coziness lodged itself between the high-powered government district and the wealthy Eiffel Tower and Invalides areas, I'll never know. This is a neighborhood of wide, tree-lined boulevards, stately apartment buildings, and lots of Americans. The American Church, American library, American University, and many of my readers call this area home.

Become a local at a rue Cler café for breakfast or join the afternoon crowd for *une bière pression* (a draft beer). On rue Cler you can eat and browse your way through a street full of tart shops, delis, cheeseries, and colorful outdoor produce stalls. For an after-dinner cruise on the Seine, it's just a short walk to the river and the Bâteaux Mouches (see page 28).

Your neighborhood tourist office is at the Eiffel Tower (May–Sept daily 11:00–18:00, tel. 01 45 51 22 15). The Métro station (École Militaire) and a **post office** are at the end of rue Cler on avenue de la Motte Piquet, and there's a handy SNCF office under the *Aérogare* at the Invalides Métro stop, where you can get information, buy tickets, and make seat reservations. The nearest **Internet access** is at the splashy Toyota Cybercafé (79 avenue Champs-Élysées, Mo: George V, tel. 01 56 89 29 79). Taxi stands are on avenue de Tourville at avenue la Motte Piquet (near Métro stop) and on avenue Bosquet at rue St. Dominique. The Banque Populaire (across from Hôtel Leveque) changes money. Rue St. Dominique is the area's boutique-browsing street. The Épicerie de la Tour **grocery** is open until midnight (197 rue de Grenelle).

The **American Church and College** is the community center for Americans living in Paris and should be one of your first stops if you're planning to stay a while (reception open Mon–Sat 9:00–22:30, Sun 9:00–19:30, 65 quai d'Orsay, tel. 01 40 62 05 00). Pick up copies of the *Free Voice* for a monthly review of Paris entertainment, and *France-U.S.A. Contacts* for information on housing and employment through the community of 30,000 Americans living in Paris. The interdenominational service at 11:00 on Sunday, the coffee hour after church, and the free Sunday concerts (18:00, not every week) are a great way to make some friends and get a taste of émigré life in Paris.

Afternoon *boules* (lawn bowling) on the esplanade des Invalides is a relaxing spectator sport. Look for the dirt area to the upper right as you face the Invalides.

You should try at least one of these helpful **bus routes:** Line #69 runs along rue St. Dominique and serves Les Invalides, Orsay, Louvre, Marais, and Père-Lachaise cemetery. Line #92 runs along avenue Bosquet and serves the Arc de Triomphe and Champs-Élysées in one direction and the Montparnasse tower in the other. Line #87 runs on avenue de la Bourdonnais and serves St. Sulpice, Luxembourg Gardens, and the Sevres-Babylone shopping area. Line #49 runs on boulevard La Tour Maubourg and serves the St. Lazare and Gare du Nord stations.

Sleeping in the Rue Cler Neighborhood
**(7th *arrondissement*, Mo: École Militaire,
zip code: 75007)**
Rue Cler is the glue that holds this pleasant neighborhood together. From here you can walk to the Eiffel Tower, Napoleon's Tomb, the Seine, and the Orsay and Rodin Museums.

Many of my readers stay in this neighborhood. If you want to disappear into Paris, you'll do it better at the hotels away from the rue Cler, or in the other neighborhoods I list. And if nightlife matters, seriously consider sleeping elsewhere (this area is dead at night). The first seven hotels listed below are within Camembert-smelling distance of rue Cler; the others are within a 5- to 10-minute stroll. Warning: The first two hotels are popular with my readers.

Hôtel Leveque** is ideally located, with an air-conditioned lobby (and ice machine), helpful staff, and a singing maid. It's a big place with well-designed rooms that have ceiling fans, cable TV, hair dryers, direct phone lines, safes, and French modem outlets (S-300F, Db-400–500F, Tb-600F, CC:VMA, breakfast-40F, first breakfast free for readers of this book, 29 rue Cler, tel. 01 47 05 49 15, fax 01 45 50 49 36, www.hotel-leveque.com, e-mail: info@hotelleveque.com).

Hôtel du Champ de Mars**, with charming, pastel rooms and helpful English-speaking owners Françoise and Stephane, is a cozier rue Cler option. The hotel has a Provence-style, small-town feel from top to bottom. Rooms are comfortable and a very good value. Single rooms can work as tiny doubles (Sb-400F, Db-440–470F, Tb-560F, CC:VMA, cable TV, hair dryers, 30 meters off rue Cler at 7 rue de Champ de Mars, tel. 01 45 51 52 30, fax 01 45 51 64 36, www.hotel-du-champ-de-mars.com, e-mail: stg@club-internet.fr).

Hôtel Cadran*** charges too much for its fine location and cozy lobby. Rooms are tight and narrow but air-conditioned (Sb or Db-900–980F, 10 rue de Champs de Mars, tel. 01 40 62 67 00, fax 01 40 62 67 13, www.cadranhotel.com).

Hôtel Relais Bosquet*** is modern, spacious, and a bit upscale, with snazzy, comfortable rooms and big beds (Sb-600–800F, Db-650–1,000F, most at 850F, more expensive rooms with air-conditioning, CC:VMA, cable TV, 19 rue de Champ de Mars, tel. 01 47 05 25 45, fax 01 45 55 08 24, www.relaisbosquet.com).

Hôtel Beaugency*** has small but comfortable rooms, a lobby you can stretch out in, and a helpful staff (Sb-680F, Db-730F, Tb-830F, includes buffet breakfast, 21 rue Duvivier, tel. 01 47 05 01 63, fax 01 45 51 04 96).

Hôtel Valadon**, on a quiet street one block west of rue Cler, will be spiffed up for 2001 by new owners (Sb-400F, Db-510–560F, CC:VMA, 16 rue Valadon, tel. 01 47 53 89 85, fax 01 44 18 90 56, www.hotelvaladon.com).

Hôtel la Motte Piquet**, at the end of rue Cler on a busy street, is pleasant with reasonable rates and a helpful owner (Ss-355F, Sb-375–435F, Ds-400F, Db-420–490F, duplex suites-670–780F, extra bed-100F, CC:VM, 30 avenue de la Motte Piquet, tel. 01 47 05 09 57, fax 01 47 05 74 36).

Near rue Cler: The following listings are a 5- to 10-minute walk west of rue Cler and are listed in order of proximity.

Hôtel Prince**, just across avenue Bosquet from the École Militaire Métro stop, has fair-value rooms, many overlooking a busy street (Db-470–625F, CC:VMA, 66 avenue Bosquet, tel. 01 47 05 40 90, fax 01 47 53 06 62).

Hôtel le Tourville**** is the most classy and expensive of

RUE CLER HOTELS

1. TAXIS
2. HOTEL LEVEQUE
3. HOTEL DU CHAMPS DE MARS
4. HOTEL RELAIS BOSQUET
5. HOTEL VALADON
6. HOTEL PRINCE
7. HOTEL DE L'ALMA
8. HOTEL LONDRES EIFFEL
9. MARS HOTEL
10. HOTEL LA TOUR MAUBOURG
11. HOTEL JARDINS EIFFEL
12. HOTEL KENSINGTON
13. HOTEL DE LA TULIPE
14. HOTEL LE PAVILLION
15. HOTEL ROYAL PHARE
16. HOTEL DE LA MOTTE PIQUET
17. HOTEL DE LA PAIX
18. HOTEL BEAUGENCY
19. HOTEL DE LA TOUR EIFFEL
20. HOTEL DE LA BOURDONNAIS
21. HOTEL DE L'EMPEREUR
22. HOTEL MUGUET
23. HOTEL CADRAN
24. HOTEL TOURVILLE
25. HOTEL TURENNE
26. HOTELS SPLENDID & DERBY

my Paris listings. This four-star gem is surprisingly intimate and friendly, from its welcoming lobby to its air-conditioned, pastel rooms and vaulted breakfast area (small standard Db-890F, superior Db-1,090F, Db with private terrace-1,350F, extra bed-100F, 16 avenue de Tourville, Mo: École Militaire, tel. 01 47 05 62 62, fax 01 47 05 43 90, e-mail: hotel@tourville.com).

Hôtel de Turenne**, with small air-conditioned rooms, is a good value when it's hot (Sb-370F, Db-440–510F, Tb-600F, extra bed-60F, CC:VM, cable TV, 20 avenue de Tourville, tel. 01 47 05 99 92, fax 01 45 56 06 04, e-mail: hotel.turenne.paris7@ wanadoo.fr).

Hôtel de l'Alma*** is a fair value, with 32 small but pleasant look-alike rooms with cable TVs and mini-bars and a tiny lobby (Sb-450F, Db-500F, no triples but a kid's bed can be moved in for free, CC:VMA, includes breakfast, 32 rue de l'Exposition, tel. 01 47 05 45 70, fax 01 45 51 84 47, e-mail: almahotel@minitel.net).

Hôtel Londres Eiffel*** may have rooms when others don't. The helpful staff takes good care of its guests and offers small but thoughtfully appointed rooms and cozy public spaces (Sb-545F, Db-645F, Tb-825F, extra bed-70F, CC:VMA, use handy bus #69 or the RER Alma stop, 1 rue Augerau, tel. 01 45 51 63 02, fax 01 47 05 28 96, www.Londres-Eiffel.com).

Mars Hôtel** is a formal Parisian place, with spacious rooms, thin walls, reasonable rates, and a beam-me-up-Jacques, coffin-sized elevator. Front rooms are noisier but have views of the Eiffel Tower (large Sb-350F, Db-410F, Twin/b-510F, CC:VM, 117 avenue de la Bourdonnais, tel. 01 47 05 42 30, fax 01 47 05 45 91).

Hôtel de la Bourdonnais***, more famous for its highly respected restaurant, is a superb three-star hotel. This perfectly Parisian place mixes Old World elegance with top-notch service, spacious rooms, and pleasant public spaces (Sb-690F, Db-790F, Tb-850F, Qb-910F, Qb suite-1,500F, CC:VMA, cable TV, 111 avenue de la Bourdonnais, tel. 01 47 05 45 42, fax 01 45 55 75 54, e-mail: otlbourd@clubinternet.fr).

Hôtel Kensington** has warmly decorated rooms at a fair value, but a cold staff (Sb-325F, Db-410–510F, extra bed-80F, CC:VMA, 79 avenue de la Bourdonnais, tel. 01 47 05 74 00, fax 01 47 05 25 81, www.hotel-kensington.com).

Hôtel de la Tulipe** is a unique place two blocks from rue Cler toward the river, with artistically decorated rooms (each one different) surrounding a wood-beamed lounge and a peaceful, leafy courtyard (Sb-570F, Db-680F, extra bed-150F, no elevator, cable TV, 33 rue Malar, tel. 01 45 51 67 21, fax 01 47 53 96 37, www .hoteldelatulipe.com).

Near Metro stop La Tour Maubourg: The next four listings are within two blocks of the intersection of avenue de la Motte Piquet and Les Invalides.

Hôtel Les Jardins Eiffel*** merits its three stars with professional service, a spacious lobby, outdoor patio, and comfortable, air-conditioned rooms—some with private balconies. Ask for a room *avec petit balcon* (Sb-600–840F, Db-700–1,000F, extra bed-135F, CC:VMA, parking-110F/day, 8 rue Amelie, tel. 01 47 05 46 21, fax 01 45 55 28 08, e-mail: Eiffel@unimedia.fr).

Hôtel La Tour Maubourg*** feels like a slightly faded, elegant manor house with spaciously comfortable Old World rooms. It overlooks a cheery green lawn within sight of Napoleon's tomb (Sb-700F, Db-800–900F, suites for up to 4 people-1,100–1,800F, prices reduced mid-July–mid-Aug, CC:VM, includes breakfast with freshly squeezed juice, immediately at La Tour Maubourg Métro stop, 150 rue de Grenelle, tel. 01 47 05 16 16, fax 01 47 05 16 14, www.latour-maubourg.fr).

Hôtel de l'Empereur** is a big, modern place with all the comforts (Sb-430F, Db-470–500F, Tb-650F, Qb-750F, CC:VM, 2 rue Chevert, tel. 01 45 55 88 02, fax 01 45 51 88 54).

Hôtel Muguet** is peaceful, overlooked, and very sharp. Here you get three-star comfort for the price of two, a pleasant owner, quiet and air-conditioned rooms, and a small garden courtyard (Sb-560F, Db-600F, Tb-780F, CC:VMA, 11 rue Chevert, tel. 01 47 05 05 93, fax 01 45 50 25 37, www.hotelmuguet.com).

Lesser values: Given this fine area, these are acceptable last choices. **Derby Eiffel Hôtel***** (Db-750F–900F, CC:VMA, air-con, 5 avenue Duquesne, tel. 01 47 05 12 05, fax 01 47 05 43 43, www.derbyeiffelhotel.com); **Hôtel Splendid***** (Db-790–930F, 29 avenue Tourville, tel. 01 45 51 24 77, fax 01 44 18 94 60, e-mail: splendid@club-internet.fr); **Hôtel de la Tour Eiffel**** (Sb-370F, Db-420F, Tb-520F, CC:VMA, 17 rue de l'Exposition, tel. 01 47 05 14 75, fax 01 47 53 99 46, Muriel speaks English); the quiet but tired **Hôtel le Pavillon**** (has unrealized potential and a small courtyard; Db-460F, family suites-575F, 54 rue St. Dominique, tel. 01 45 51 42 87, fax 01 45 51 32 79, e-mail: PatrickPavillon@aol.com); **Hôtel Royal Phare**** (Db-390–460F, CC:VMA, facing École Militaire Métro stop, 40 avenue de la Motte Piquet, tel. 01 47 05 57 30, fax 01 45 51 64 41); the simple, quiet **Hôtel de la Paix** (S-180F, Ds-330F, Db-350F, Tb-480F, no elevator, 19 rue du Gros-Caillou, tel. 01 45 51 86 17, fax 01 45 55 93 28); and the basic, overpriced **Hôtel La Serre*** (Db-500F, has superb location on rue Cler but generates readers' complaints for its rude staff and bizarre hotel practices—you can't see room in advance or get a refund, 24 rue Cler, across from Hôtel Leveque, Mo: École Militaire, tel. 01 47 05 52 33, fax 01 40 62 95 66).

Marais Orientation

Those interested in a more Soho-Greenwich Village locale should make the Marais their Parisian home. The Marais is a more happening area than rue Cler, with great access to many museums: Picasso, Carnavalet, Jewish History, and Pompidou Center. It's narrow, medieval Paris at its finest, where elegant stone mansions sit side by side with trendy bars, antique shops, and slick boutiques. Only 15 years ago it was a forgotten Parisian backwater, but now the Marais is one of Paris' most popular residential and shopping areas.

The nearest **tourist offices** are in the Louvre and Gare de Lyon (arrival level, daily 8:00–20:00, tel. 01 43 43 33 24). The **Banque de France** changes money, offering good rates and sometimes long lines (Mon–Fri 9:00–11:45, 13:30–15:30, at corner of rue St. Antoine and place de la Bastille). Most banks and other services are on the main drag, rue de Rivoli/St. Antoine. You'll find one **taxi stand** on the north side of rue St. Antoine, where it meets rue Castex, and another on the south side of St. Antoine, in front of the St. Paul church.

The new Bastille opera house, Promenade Plantée Park, place des Vosges (Paris' oldest square), and the Jewish Quarter (rue des Rosiers) are all nearby. Be sure to stroll into place des Vosges after dark. The massive budget **department store** is BHV, next to Hôtel de Ville. Marais **post offices** are on rue Castex and on the corner of rues Pavée and Francs Bourgeois. The handiest **Internet cafés** are the Café du Hamman (4 rue des Rosiers) and the Quick Cybercafé (66 rue de Rivoli, Mo. Chatelet, tel. 01 48 87 78 43).

Helpful **bus routes**: Line #69 on rue St. Antoine takes you to the Louvre, Orsay, Rodin, and Napoleon's Tomb and ends at the Eiffel Tower. Line #86 runs down boulevard Henri IV, crossing Île St. Louis and serving the Latin Quarter along boulevard St. Germain. Line #96 runs on rues Turenne and Francois Miron and serves the Louvre and boulevard St. Germain (near Luxembourg Gardens). Line #65 serves the train stations Austerlitz, Est, and Nord from place de la Bastille.

Sleeping in the Marais Neighborhood
(4th arrondissement, Mo: St. Paul or Bastille, zip code: 75004)

The Marais runs from the Pompidou Center to the Bastille (a 15-min walk), with most hotels located a few blocks north of the main east-west drag, rue de Rivoli/St. Antoine. It's about 15 minutes on foot from any hotel in this area to Notre-Dame, Île St. Louis, and the Latin Quarter. Strolling home (day or night) from Notre-Dame along the Île St. Louis is marvelous.

The St. Paul Métro stop puts you right in the heart of the

Marais, while the Hôtel de Ville stop serves its western end and the Bastille stop serves its eastern limit.

Hôtel Castex** is a clean, well-run, and cheery place— a great value with comfortable rooms, many stairs, and a good location on a relatively quiet street. Reserve by phone and leave your credit-card number (Sb-310F, Db-360–380F, Tb-480F, CC:VM, no elevator, just off place de la Bastille and rue St. Antoine, 5 rue Castex, Mo: Bastille, tel. 01 42 72 31 52, fax 01 42 72 57 91, e-mail: info@castexhotel.com). The owners have another good-value hotel two Métro stops away in a less-appealing location that often has rooms when others don't: **Hôtel de la République**** (Sb-350F, Db-400F, cable TV, 31 rue Albert Thomas, 75010 Paris, Mo: République, tel. 01 42 39 19 03, fax 01 42 39 22 66, www.republique.com).

Grand Hôtel Jeanne d'Arc**, a warm, welcoming place with thoughtfully appointed rooms and cozy public spaces, is ideally located for connoisseurs of the Marais. Rooms on the street can be noisy until the bars close. Sixth-floor rooms have a view and corner rooms are wonderfully bright in the City of Light. Reserve this place way ahead (small Db-320F, Db-435–500F, Tb-550F, family friendly Qb-620F, extra bed-75F, CC:VM, 3 rue Jarente, Mo: St. Paul, tel. 01 48 87 62 11, fax 01 48 87 37 31).

Hôtel Bastille Speria***, a short block off the Bastille, feels family-run while offering serious, business-type service. Its spacious lobby and 45 rooms are modern, cheery, and pastel. It's English-language friendly, from the *Herald Tribune*s in the lobby to the history of the Bastille posted in the elevator (Sb-540–580F, Db-600–720F, Tb-830F, extra bed-110F, CC:VMA, 1 rue de la Bastille, Mo: Bastille, tel. 01 42 72 04 01, fax 01 42 72 56 38, e-mail: speria@micronet.fr).

Hôtel Lyon-Mulhouse**, on a busy street just off place de la Bastille, is a good value, with pleasant, modern rooms and helpful owners (Sb-345–435F, Db-370–540F, Tb-545–575F, Qb-600–640F, CC:VM, 8 boulevard Beaumarchais, tel. 01 47 00 91 50, fax 01 47 00 06 31, e-mail: hotelyonmulhouse@wanadoo.fr).

Hôtel de la Place des Vosges**, quasi-classy with a linoleum/antique feel, is ideally located on a quiet street (Sb-495F, Db-660–690F, CC:VMA, elevator begins on 2nd floor, just off elegant place des Vosges and just as snooty, 12 rue de Biraque, Mo: St. Paul, tel. 01 42 72 60 46, fax 01 42 72 02 64, e-mail: hotel.place.des.vosges@gofornet.com).

Hôtel des Chevaliers***, one block northwest of place des Vosges, offers small, pleasant, and comfortable rooms, with modern comforts from hair dryers to cable TV. Rooms off the street are quiet (Db-660–850F, CC:VMA, skip overpriced

MARAIS HOTELS

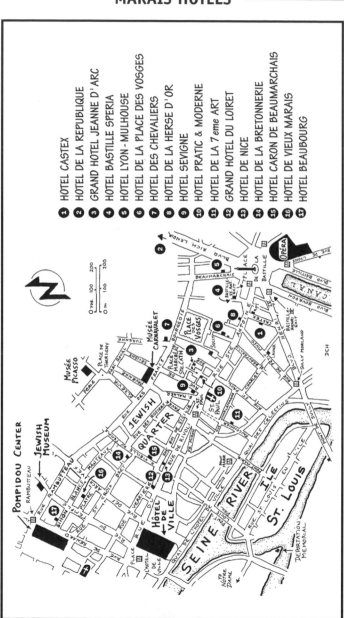

1. HOTEL CASTEX
2. HOTEL DE LA REPUBLIQUE
3. GRAND HOTEL JEANNE D'ARC
4. HOTEL BASTILLE SPERIA
5. HOTEL LYON-MULHOUSE
6. HOTEL DE LA PLACE DES VOSGES
7. HOTEL DES CHEVALIERS
8. HOTEL DE LA HERSE D'OR
9. HOTEL SEVIGNE
10. HOTEL PRATIC & MODERNE
11. HOTEL DE LA 7eme ART
12. GRAND HOTEL DU LOIRET
13. HOTEL DE NICE
14. HOTEL DE LA BRETONNERIE
15. HOTEL CARON DE BEAUMARCHAIS
16. HOTEL DE VIEUX MARAIS
17. HOTEL BEAUBOURG

breakfast, 30 rue de Turenne, Mo: St. Paul, tel. 01 42 72 73 47, fax 01 42 72 54 10).

Hôtel de la Herse D'Or is industrial-strength, three-coats-of-paint simple, with a good location, tortured floor plan, and hard-to-beat prices for its relatively comfortable rooms (S-180F, D-220F, Db-310F, extra bed-50F, showers-10F, no elevator, 20 rue St. Antoine, Mo: Bastille, tel. 01 48 87 84 09, fax 01 48 87 94 01).

Hôtel Sévigné** provides two-star comfort at fair prices with the cheapest breakfast in Paris—20F (Sb-360F, Db-380–400F, Tb-512F, CC:VM, 2 rue Malher, Mo: St. Paul, tel. 01 42 72 76 17, fax 01 42 78 68 26).

Hôtel Pratic* is in a fantastic spot on a great, people-friendly square. Its pricey rooms are modern (single rooms are tiny) and its stairs are many (St-250F, Dt-280F, Ds-390F, Db-460F, no elevator, 9 rue d'Ormesson, Mo: St. Paul, tel. 01 48 87 80 47, fax 01 48 87 40 04).

The bare-bones and dumpy **Hôtel Moderne**, next to Hôtel Pratic, might be better than a youth hostel if you need privacy. The only thing *moderne* about it is the name, which is illegible on the broken sign (S-170F, D-190F, Db-340F, 3 rue Caron, Mo: St. Paul, tel. 01 48 87 97 05).

Hôtel de 7ème Art**, two blocks south of rue St. Antoine, is a relaxed, Hollywood-nostalgia place, run by young, friendly, hip Marais types, with a full service café/bar and Charlie Chaplin murals. Most rooms are average, but the few large double rooms at 690F are very nice (Sb-300F, Db-430–570F, large Db-690F, extra bed-100F, CC:VMA, 20 rue St. Paul, Mo: St. Paul, tel. 01 44 54 85 00, fax 01 42 77 69 10).

MIJE Youth Hostels: The Maison Internationale de la Jeunesse des Étudiants (MIJE) runs three classy old residences clustered a few blocks south of rue St. Antoine. Each offers simple, clean, single-sex, one- to four-bed rooms for families and travelers under the age of 30 (exceptions are made for families). Prices are per person; you can pay more to have your own room or be roomed with as many as three others (Sb-225F, Db-175F, Tb-155F, Qb-145F; includes breakfast but not towels, which you can get from a machine; required membership card-15F extra/person; rooms locked 12:00–15:00 and at 01:00). **MIJE Fourcy** (cheap dinners, 6 rue de Fourcy, just south of rue Rivoli), **MIJE Fauconnier** (11 rue Fauconnier), and the best, **MIJE Maubisson** (12 rue des Barres), share the same contact information (tel. 01 42 74 23 45, fax 01 40 27 81 64, www.mije.com) and Métro stop (St. Paul). Reservations are accepted.

Near Pompidou Center: The remaining hotels are farther west and closer to the Pompidou Center than to place Bastille.

Hôtel de Nice** is a cozy "Marie Antoinette does tie-dye" place with lots of thoughtful touches on the Marais' busy main drag. Twin rooms, which cost the same as doubles, are roomier but on the street side—with effective double-paned windows (Sb-380F, Db-550F, Tb-680F, CC:VM, 42 bis rue de Rivoli, Mo: Hôtel de Ville, tel. 01 42 78 55 29, fax 01 42 78 36 07).

Hôtel de la Bretonnerie***, three blocks north and east of the Hôtel de Ville, is a fine Marais splurge. It has elegant decor, tastefully decorated and spacious rooms with an antique, open-beam coziness, and an efficient, helpful staff (standard Db-660F, Db with character-830F, the standard Db has enough character for me, family-friendly suites-1,050F, CC:VMA, between rue du Vielle du Temple and rue des Archives at 22 rue Sainte Croix de la Bretonnerie, Mo: Hôtel de Ville, tel. 01 48 87 77 63, fax 01 42 77 26 78, www.laBretonnerie.com).

Grand Hôtel du Loiret**, just north of rue de Rivoli, is a fair enough value. It has laid-back management and is popular with American students (S-190F, Sb-270–350F, D-230F, Db-310–410F, Tb-515F, Qb-600F, CC:VMA, 8 rue des Garçons Mauvais, Mo: Hôtel de Ville, tel. 01 48 87 77 00, fax 01 48 04 96 56, e-mail: HOTELLOIRET@aol.com).

Hôtel Caron de Beaumarchais***, an 18th-century Marais manor house, charges top prices for its precious, comfortable, and air-conditioned rooms (Db-790–870F, CC:VMA, 12 rue Vielle du Temple, Mo: Hôtel de Ville, tel. 01 42 72 34 12, fax 01 42 72 34 63).

Hôtel de Vieux Marais**, tucked away on a quiet street two blocks east of the Pompidou Center, offers spotless and fairly spacious rooms with air-conditioning, pleasing decor, and we-try-harder owners. Make sure to greet Leeloo, the hotel hound (Sb-600–660F, Db-695–720F, extra bed-150F, CC:VM, cable TV, just off rue des Archives at 8 rue du Platre, Mo: Rambuteau/Hôtel de Ville, tel. 01 42 78 47 22, fax 01 42 78 34 32).

Hôtel Beaubourg*** is an excellent three-star value within spitting distance of the Pompidou Center on a small street. The comfortable rooms are wood-beam cozy and public spaces are warm and pleasant (Db-520–590F, Db with private terrace-690F, CC:VM, 11 rue Simon Lefranc, Mo: Rambuteau, tel. 01 42 74 34 24, fax 01 42 78 68 11, e-mail: htlbeaubourg@hotellerie.net).

Contrescarpe Orientation

This lively, colorful neighborhood is like Montmartre without all the tourists. It's just south of the Latin Quarter, encompassing the area between the Luxembourg Gardens and rue Monge.

The nearest **tourist office** is at the Louvre Museum.

The **post office** (PTT) is between rue Mouffetard and rue Monge at 10 rue de l'Épée du Bois. Place Monge hosts a colorful **outdoor market** on Wednesday, Friday, and Sunday until 13:00. The **street market** at the bottom of rue Mouffetard bustles daily except Monday (Tue–Sat 8:00–12:00, 15:30–19:00, Sun 8:00–12:00, 5 blocks south of place Contrescarpe). The lively place Contrescarpe hops in the afternoon and evening until the wee hours. **Bus** #47 runs along rue Monge north to Notre-Dame, the Pompidou Center, and Gare du Nord.

The flowery Jardin des Plantes park is just east and the sublime Luxembourg Gardens are just west. Both are ideal for afternoon walks, picnics, and naps. The doorway at 49 rue Monge leads to a hidden Roman arena (Arènes de Lutèce). Today, *boules* players occupy the stage while couples cuddle on the seats. Admire the Panthéon from the outside (it's not worth paying to go in), and go into the exquisitely beautiful St. Étienne-du-Mont church.

Sleeping in the Contrescarpe Neighborhood
(5th *arrondissement*, Mo: place Monge, zip code: 75005)

Hotels here are a 20-minute walk from Notre-Dame, Île de la Cité, and Île St. Louis, and a 5- to 10-minute walk to the Luxembourg Gardens and the grand boulevards St. Germain and St. Michel. Fewer tourists sleep in Contrescarpe, and I find the hotel values generally better than in most other neighborhoods. Most hotels listed are on or very near rue Mouffetard, the spine of this area, running from the perfectly Parisian place Contrescarpe south to rue Bazelles. Two thousand years ago, rue Mouffetard was the principal Roman road south to Italy. Today this small, meandering street has a split personality. The lower part thrives in the daytime as a pedestrian market street. The upper part sleeps during the day but comes alive after dark, teeming with bars, restaurants, and nightlife. These hotels are listed in order of proximity to the Seine and Notre-Dame.

The low-energy, no-frills **Hôtel du Commerce** is run by Monsieur Mattuzzi, who must be a pirate gone good. This 300-year-old place (with vinyl that looks it) is a great rock-bottom deal and as safe as any dive next to a police station can be. In the morning, the landlady will knock and chirp, "*Restez-vous?*"—Are you staying tonight? (S-135F, D-155F, Ds-175F, Ts-225F, Qs-290F, showers-15F, no elevator, takes no reservations, call at 10:00 and monsieur will say "*oui*" or "*non*," 14 rue de La Montagne Ste. Geneviève, Mo: Maubert-Mutualité, tel. 01 43 54 89 69).

Hôtel Central* is unpretentious, with a charming location, a steep and slippery castlelike stairway, simple rooms (all with

CONTRESCARPE HOTELS

1 HOTEL DU COMMERCE

2 HOTEL CENTRAL

3 HOTEL DES GRANDES ÉCOLES

4 Y & H HOSTEL

5 HOTEL DE L'ESPERANCE

6 HOTEL DE FRANCE

7 HOTEL PORT ROYAL

8 LE JARDIN D'ARTEMIS

9 RESTAURANT L'ÉPOQUE

10 SAVANNAH CAFE

11 LE JARDIN DES PATES

12 BRASSERIE LA CHOPE

13 CAFE LE MOUFFETARD

14 CAVE DE LA BOURGOGNE

15 CAFE DE LA MOSQUE

16 HOTEL DES GRANDES HOMME

17 HOTEL SENLIS

18 HOTEL MEDICIS

19 HOTEL BRESIL

20 HOTEL ELYSA-LUXEMBOURG

21 LE PORT DE SALUT

showers, though toilets are down the hall), so-so beds, and plenty of smiles. It's a fine budget value (Ss-165–213F, Ds-240–276F, no elevator, 6 rue Descartes, Mo: Cardinal Lemoine, tel. 01 46 33 57 93).

Hôtel des Grandes Écoles*** is simply idyllic. A short alley leads to three buildings that protect a flowering garden courtyard, preserving a sense of tranquility that is rare in a city this size. Rooms are spacious and comfortable with large beds. This romantic place is deservedly popular, so call up to four months in advance (Db-555–720F, extra bed-100F, 75 rue de Cardinal Lemoine, Mo: Cardinal Lemoine, tel. 01 43 26 79 23, fax 01 43 25 28 15, www.hotel-grandes-ecoles.com, mellow Marie speaks English).

Between the Panthéon and Luxembourg Gardens: The following five hotels are a five-minute walk from the rue Mouffetard. For these listings, the RER stop Luxembourg is closer than the nearest Métro stop, Maubert Mutualité.

At **Hôtel des Grandes Hommes*****, spacious, wood-beamed rooms stare across the street at the Panthéon and offer all the comforts you'd expect for the price, including air-conditioning, cable TV, and mini-bar. Some rooms have terraces (Db-850F, suite-1,100F, CC:VM, 17 place du Panthéon, tel. 01 46 34 19 60, fax 01 43 26 67 32, e-mail: henri4@hotellerie.net).

Hôtel Senlis** hides quietly two blocks from the Luxembourg Gardens with simple but comfortable rooms, all with beamed ceilings and TVs (Sb-420F, Db-450–530F, Tb-530–580F, Qb-680F, CC:VMA, 7 rue Malebranche, tel. 01 43 29 93 10, fax 01 43 29 00 24).

Hôtel Brésil** lies one block from Luxembourg Gardens and offers unimaginative but comfortable and modern rooms at reasonable rates (Sb-375F, Db-400–500F, CC:VM, 10 rue le Goff, tel. 01 43 54 76 11, fax 01 46 33 45 78).

Hôtel Medicis is as cheap, stripped-down, and basic as it gets with a helpful owner and great location (S-100F, D-190–200F, 214 rue St. Jacques, tel. 01 43 54 14 66).

Hôtel Elysa-Luxembourg*** sits on a busy street at Luxembourg Gardens and charges top franc for its air-conditioned, impressively decorated rooms (Sb-680F, Db-800F, Tb-900F, CC:VMA, 6 rue Gay Lussac, tel. 01 43 25 31 74, fax 01 46 34 56 27).

At the bottom of rue Mouffetard: Of my recommended accommodations in the Contrescarpe neighborhood, these are farthest from the Seine. They may have rooms when others don't.

Y&H Hostel offers a great location, easygoing English-speaking management, Internet access, kitchen facilities, and basic but acceptable hostel-like conditions (beds in 4-bed rooms-117F, beds in double rooms-137F, sheets-15F, rooms closed 11:00–16:00

but reception stays open, 02:00 curfew, reservations must be paid in advance, 80 rue Mouffetard, Mo: Cardinal Lemoine, tel. 01 45 35 09 53, fax 01 47 07 22 24, e-mail: smile@youngandhappy.fr).

Hôtel de l'Esperance, located at the bottom of rue Mouffetard, gives you nearly three stars for the price of two. It's quiet, pink, fluffy, and comfortable, with thoughtfully appointed rooms complete with canopy beds, hair dryers, cable TV, and a flamboyant owner (Sb-440F, Db-450–550F, small Tb-600F, CC:VM, 15 rue Pascal, Mo: Censier-Daubenton, tel. 01 47 07 10 99, fax 01 43 37 56 19).

Hôtel de France, set on a busy street, has fine, modern rooms and hardworking, helpful owners (Jean and Christine). The best and quietest rooms are *sur le cour* (on the courtyard), though streetside rooms are fine (Sb-390F, Db-435–455F, CC:VM, 108 rue Monge, Mo: Censier-Daubenton, tel. 01 47 07 19 04, fax 01 43 36 62 34, e-mail: hotel.de.fce@wanadoo.fr).

Hôtel Port Royal is well run (by the same family for 66 years), with a small, pleasant courtyard and incredibly clean, comfortable rooms at fair prices. Ask for a room off the street (S-210–260F, D-260F, Db-405F, no CC, climb stairs from rue Pascal to busy boulevard de Port Royal, 8 boulevard de Port Royal, Mo: Gobelins, tel. 01 43 31 70 06, fax 01 43 31 33 67).

Sleeping near Paris, in Versailles

For a laid-back alternative to Paris within easy reach of the big city by RER train (5/hrly, 30 min), Versailles, with easy, safe parking and reasonably priced hotels, can be a good overnight stop (see map on page 192). Park in the château's main lot while looking for a hotel or leave your car there overnight (acceptable rates). Get a map of Versailles at your hotel or at the tourist office and be sure to explore the pleasant town center around place du Marché Notre-Dame (15-min walk veering left out of the château), where you'll find a variety of reasonable restaurants, cafés, and a few cobbled lanes (market days Sun, Tue, and Fri until 13:00). Rue Satory near the recommended Hôtel d'Angleterre (10-min walk veering right out of the château) is another pedestrian-friendly street with restaurants.

Hôtel Le Cheval Rouge, built in 1676 as Louis XIV's stables, now houses tourists. It's a block behind place du Marché in a quaint corner of town on a large, quiet courtyard with free, safe parking and simple but adequate rooms (Ds-300F, Db-360–410F, extra bed-90F for 1 person, 120F for 2, CC:VMA, cable TV, 18 rue Andre Chenier, tel. 01 39 50 03 03, fax 01 39 50 61 27).

Ibis Versailles, a slick business-class place, offers all the comfort with none of the character (Db-425F, cheaper weekend rates available but can't be reserved ahead, CC:VMA, across from RER station, 4 avenue du General de Gaulle, tel. 01 39 53 03 30, fax 01 39 50 06 31, e-mail: accorhotel.com).

Hôtel du Palais, facing the RER station, has cheap and handy beds; ask for a quiet room off the street. It's a pink and funky place—dumpy enough to lack even one star but proud enough to put candy on the beds (D-180F, Ds-250F, Db-250–280F, extra person-70F, miles of stairs, 6 place Lyautey, tel. 01 39 50 39 29, fax 01 39 50 80 41).

Hôtel d'Angleterre** is a tranquil old place with comfortable and spacious rooms. Park nearby in the palace lot (Db-350–450F, extra bed-100F, CC:VMA, cable TV, mini-bar, just below palace to the right as you exit, 2 rue de Fontenay, tel. 01 39 51 43 50, fax 01 39 51 45 63).

For Longer Stays

Staying a week or longer? Consider the advantages that come with renting a furnished apartment. Complete with a small, equipped kitchen and living room, this option is great for families. Among the many English-speaking organizations ready to help, the following have proven most reliable. Their Web sites are generally excellent and essential to understanding your options.

Paris Appartements Services rents studios and one-bedroom apartments in the Opéra, Louvre, and Marais neighborhoods (2 rue d'Argout, 75002 Paris, tel. 01 40 28 01 28, fax 01 40 28 92 01, www.paris-appartements-services.fr).

Apalachee Bay is British-owned and offers an extensive range of carefully selected, furnished apartments (21 rue de Madrid, 75008 Paris, tel. 01 42 94 13 13, fax 01 42 94 83 01, www.apalachee.com).

Localflat offers accommodations ranging from studios to five-room apartments (tel. 01 43 06 78 79, fax 01 40 56 99 69, www.localflat.com).

EATING
IN PARIS

Paris is France's wine and cuisine melting pot. While it lacks a style of its own (only French onion soup is truly Parisian), it draws from the best of France. Paris could hold a gourmet's Olympics and import nothing.

Picnic or go to bakeries for quick take-out lunches, or stop at a café for a lunch salad or *plat du jour*, but linger longer over dinner. You can eat well, restaurant style, for 100F to 150F. Your hotel can usually recommend nearby restaurants in the 80F-to-100F range. Remember, cafés are happy to serve a *plat du jour* (garnished plate of the day, about 70F) or a chef-like salad (60F) day or night. Famous places are often overpriced, overcrowded, and overrated. Find a quiet neighborhood and wander, or follow a local recommendation. Restaurants open for dinner around 19:00, and small local favorites get crowded after 21:00.

To save piles of francs, review the budget eating tips in this book's introduction and consider dinner picnics (great take-out dishes available at *charcuteries*). My recommendations are centered around the same three great neighborhoods listed in the Sleeping chapter; you can come home exhausted after a busy day of sightseeing and have a good selection of restaurants right around the corner. And evening is a fine time to explore any of these delightful neighborhoods, even if you're sleeping elsewhere.

Restaurants

The Parisian eating scene is kept at a rolling boil. Entire books (and lives) are dedicated to the subject. If you are traveling outside of Paris, save your splurges for the countryside, where you'll enjoy regional cooking for less money. I've listed places that conveniently fit a busy sightseeing schedule and places near recommended hotels. If you'd like to visit a district specifically to eat, consider the many romantic restaurants that line the cozy Île St. Louis' main street and the colorful, touristy-but-fun string of eateries along rue Mouffetard behind the Panthéon (in the Contrescarpe neighborhood). Beware: Many restaurants close Sunday and Monday.

Cafeterias and Picnics

Many Parisian department stores have huge supermarkets hiding in the basement and top-floor cafeterias offering not really cheap but low-risk, low-stress, what-you-see-is-what-you-get meals.

For lunch and dinner picnics, you'll find handy little groceries (*épiceries*) and delis (*charcuteries*) all over town but rarely near famous sights. Good picnic fixings include roasted chicken, drinkable yogurt, fresh bakery goods, melons, and exotic pâtés and cheeses. Great take-out deli-type foods like gourmet salads and quiches abound. *Boulangeries* make good, cheap mini-quiches and sandwiches. While wine is taboo in public places in the United States, it's *pas de problème* in France.

Romantic Picnic Spots: My favorite dinner-picnic places are the pedestrian bridge (Pont des Arts) across from the Louvre, with unmatched views and plentiful benches; the Champ de Mars park under the Eiffel Tower; and the western tip of Île St. Louis, overlooking Île de la Cité. Bring your own dinner feast and watch the riverboats or the Eiffel Tower light up the city for you. The Palais Royal (across the street from the Louvre) is a good spot for a peaceful, royal picnic, as is the little triangular Henry IV Park on the west tip of Île de la Cité. For lunch picnics with great people watching, try the Pompidou Center (by the *Homage to Stravinsky* fountain), the elegant place des Vosges (closes at dusk), the gardens at the Rodin Museum, and Luxembourg Gardens.

Eating in the Rue Cler Neighborhood

The rue Cler neighborhood isn't famous for its restaurants. That's why I enjoy eating here. Several small family-run places serve great dinner *menus* for 100F and *plats du jour* for 60F to 80F. My first two recommendations are easygoing cafés, ideal if what you want is a light dinner (good dinner salads) or more substantial but simple meals.

Café du Marché, with the best seats, coffee, and prices on rue Cler, serves hearty salads and good 60F *plats du jour* for lunch or dinner to a trendy, mainly French crowd. Arrive before 19:30 or wait at the bar. A chalkboard listing the plates of the day—each a meal—will momentarily be hung in front of you (at the corner of rue Cler and rue Champ de Mars). You'll find the same menu and prices with better (but smoky) indoor seating at their other restaurant, **Le Comptoir du**

Septième, at the École Militaire Métro stop (39 avenue de la Motte Piquet, tel. 01 45 55 90 20).

Café le Bosquet's friendly owner Jean Francois will make you feel welcome at his classic Parisian brasserie. Come here for a bowl of French onion soup, a salad, or a three-course set *menu* (98F *menu*, many choices, 46 avenue Bosquet, tel. 01 45 51 38 13).

Leo le Lion, run by Mimi for 20 years, is an easygoing place. A warm, charming souvenir of old Paris, it's popular with locals. The 115F *menu* comes with a first course that could feed two for an entire meal (but no splitting) and a fully garnished main course (closed Sun, 23 rue Duvivier, tel. 01 45 51 41 77).

Vegetarians will appreciate the Mediterranean cuisine at **7ème Sud** (closed Sun, at the corner of rue de Grenelle and rue Duvivier).

Closer to Invalides, the friendly **Le Bistrot du 7ème** opens its cozy interior onto a broad sidewalk and serves a decent 98F *menu* with many choices (open daily, 56 boulevard Latour-Maubourg, tel. 01 45 51 93 08). **La Bressanne** is a country-warm place with a good 130F *menu* (16 avenue de la Motte Piquet, tel. 01 47 05 98 37). The tiny **Au Petit Tonneau** is a totally Parisian experience, where the owner/chef prepares everything herself (open daily, 20 rue Surcouf, tel. 01 47 05 09 10).

Thoumieux, the neighborhood's classy, traditional Parisian brasserie, is deservedly popular (skippable 82F but fine 160F *menu*, complete à la carte, 79 rue St. Dominique, tel. 01 47 05 49 75).

For a special dinner, survey the handful of fine places that line rue de l'Exposition one block west of avenue Bosquet between rue St. Dominique and rue de Grenelle: **Restaurant La Serre**, at #29, has fun ambience and usually great food, but an unpredictable staff (*plats* 50–70F, daily from 19:00, often a wait after 21:00, good onion soup and duck specialties, tel. 01 45 55 20 96, Marie-Alice and intense Philippe speak English). **Le P'tit Troquet**, across the street at #28, is delightfully Parisian, popular with locals, and ideal for a last-night splurge—allow 160F per person for dinner (closed Sun–Mon, tel. 01 47 05 80 39). The quieter **La Maison de Cosima** at #20 offers refined, creative French cuisine and excellent 100F and 160F *menus* that include a vegetarian option (closed Sun, tel. 01 45 51 37 71, run by friendly Helene). The softly lit tables and red velvet chairs of **Auberge du Champ de Mars**, at #18, draw a romantic crowd (no inexpensive wines, closed Mon). For top à la carte–only cuisine, locals reserve early for the charmingly situated **La Fontaine de Mars** (allow 250F per person with wine, 129 rue St. Dominique, tel. 01 47 05 46 44). Just off rue de Grenelle, the friendly and unpretentious **La Varanque** is a good budget bet, with 60F *plats* and an 80F *menu* (27 rue Augereau, tel. 01 47 05 51 22).

RUE CLER RESTAURANTS

1. CAFE DU MARCHE
2. COMPTOIR DU SEPTIEME
3. CAFE LA ROUSSILLON
4. CAFE LE BOSQUET
5. LEO LE LION
6. 7eme SUD
7. THOUMIEUX
8. LA SERRE
9. P'TIT TROQUET, COSIMA &
   AUBERGE DU CHAMPS DE MARS
10. LA FONTAINE DE MARS
11. LA VARANQUE
12. AMBASSADE DU SUD-OUEST
13. L'AMI DE JEAN
14. TARTE JULIE
15. FLO PRESTIGE
16. REAL McCOY
17. O'BRIEN'S PUB
18. CAFE THOUMIEUX

Ambassade du Sud-Ouest, a wine and food boutique/
restaurant, specializes in southwestern French cuisine such as
daubes de canard (duck meatballs) and cassoulet (46 avenue de
la Bourdonnais, tel. 01 45 55 59 59). **L'Ami de Jean** is a lively
place to sample Basque cuisine (closed Sun, 27 rue Malar, tel.
01 47 05 86 89).

Picnicking: The rue Cler is a moveable feast that gives "fast
food" a good name. The entire street is clogged with connoisseurs
of good eating. Only the health-food store goes unnoticed. A
festival of food, the street is lined with people whose lives seem
to be devoted to their specialty: stacking polished produce, rotisserie chicken, crêpes, or cheese squares.

For a magical picnic dinner at the Eiffel Tower, assemble it in
no fewer than five shops on rue Cler and lounge on the best grass
in Paris (the police don't mind after dusk), with the dogs, Frisbees,
a floodlit tower, and a cool breeze in the Parc du Champ de Mars.

The **crêpe stand** next to Café du Marché does a wonderful
top-end dinner crêpe for 25F. An Asian deli, **Traiteur Asie** (many
in the area, one across from Hôtel Leveque), has tasty low-stress,
low-price take-out treats. Its tables offer the cheapest place to sit,
eat, and enjoy the rue Cler ambience. For quiche, cheese pie, or a
pear/chocolate tart, try **Tarte Julie's** (take-out or stools, 28 rue
Cler). The elegant **Flo Prestige** *charcuterie* (at the École Militaire
Métro stop) is open until 23:00 and offers mouthwatering meals to
go. **Real McCoy** is a little shop selling American food and sandwiches (194 rue de Grenelle). A good, small, late-night grocery is
at 197 rue de Grenelle.

The bakery (*boulangerie*) on the corner of rue Cler and rue de
Champ de Mars is the place for a fresh baguette, sandwich, tiny
quiche, or *pain au chocolat*, but the almond croissants at the *boulangerie* on rue de Grenelle at rue Cler make my day. The bakery at
112 rue St. Dominique is in a league by itself and worth the detour,
with classic decor and tables to enjoy your *café au lait* and croissant.

Cafés and Bars: If you want to linger over coffee or a drink
at a sidewalk café, try **Café du Marché** (see above), **Petite
Brasserie PTT** (local workers eat here, opposite 53 rue Cler), or
Café le Bosquet (46 avenue Bosquet, tel. 01 45 51 38 13). **Café
La Roussillon**, peopled and decorated belle epoque, also offers a
quintessential café experience (at the corner of rue de Grenelle
and rue Cler). **Le Sancerre** wine bar/café is wood-beam warm and
ideal for a light lunch or dinner, or just a glass of wine after a long
day of sightseeing. The owner's cheeks are the same color as his
wine (open until 21:30, great omelets, 22 avenue Rapp, tel. 01 45
51 75 91). **Maison Altmayer** is a hole-in-the-wall place good
for a quiet drink (9:00–19:30, next to Hôtel Eiffel Rive Gauche,

6 rue du Gros Caillou). Cafés like this originated (and this one still functions) as a place where locals enjoyed a drink while their heating wood, coal, or gas was prepared for delivery.

Nightlife: This sleepy neighborhood is not the place for night owls, but there are four notable exceptions: **Café du Marché** and its brother, **Le Comptoir du Septième** (both listed above), hop with a Franco-American crowd until about midnight. **O'Brien's Pub** is a relaxed, Parisian rendition of an Irish pub (77 St. Dominique). **Café Thoumieux** is a sophisticated place with big-screen sports and a trendy young crowd (4 rue de la Comete, Mo: Latour Maubourg).

Eating in the Marais Neighborhood

The windows of the Marais are filled with munching sophisticates and crowd-pleasing eateries. And with Île St. Louis a short walk away (see below), those sleeping in the Marais have a great selection of good-value restaurants.

You'll find several good places at place du Marché Ste. Catherine, a tiny square just off rue St. Antoine between the St. Paul Métro stop and place des Vosges. **Le Marais Ste. Catherine** is a good value (110F *menu*, daily from 19:00, nonsmoking, extra seating in candlelit cellar, 5 rue Caron, tel. 01 42 72 39 94), but if it's warm, you may prefer the outdoor tables at **Le Marché** (130F *menu*, 2 place Marché Ste. Catherine, tel. 01 42 77 34 88). Just off the square, **L'Auberge de Jarente** offers a well-respected cuisine with Basque specialties (120F *menu*, closed Sun–Mon, 7 rue Jarente, tel. 01 42 77 49 35).

Dinners under the candlelit arches of the place des Vosges are *très* romantic. **Nectarine**, at #16, serves salads, quiches, and reasonable *plats du jour* daily and nightly (no CC), while **Ma Bourgogne** is where locals go for a splurge (open daily, reserve dinner ahead, no CC, at northwest corner, tel. 01 42 78 44 64).

For a fast, cheap change of pace, eat at (or take out from) the Chinese/Japanese **Delice House**. Two can split 200 grams of chicken curry (or whatever, 30F) and rice (20F). There's lots of seating, with pitchers of water at the ground-floor tables and a roomier upstairs (open until 21:00, 81 rue St. Antoine).

The **Crêperie** at 6 rue Castex serves a 60F all-crêpe menu (closed Sun–Mon), and the cozy restaurant **de la Poste** (13 rue Castex) offers 60F *plats du jour* (closed Sun). **La Bastoche**'s warm ambience and reasonable 90F *menu* make it a popular place (7 rue St. Antoine, tel. 01 48 04 74 34). Across the street, **Le Paradis de Fruit** serves salads and organic foods to a young local crowd (on small square at rues Tournelle and St. Antoine). **Gaspard de le Nuit** is a cozy step up with a fine 152F *menu* (6 rue des Tournelles, tel. 01 42 77 90 53).

MARAIS RESTAURANTS

1. MARAIS STE. CATHERINE & LE MARCHE
2. AUBERGE DE JARENTE
3. NECTARINE
4. MA BOURGOGNE
5. CREPERIE
6. CAFE DE LA POSTE
7. LA BASTOCHE
8. FLO PRESTIGE & PARADIS DE FRUIT
9. L'EXCUSE
10. L'ENOTECA
11. AU BOURGUIGNON DU MARAIS
12. PICOLO TEATRO
13. L'AS DU FALAFEL
14. PETITE GAVROCHE
15. CAFE HAMMAN
16. AU TEMPS DES CERISES
17. LE VIEUX COMPTOIR
18. LA PERLA
19. QUIET MAN

Near Hôtel du 7ème Art, splurge at the romantic, traditional **L'Excuse** (190F *menu*, closed Sun, call ahead, 14 rue Charles V, tel. 01 42 77 98 97). Across the street, **L'Énoteca** (wine bar) has lively and reasonable Italian cuisine in a relaxed, open setting (closed Sun, 20 rue St. Paul, tel. 01 42 78 91 44).

Wine lovers shouldn't miss the superb Burgundy wines and exquisite, though limited, menu selection at **Au Bourguignon du Marais** (closed Sat–Sun, call by 19:00 to reserve, 52 rue Francois Miron, tel. 01 48 87 15 40).

Vegetarians will appreciate the excellent cuisine at the popular **Picolo Teatro** (closed Mon, 6 rue des Ecouffes, tel. 01 42 72 17 79) and **L'As du Falafel**, serving the best falafel on rue Rosier at #34.

Picnicking: Picnic at the peaceful place des Vosges (closes at dusk). Hobos stretch their francs at the supermarket in the basement of the **Monoprix** department store (close to place des Vosges on rue St. Antoine), and connoisseurs prefer the gourmet take-out places all along rue St. Antoine, such as **Flo Prestige** (open until 23:00, on the tiny square where rue Tournelle and rue St. Antoine meet). A few small grocery shops are open until 23:00 on rue St. Antoine (near intersection with rue Castex). An **open-air market**, held Sunday morning, is just off place de la Bastille on boulevard Richard Lenoir.

For a cheap breakfast, try the tiny *boulangerie/pâtisserie* where the hotels buy their croissants (coffee machine-3F, baby quiches-10F, *pain au chocolat*-5F, 1 block off place de la Bastille, corner of rue St. Antoine and rue de Lesdiguieres).

Cafés and Bars: The trendiest cafés and bars are clustered on rues Vielle du Temple, Archives, and Ste. Croix de la Bretonniere (open generally till 02:00), and are popular with gay men. The *très* local wine bar at **Au Temps des Cerises** is amiably run and a welcoming, if smoky, place (around the corner from Hôtel Castex, rue du Petit Musc and rue de Cerisaie).

Nightlife: Le Vieux Comptoir is tiny, lively, and not too hip (just off place des Vosges at 8 rue Biraque). **La Perla** is trendy and full of Parisian yuppies in search of the perfect margarita (26 rue Francois Miron). **The Quiet Man** is a traditional Irish pub with happy hour from 16:00 to 20:00 (5 rue des Haudriettes).

Eating in the Contrescarpe Neighborhood

Rue Mouffetard and rue du Pot-de-Fer are lined with inexpensive, lively, and forgettable restaurants. Study the many *menus*, compare crowds, then dive in (see map on page 242). **Le Jardin d'Artemis** is one of the better values on rue Mouffetard at #34 (89F *menu*). **Restaurant l'Époque**, a fine neighborhood restaurant, has excellent

menus at 78F and 118F (a block off place Contrescarpe at 81 rue
Cardinal Lemoine, tel. 01 46 34 15 84). **Savannah Café**'s creative
Mediterranean cuisine attracts a loyal, artsy crowd (27 rue Descartes, tel. 01 43 29 45 77). **Le Jardin des Pates** is popular with
vegetarians, serving pastas and salads at fair prices (near Jardins
des Plantes, 4 rue Lacepede, tel. 01 43 31 50 71). **Le Port de Salut**,
one block from the Panthéon, has ambience and inexpensive *menus*
(closed Sun–Mon, 163 bis rue St. Jacques, tel. 01 46 33 63 21).

   Cafés: Brasserie La Chope, a classic Parisian brasserie right
on place Contrescarpe, is popular until the wee hours. Sit indoors
or outdoors for good people watching. **Café Le Mouffetard** is in
the thick of the street-market hustle and bustle (at the corner of
rue Mouffetard and rue de l'Arbalete). The outdoor tables at **Cave
de la Bourgogne** are picture-perfect (at the bottom of rue Mouffetard on rue Bazelles). At **Café de la Mosque** you'll feel like
you've been beamed to Morocco. In this purely Arab café, order a
mint tea, pour in the sugar, and enjoy the authentic interior and
peaceful outdoor terrace (behind mosque, 2 rue Daubenton).

Eating on Île St. Louis
Cruise the island's main street for a variety of good options, from
cozy *crêperies* to romantic restaurants. Sample Paris' best sorbet
and ice cream at any place advertising "les glaces Berthillon";
the original Berthillon shop is at 31 rue St. Louis en l'Île.

   All listings below are on rue St. Louis en l'Île and are listed
starting at the end of the island closest to the Île de la Cité. **Café
Med**, at #73, serves inexpensive salads, crêpes, and lighter *menus*
in a cheery setting. **La Castafiore**, at #51-53, serves fine Italian
dishes in a cozy atmosphere (160F *menu*). Farther down lie two
fine romantic splurges: **Le Tastevin** (150F and 220F *menus*, #46,
tel. 01 43 54 17 31) and, next door, **Au Gourmet de l'Isle** (150F
and 185F *menus*, closed Mon–Tue).

   For a crazy, touristy, cellar atmosphere and hearty, fun food,
feast at **La Taverne du Sergeant Recruiter**. The "Sergeant
Recruiter" used to get young Parisians drunk and stuffed here,
then sign them into the army. It's all-you-can-eat, including wine
and service, for 190F (daily from 19:00, #41, tel. 01 43 54 75 42).
There's a near-food-fight clone next door at **Nos Ancêtres Les
Gaulois** ("Our Ancestors the Gauls," 190F *menu*, daily from
19:00, tel. 01 46 33 66 07).

Elegant Dining on the Seine
La Plage Parisienne is a nearly dress-up riverfront place popular
with locals, serving elegant, healthy meals at good prices (Port de
Javel-Haut, Mo: Javel, tel. 01 40 59 41 00).

LES GRANDS CAFÉS DE PARIS

Please see "Café Culture" (page 14) in this book's Introduction for tips on Parisian cafés.

History of Cafés in Paris

The first café in the Western world was in Paris—established in 1686 at Le Procope (still a restaurant today). The French had just discovered coffee. And at about the same time, La Comedie Française theater was inaugurated, creating the necessary artsy, coffee-sipping crowds. France's robust economy was growing a population of pleasure seekers and thinkers looking for places to be seen, to exchange ideas, and to plot revolutions political and philosophical. By 1700 more than 300 cafés had opened their doors; at the time of the Revolution (1789), there were over 1,800 cafés in Paris. Revolutionaries from Marat to Napoleon to Dalí enjoyed the spirit of free thinking that the cafés engendered.

Café society took off in the early 1900s. Life was changing rapidly with the Industrial Revolution and wars on a global scale. Many retreated to Parisian cafés to try to make sense out of the confusion. Vladimir Lenin, Leon Trotsky, Igor Stravinsky, Ernest Hemingway, Scott Fitzgerald, James Joyce, Albert Einstein, Jean Paul Sartre, Gene Openshaw, and Albert Camus were among the devoted café society. Some virtually lived at their favorite café, keeping their business calendars, entertaining friends, and having every meal. Parisian apartments were small, walls were thin (still often the case), and heating (particularly during war times) was minimal, making the warmth of cafés all the harder to leave.

There are more than 12,000 cafés in Paris today. They're still used for business meetings, encounter sessions, and political discussions. Most Parisians are loyal to their favorites and know their waiter's children's names. And with the recently approved 35-hour workweek, most will have even more time to linger longer over their *café crème*.

Here's a short list of grand Parisian cafés, worth the detour only if you're not in a hurry and don't mind paying outrageous prices for a shot of espresso. Think of these cafés as museums. Try to understand why they matter just as much today as they did yesterday.

Grand Cafés by Neighborhood

St. Germain

Where the boulevard St. Germain meets rue Bonaparte (Mo: St. Germain-des-Prés), you'll find two famous cafés. **Les Deux Magots** offers great outdoor seating and a warm, wood-paneled interior. Once a favorite of Ernest Hemingway (in the *Sun Also Rises*, Jake met Brett here) and of Jean Paul Sartre (he and Simone de Beauvoir met here), today's café is filled with tourists. **Le Café de Flore**, right next door, feels more local, hip, and literary—wear your black turtleneck. Picasso was a regular here while painting *Guernica*. The smoky interior is popular with Europeans.

For great outdoor seating at almost half the price, skip these places and set up at **Café Bonaparte** (from Les Deux Magots 1 block down rue Bonaparte toward the river). You're farther from the large boulevards and exhaust fumes here but still in the thick of this pleasant café-sitting area. Skip the inside tables.

Boulevard Montparnasse

An eclectic assortment of historic cafés gather along the boulevard Montparnasse, just a few blocks from Luxembourg Gardens at the intersection with boulevard Raspail (Mo: Vavin).

La Coupole, built in the 1920s, was decorated by aspiring artists (Leger, Brancusi, and Chagall, among others) in return for free meals. This cavernous place feels like a classy train station, with grand chandeliers, red velvet booths, brass decor, and waiters by the dozen. Bring your friends and make noise. The food is fine but not the reason you came. In fact, I prefer coffee and drinks rather than dinner here (102 boulevard Montparnasse, tel. 01 43 26 70 50).

Le Dome sits right at the intersection of Raspail and Montparnasse and forms a dramatic contrast to the party atmosphere of La Coupole. Smaller, more elegant, and refined in every way, this place makes me want to dress up and look better than I do. The sumptuous decor is pure 1920s, and the best tables are just inside, facing the sidewalk. While La Coupole is not known for its cuisine, Le Dome is. Come here for a splurge dinner (figure 250F per person, tel. 01 43 35 25 81).

Le Select was popular with the more rebellious types—Leon Trotsky, Jean Cocteau, and Pablo Picasso loved it. It feels more conformist today, with good salads from 50F to 60F, outdoor seating, and pleasant tables just inside the door (99 boulevard Montparnasse, across from La Coupole).

Champs-Élysées

Le Fouquet's, which opened in 1899, served as James Joyce's dining room. Today it's known as the film stars' place to go. Those golden plaques at the entry are from winners of France's version of our Oscar awards, the Cesars. While the intimidating interior is impressive, the outdoor setting is Champs-Élysées great—and you can buy the most expensive shot of espresso I found in Paris (29F). Fouquet's was recently saved from foreign purchase and eventual destruction when the government declared it a historic monument (99 Avenue du Champs-Élysées, Mo: George V).

Near the Louvre
Within a short walk of the Louvre, you'll find two melt-in-your-chair cafés (Mo: Palais Royal/Musée du Louvre). The staunchly Parisian **Café Le Nemours** is tucked into the corner of Palais Royal adjacent to Comedie Francaise. Brass-and-art-deco elegant, with outdoor tables under an arcade two minutes from the pyramid, this place makes a great post-Louvre retreat (2 place Colette). **Café de l'Époque**, inside a classy pedestrian mini-mall, is softly lit and elegantly appointed—a tranquil escape from the city's street noise (2 rue du Bouloi).

On Place de la Concorde
Hotel de Crillon's four-star elegance can be yours for an afternoon. Considered the most exclusive hotel in Paris (and the last of the great hotels to be French-owned), this is the place to experience château life. Wear the best clothes you packed, arrive after 15:00, let the bellhop spin the door, and settle into the royal blue chairs in the *salon du thé* (45F for a pot of tea or double café au lait, 155F for high tea). You'll be serenaded by a harpist and surrounded by famous people you won't recognize.

PARIS WITH
CHILDREN

Paris is surprisingly kid friendly. With so many parks, squares, and pedestrians and such a variety of kid-friendly sights, your children may want to return to Paris before you do. Consider these tips:

- Hotel selection is critical. Stay in a kid-friendly area near a park. The rue Cler neighborhood is ideal. If you're staying a week or more, rent an apartment (see "For Longer Stays," page 245).
- Eat dinner early (19:30 at restaurants, earlier at cafés). Skip famous places. Try relaxed cafés (or fast-food restaurants) where kids can move around without bothering others. Picnics work well.
- Follow this book's crowd-beating tips to a tee. Kids (and parents) don't like to stand in long lines.
- Don't overdo it. Tackle one key sight each day (Louvre, Orsay, Versailles) and mix with a healthy dose of fun activities (ideas listed below).
- Get your kids in the spirit (rent or read Madeleine stories, *The Hunchback of Notre-Dame*, or *The Man in the Iron Mask*).
- The best, cheapest toy selection is in the large department stores, such as Bon Marché (see Shopping chapter, page 262).
- French marionette shows, called *guignols*, are fun for the entire family. They take place in several locations in Paris, mostly in big parks. See *Pariscope* or *L'Officiel des Spectacles* under "Marionettes" for times and places. The plots, while in French, are easy to follow. Arrive 20 minutes early for good seats.

TOP TEN KIDS' SPOTS IN PARIS

1. Luxembourg Gardens: This is my favorite place to mix kid business with pleasure. This perfectly Parisian park has it all—from an extensive big-toys play area with imaginative slides, swings, and jungle gyms (kids-16F, adults-10F, good for all day, open daily, many parents watch from chairs outside the play area), to pedal go-karts, a fun merry-go-round, toy sailboats in the main pond (18F/hr, daily in summer, otherwise Wed, Sat–Sun), and big open areas perfect for kicking a ball. Near the main building is a toddler wading pool and sandpit (free). Adults and kids enjoy the terrific puppet shows (*guignols*) held in the afternoons (Mo: St. Sulpice, Odéon, or Notre-Dame-des-Champs; tel. 01 43 26 46 47).

2. Jardin des Plantes: These pleasant, colorful gardens are short on grass but have a zoo, a maze made of plants, and several kid-friendly natural-science museums (closed Tue). Kids love the dinosaur exhibit at the Galerie d'Anatomie Comparée et de Paléontologie. There are no English explanations, but there is no real need (kids-20F, adults-30F, Wed–Mon 10:00–17:00, includes Musée de Mineralogie). From the main entrance on place Valhubert, the museums line the left side of the park (Mo: Gare d'Austerlitz or Jussieu).

3. Eiffel Tower, Trocadero, and Champ de Mars Park: All ages enjoy the view from Trocadero across the river to the Eiffel Tower, especially after dark (Mo: Trocadero). In-line skaters and skateboarders make Trocadero a teenage scene, particularly in afternoons and evenings. A ride up the tower is a hit day or night. See the video on the first floor. The vast Champ de Mars park stretches out from the tower's base; near the southwestern corner of the park (about halfway between the tower and the military school) are grassy play areas (bring your own ball, play after dusk), big toys, pony rides, and picnic-perfect benches (Mo: École Militaire). For more information on the tower, see page 34.

4. Notre-Dame, Towers, and Crypt: Paris' famous Gothic cathedral doesn't have to be dry and dull. Replay Quasimodo's stunt and climb the tower. Kids love being on such a lofty perch with an in-your-face look at a gargoyle. The crypt on the square in front of Notre-Dame is quick and interesting. Kids can push buttons to highlight remains of Roman Paris and leave with a better understanding of how different civilizations build on top of each other. The small but beautiful park along the river and behind Notre-Dame has sandboxes, picnic benches, and space to run (Mo: Cité). ⭐ See Historic Paris Walk, page 43.

5. Seine River Boat Rides: A variety of boats offer one-hour Seine cruises on huge glass-domed boats, with departures until 23:00. Or hop on a Bâteau-Bus, a river bus connecting six stops along the river: Eiffel Tower, Orsay/place de la Concorde, Louvre, Notre-Dame, Hôtel de Ville, and St. Germain-des-Près. Use the Bâteau-Bus by day, and take a twilight cruise on a Bateau-Mouche. See "Boat Tours," page 28.

6. Arc de Triomphe and Champs-Élysées: Watch the crazy traffic rush around the Arc de Triomphe for endless entertainment, then stroll the Champs-Élysées with its car dealerships (particularly Renault's, with its antique car museum), Virgin Megastore, Disney Store, and the river of humanity that flows along its broad sidewalks. Take your teenager to see a movie on the Champs-Élysées ("v.o." next to the show time means original-version language). ★ See Champs-Élysées Walk, page 61.

7. Versailles: This huge complex of palaces, gardens, fountains, and forest is a great Parisian family getaway. My kids even enjoy the 30-minute train ride to Versailles. Rent a bike for the gardens or a rowboat for the canal. Come on Sunday, when the fountains are flowing. The Hameau has barnyard animals nearby. Visit the palace at the end of the day and you can do cartwheels in an empty Hall of Mirrors. ★ See Versailles Tour, page 191.

8. Pompidou Center: The Pompidou Center appeals more to teens with its crazy outdoor entertainers, throngs of young people, happening cafés, and fun fountains next door. Inside, the temporary exhibits on the main floor are visually impressive. The *Star Wars* escalator to the top is fun for all ages, but you need to have a museum pass or a ticket for the museum (Modern Art) to escalate (Mo: Rambuteau).

9. The Cité des Sciences in the Parc de la Vilette: This is like a city of its own, filled with hands-on science museums (closed Mon). It's brilliantly organized with something for all ages and provides helpful information in English for most exhibits. Walk up from the Métro Porte de la Vilette into the huge metal building and stop at the information desk to understand your options. Pick up the essential brochure ("The Keys to the Cité") explaining the exhibits, which include separate discovery/play areas for kids ages 3 to 5 and 5 to 11, and a Technocité for those ages 12 and up (each 25F); the most important Explora museum (55F, helpful English audioguide available for 25F); an aquarium (35F); the Geode (a giant spherical movie screen, 45F); and a planetarium (35F). Whew, you could go broke if you don't focus— the Explora museum and the Geode are the most fam-ous. Most of these areas have alloted times when you can enter, generally limited to 90 minutes per area (Tue–Sat 10:00–18:00, Sun until 19:00, closed Mon, tel. 01 40 05 12 12).

10. La Butte Chaumont Park: Rather than manicured gardens, this is a big park where your kids can explore hills, lakes, trails, and a waterfall. Baron Haussmann converted this one-time city dump into a remarkable mix of cafés and outdoor fun (Mo: Buttes-Chaumont).

SHOPPING
IN PARIS

Consider three ways to shop in Paris:

1) If you just need souvenirs, hit a souvenir shop.
2) For more elaborate purchasing plans, the city's large department stores offer relatively painless one-stop shopping in elegant surroundings.
3) Neighborhood boutiques offer the greatest reward at the highest risk. While clerks and prices can be intimidating, the selection is generally more original and the experience totally Parisian.

Tips

Before you enter a Parisian store, remember:

- The customer is not always right. In fact, figure the clerk is doing you a favor by waiting on you.
- Except for department stores, it's not normal for the customer to handle clothing. Ask first if you can look at an item.
- Forget returns (and don't count on exchanges).
- Saturdays are busiest.
- Observe French shoppers. Then imitate.

Souvenir Shops

Avoid souvenir carts in front of famous monuments. Prices and selection are better in shops. Look under the arcades of rue de Rivoli (across from Tuileries Gardens), around the Pompidou Center, on the streets of Montmartre, and in department stores (see below). The riverfront stalls near Notre-Dame sell a variety of used books, magazines, and tourist paraphernalia in the most romantic setting.

Department Stores *(Les Grandes Surfaces)*

Like cafés, department stores were invented here (surprisingly, not in America). While the stores seem overwhelming at first, they

Key Phrases

Just looking. - *Je regards.* (zhuh ruh-gar)

How much is it? - *Combien?* (kohm-bee-en)

Too big/small/expensive. - *Trop grand/petit/cher.* (troh grahn/puh-tee/sher)

May I try it on? - *Je peut l'essayer?* (zhuh puh luh-say-yay)

Can I see more? - *Puis-je en voir d'autres?* (pweezh en vwahr doh-truh)

I'll think about it. - *Je vais y penser.* (zhuh vay ee pahn-say)

I'd like this. - *Je voudrais ça.* (zhuh voo-dray sah)

generally work like ours, and those listed here are accustomed to foreign shoppers. These stores are not only beautiful monuments to more elegant times, but also a great lesson on how others live. Most have spectacular perfume sections, a good selection of souvenirs and toys at fair prices, great view terraces, reasonably priced restaurants, and helpful information desks (near the front door). Stores are generally open Monday through Saturday from 10:00 to 19:00. Choose from these four great Parisian department stores:

Galeries Lafayette and Printemps
You'll find both Galeries Lafayette and Printemps (pran-tom) department stores in many Parisian neighborhoods. The most convenient and busiest are side by side behind the old Opéra (Mo: Chaussee d'Antin, Havre-Caumartin, or Opéra). Both Galeries Lafayette and Printemps sprawl over three buildings and consume entire city blocks. The selection is huge. Don't miss the belle epoque dome at Galeries Lafayette. Continue your shopping by walking from this area to the place Vendôme (see "Boutiques," below).

Samaritaine
Samaritaine (sah-mah-ree-ten) is Paris' most central department store (on the Seine at Pont Neuf, Mo: Pont Neuf, see Historic Paris Walk, page tk). Old World elegant yet not high priced, this is a handy place to take care of business and enjoy one of the best views of Paris. Review the history of the store in dioramas at the top of the elevator. Then climb to the panorama terrace on the 11th floor.

Bon Marché
Combine this fine department store with a great neighborhood shopping experience (Mo: Sevres-Babylone). Bon Marché, quieter and more relaxed than the others, is surrounded by pleasant

shopping streets (see "Boutiques," below). Graze through the gourmet grocery store in the basement.

Boutiques

I enjoy window shopping on city streets, pausing at cafés, and observing the rhythm of neighborhood life. While the shops are more intimate, sales clerks can be in-your-face intimidating. Here are three very different areas to try:

Sevres-Babylone to St. Sulpice

Start at the elegant Bon Marché department store, described above (Mo: Sevres-Babylone), then shop the smart boutiques that line the streets between Bon Marché and St. Sulpice Church. The rue de Sevres (turns into rue du Four) is the spine of this upscale area. Explore rues du Dragon, Cherche Midi, Bonaparte, and Vieux Colombier. End your shopping stroll in the Luxembourg Gardens or at a grand café on the boulevard St. Germain (see "Les Grands Cafés de Paris," on page 255).

Le Marais

For more eclectic, avant-garde stores, peruse the shops between the Pompidou Center and place des Vosges. Stick to the east-west axis formed by rue des Francs Bourgeois, rue des Rosiers, and rue Ste. Croix de la Bretonniere. (These streets are part of the Marais Walk on page 68.) On Sunday afternoons this trendy area pulses with shoppers and café crowds.

Place Vendôme

The ritzy streets connecting the Galeries Lafayette with place de la Concorde are a miracle mile of jewelry stores, four-star hotels, perfumeries, and exclusive clothing boutiques.

From place de l'Opéra (Mo: Opéra), walk down rue de la Paix to place Vendôme. The *très* elegant place Vendôme is home to the Ritz Hôtel (Hemingway liberated the bar in World War II) and equally exclusive boutiques. The square was created by Louis XIV in the 17th century as a setting for a statue of himself. One hundred and fifty years later, Louis was replaced by a statue of Napoleon.

Continue on rue Castiglione, window-shopping the arcades, to rue de Rivoli. Turn right on Rivoli, passing Paris' largest English bookstore, W. H. Smith, at #248, to reach place de la Concorde.

PARIS AT
NIGHT

Paris is brilliant after dark. Save energy from your day's sight-seeing and get out at night. Whether it's a concert at Sainte-Chapelle, a boat ride on the Seine, an elevator up the Arc de Triomphe, or a late-night café, experience the City of Light lit. *Pariscope* magazine (3F at any newsstand, in French) offers a complete weekly listing of music, cincma, theater, opera, and other special events—I decipher this useful periodical for you below. The *Free Voice* newspaper, in English, has a monthly review of Paris entertainment (available at any English-language bookstore, French-American establishments, or the American Church).

A Tour of *Pariscope*

The weekly *Pariscope* (3F) or *L'Officiel des Spectacles* (2F) are both cheap and essential if you want to know what's happening. Pick one up and page through it. For a head start, *Pariscope* has a Web site: www.pariscope.fr (in French).

Each begins with culture news. Skip the bulky "Théatres" and "Dîners/Spectacles" sections and anything listed as "des environs" (outside of Paris). "Musique" or "Concerts Classiques" follow, listing each day's events (program, location, time, and price). Venues with phone numbers and addresses are listed in an "Adresses des Salles de Concerts" sidebar. Touristic venues (such as Sainte-Chapelle and Église de la Madeleine) are often featured in display ads. "Opéras, Musique Traditionelle, Ballet/ Danse," and "Jazz/Rock" listings follow.

Half of these magazines are devoted to cinema—a Parisian forte. After the "Films Nouveaux" section trumpets new releases, the "Films en Exclusivite" pages list all the films playing in town. While a code marks films as "Historique, Karate, Erotisme," and so on, the key mark for tourists is "v.o.," which means *version originale* (American films have their English soundtracks). Films are listed alphabetically, with theaters and their *arrondissements* at the end of each entry. Then films are listed by neighborhood ("Salles Paris") and by genre. First-runs are shown at cinemas on the Champs-Elysées and on place de l'Odéon; art films and older films are best found in the Latin Quarter. To find a showing near your hotel, simply match the *arrondissement*. (But don't hesitate to hop on the Métro for the film you want.) "Salles Périphérie" is out in the suburbs.

Pariscope has a small English "Time Out" section listing the week's events. The "Musées" sections ("Monuments," "Jardins," "Autres Curiosites," "Promenades," "Activites Sportives," "Piscines") give the latest hours of the sights, gardens, curiosities, boat tours, sports, swimming pools, and so on. "Clubs de Loisirs" are various athletic and social clubs. "Pour les Jeunes" is for young people (kids' films, animations/cartoons, marionettes, circuses, and amusement parks such as Asterix and Disney). Conferences are mostly lectures. For cancan mischief, look under "Paris la Nuit," "Cabarets," or the busty "Spectacles Erotiques."

Finally, you'll find a TV listing. Paris has four countrywide stations: TF1, France 2, France 3, and the new Arte station (a German/French cultural channel). M6 is filled with American series. Canal Plus (channel 4) is a cable channel that airs an American news show at seven in the morning and an American sports event on Sunday evening.

Music

Jazz Clubs: With a lively mix of American, French, and international musicians, Paris has been an internationally acclaimed jazz capital since World War II. You'll pay from 40F to 160F to enter a jazz club (1 drink may be included; if not, expect to pay 30–60F per drink; beer is cheapest). See *Pariscope* magazine under "Musique" for listings, or better, the American Church's *Free Voice* paper for a good monthly review (in English), or drop by the clubs to check out their calendars posted on the front door. Music starts after 22:00 in most clubs. Some offer dinner concerts from about 20:30 on. Here are a few good bets:

Caveau de la Huchette, a characteristic old jazz club for visitors, fills an ancient Latin Quarter cellar with live jazz and frenzied dancing every night (65F weekday, 80F weekend admission, 30F drinks, Tue–Sun 21:30–02:30 or later, closed Mon, 5 rue de la Huchette, recorded info tel. 01 43 26 65 05).

For a hotbed of late-night activity and jazz, go to the two-block-long rue des Lombards, at boulevard Sebastopol, midway between the river and Pompidou Center (Mo: Chatelet).

Au Duc des Lombards, right at the corner, is one of the most popular and respected jazz clubs in Paris with concerts generally at 21:30 (42 rue des Lombards, tel. 01 42 33 22 88, www.jazzvalley .com/duc). **Le Sunset**, a block west, offers more traditional jazz— Dixieland, big band—and fewer crowds with concerts generally at 21:00 and 02:00 (60 rue des Lombards, tel. 01 40 26 46 60).

At the more down-to-earth and mellow **Le Cave du Franc Pinot**, you can enjoy a glass of Chardonnay at the main-floor wine bar, then drop downstairs for a cool jazz scene (good dinner values as well, located on Île St. Louis where Pont Marie meets the island, 1 quai de Bourbon, Mo: Pont Marie, tel. 01 46 33 60 64).

The **American Church** regularly plays host to fine jazz musicians for the best price in Paris (free, 65 quai d'Orsay, Mo: Invalides, RER-C: Pont de l'Alma, tel. 01 40 62 05 00).

Classical Concerts: For classical music on any night, consult *Pariscope* magazine; the "Musique" section under "Concerts Classique" lists concerts (free and fee). Look for posters at the churches. Churches that regularly host concerts include St. Sulpice, St. Germain-des-Près, Basilique de Madeleine, St. Eustache, and Sainte-Chapelle. It's worth the 100F to 150F entry for the pleasure of hearing Mozart surrounded by the stained glass of the tiny Sainte-Chapelle. Even the Galeries Lafayette department store offers concerts. Many are free (*entrée libre*), such as the Sunday atelier concert sponsored by the American Church (18:00, 65 quai d'Orsay, Mo: Invalides, RER: Pont de l'Alma, tel. 01 40 62 05 00).

Opera: Paris is home to two well-respected operas. The Opéra Garnier, Paris' first opera house, hosts opera and ballet performances. Come here for less expensive tickets and grand belle epoque decor (Mo: Opéra, tel. 01 44 73 13 99). The Opéra de la Bastille is the massive modern opera house that dominates place de la Bastille. Come here for state-of-the-art special effects and modern interpretations of classic ballets and operas (Mo: Bastille, tel. 01 43 43 96 96). For tickets, call 01 44 73 13 00, go to the opera ticket offices (open 11:00–18:00), or, best, reserve on the Web at www.ticketavenue.com (for both operas).

Bus Tours

Paris Illumination Tours, run by Paris Vision, connects all the great illuminated sights of Paris with a 100-minute bus tour in 12 languages. Double-decker buses have huge windows, but Moulin Rouge customers get the most desirable front seats. You'll stampede on with a United Nations of tourists, get a hand-held audioguide, and listen to a tape-recorded spiel (interesting

but occasionally hard to hear). Uninspired as it is, this provides a
fine first-night overview of the city at its floodlit and scenic best.
Left-side seats are marginally better. Visibility is fine in the rain.
You're entirely on the bus except for one five-minute cigarette
break at the Eiffel Tower viewpoint (150F-adult, 75F-ages 4–11,
free-under 3, departures at 20:30 nightly all year, also 22:00
April–Oct only, departs from Paris Vision office at 214 rue de
Rivoli, across the street from Mo: Tuileries). These trips are sold
through your hotel (brochures in lobby) or direct at the address
listed above. Look also for the same tour by minivan—pick-up
is at your hotel, the driver is a qualified guide, and there's a maximum of seven clients (295F per person, tel. for bus and minivans
01 42 60 30 01, fax 01 42 86 95 36, www.parisvision.com).

Seine River Cruises

The Bateaux-Mouches offer one-hour cruises on huge glass-
domed boats with departures from the pont de l'Alma, the centrally
located pont Neuf, and right in front of the Eiffel Tower (every
30 min 10:00–23:00; see "Organized Tours of Paris," on page 28).

Walks

Go for a walk to best appreciate the City of Light. Break for
ice cream, pause at a café, and enjoy the sidewalk entertainers as
you join the post-dinner Parisian parade. Consider these walks:
Champs-Élysées and the Arc de Triomphe—★ See Champs-
Élysées Walk, page 61. This is brilliant after dark. Start at the
Arc de Triomphe then stroll down the lively Champs-Élysées.
A right turn on avenue George V leads to the Bâteaux-Mouches
river cruises. A movie on the Champs-Élysées is a fun experience
(weekly listings in *Pariscope* under "Cinema").
Trocadero and Eiffel Tower—These monuments glimmer at
night. Take the Métro to the Trocadero stop and join the party
on place de la Trocadero for a magnificent view of the glowing
Eiffel Tower. It's a festival of gawkers, drummers, street acrobats,
and entertainers. Pass the fountains and cross the river to the base
of the tower, worth the effort even if you don't go up. See "Eiffel
Tower," page 34.

From the Eiffel Tower, you can stroll through the Parc du
Champ de Mars past Frisbees, soccer balls, and romantic couples
and take the Métro home (École Militaire stop, across avenue de
la Motte Piquet from the far southeast corner of the park). Or, if
you've had enough, there's a handy RER stop (Champ de Mars-
Tour Eiffel) two blocks west (downriver) of the Eiffel Tower.

TRANSPORTATION
CONNECTIONS

paris

This chapter covers Paris' two airports, six train stations, and main bus station.

CHARLES DE GAULLE AIRPORT

Charles de Gaulle Airport is Paris' primary airport. It has three main terminals: T-1, T-2, and T-9. Air France uses T-2; charters dominate T-9. Terminals are connected every few minutes by a free *navette* (bus), and the RER (Paris subway) stops at T-1 and T-2 terminals. There is no bag storage at the airport.

Those flying to or from the United States will probably use T-1. Here you'll find an American Express cash machine, an automatic bill changer (at baggage claim 30), and an exchange window (at baggage claim 18). A bank (with lousy rates) and an ATM are near gate 32. At the Meeting Point, you'll find the tourist office, which has free maps and information (daily 7:00–22:00), and Relais H, which sells *télécartes* (phone cards). Car-rental offices are on the arrival level from gates 10 to 22; the SNCF (train) office is at gate 22. For flight information, call 01 48 62 22 80.

Transportation between Charles de Gaulle Airport and Paris: There are plenty of choices. Three efficient public-transportation routes, taxis, and airport shuttle vans link the airport's T-1 and T-2 terminals with central Paris. At T-1 (where most land), the free *navette* runs between gate 36, the lower level (take elevator down to floor 2, walk outside, cross the street, and catch the green bus), and the **RER Roissy Rail** station, where a train zips you into Paris' subway system in 30 minutes (51F, stops at Gare du Nord, Chatelet, St. Michel, and Luxembourg Gardens). The **Roissy Bus** runs every 15 minutes between gate 30 and the old Opéra Garnier (stop is on rue Scribe, in front of American Express), costs 48F (use the automatic ticket machine), and takes 40 minutes, but can be jammed. The **Air France Bus** leaves every 15 minutes from gate 34 and serves the Arc de Triomphe and Porte Maillot in about 40 minutes for 60F, and the Montparnasse Tower in 60 minutes for 75F (from any of these stops you can reach your hotel by taxi). For most people, the RER Roissy Rail works best. A **taxi** ride with luggage costs about 230F; a taxi stand is at gate 16. The **Disneyland Express bus** departs from gate 32. (The RER Roissy Rail, Roissy Bus, and Air France bus described above serve the T-2 terminal as efficiently and economically as T-1.)

For a stress-free trip between either of Paris' airports and downtown, consider an airport shuttle minivan, ideal for single travelers or families of four or more. Reserve from home and they'll meet you at the airport. Consider **Airport Shuttle** (allow 150F for 1 person, 89F per person for 2, cheaper for larger groups and kids, plan on a 30-min wait if you ask them to pick you up at the airport, tel. 01 45 38 55 72, fax 01 43 21 35 67, www.paris-anglo.com/clients/ashuttle.html, e-mail: ashuttle @club-internet.fr) or **Paris Airport Services** (tel. 01 49 62 78 78, fax 01 49 62 78 79, www.magic.fr/pas, e-mail: pas@magic.fr).

Sleeping at or near Charles de Gaulle Airport: Those with early flights can sleep in T-1 at **Cocoon** (60 cabins, Sb-250F, Db-300F, CC:VM, tel. 01 48 62 06 16, fax 01 48 62 56 97). Take the elevator down to "boutique level" or walk down from the departure level. You get 16 hours of silence buried under the check-in level with TV and toilet. **Hôtel Ibis****, at the Roissy Rail station, offers more normal accommodations (Db-420F, CC:VMA, free shuttle bus to either terminal takes 2 min, tel. 01 49 19 19 19, fax 01 49 19 19 21), as does the similarly priced **Novotel***** (CC:VMA, tel. 01 49 19 27 27, fax 01 49 19 27 99).

ORLY AIRPORT

This airport feels small. Orly has two terminals: Sud and Ouest. International flights arrive at Sud as I assume you will. After exiting Terminal Sud's baggage claim (near gate H), you'll be greeted by signs directing you to city transportation, car rental, and so on. Turn left to enter the main terminal area, and you'll find exchange offices with bad rates, an ATM machine, the ADP (a quasi-tourist office that offers free city maps and basic sightseeing information, open until 23:00), and an SNCF French rail desk (closes at 18:00, sells train tickets and even Eurailpasses, next to the ADP). Downstairs is a sandwich bar, WCs, a bank (same bad rates), a newsstand (buy *télécarte* phone card), and a post office (great rates for cash or American Express traveler's checks). Car-rental offices are located in the parking lot in front of the terminal. For flight info on any airline serving Orly, call 01 49 75 15 15.

Transportation between Paris and Orly Airport: There are three efficient public-transportation routes, taxis, and a couple of airport shuttle services linking Orly and central Paris. The **Air France bus** (outside gate G) runs to Paris' Invalides Métro stop (45F, 5/hrly, 30 min) and is best for those staying in or near the rue Cler neighborhood (from the Invalides terminal, take the Métro 2 stops to École Militaire to reach recommended hotels). The **Jetbus #285** (outside gate F, 28F, 4/hrly) is the quickest way to the Paris subway and the best way to the recommended hotels in the Marais and Contrescarpe neighborhoods (take Jetbus to Villejuif Métro stop, buy a carnet of 10 Métro tickets, then take the Métro to the Sully Morland stop for the Marais area, or the Cardinal Lemoine stop for the Contrescarpe area). The **Orlybus** (outside gate H, 35F, 4/hrly) takes you to the Denfert-Rochereau RER-B line and the Métro, offering subway access to central Paris. The **Orlyval trains** are overpriced (57F). **Taxis** are to the far right as you leave the terminal, at gate M. Allow 170F for a taxi into central Paris.

Airport shuttle minivans are ideal for single travelers or families of four or more (see under "Charles de Gaulle Airport," above; from Orly, figure about 120F for 1 person, 80F per person for 2, less for larger groups and kids).

Sleeping near Orly Airport: The only reasonable airport hotel is **Hôtel Ibis**** (Db-420F, CC:VMA, tel. 01 46 87 33 50, fax 01 46 87 29 92). The **Hilton***** offers more comfort for more money (Db-680F, tel 01 45 12 45 12, fax 01 45 12 45 00). Both have free shuttle service to the terminal.

PARIS' TRAIN STATIONS

Paris is Europe's rail hub, with six major train stations, each serving different regions: Gare de l'Est (east-bound trains), Gare du Nord (northern France and Europe), Gare St. Lazare (northwestern France), Gare d'Austerlitz (southwest France and Europe), Gare de Lyon (southeastern France and Italy), and Gare Montparnasse (northwestern France and TGV service to France's southwest). Any train station can give you schedule information, make reservations, and sell tickets for any destination. Buying tickets is handier from an SNCF neighborhood office (e.g., Louvre, Invalides, Orsay, Versailles, airports) or at your neighborhood travel agency—worth their small fee (SNCF signs in their window indicate they sell train tickets). For schedule information call 08 36 35 35 35 (3F/min, English sometimes available).

All six train stations are connected by Métro, bus, and taxi. All have banks or change offices, information desks, telephones, cafés, lockers (*consigne automatique*), newsstands, and clever pickpockets. Each station offers two types of rail service: long distance

Key Train Phrases

accueil (ah-coy) = information assistance
billets (bee-yay) = tickets
départs (day-par) = departures
arrivées (ah-ree-vay) = arrivals
aller simple (ah-lay sam-pluh) = one way
aller-retour (ah-lay ruh-toor) = round-trip
voyageurs munis de billets = travelers with tickets
Grandes Lignes (grahnd leen) = major domestic and
    international lines
RER (air-ay-air) = suburban lines
Banlieue (bahn-lee-yuh) = suburban lines
quai (kay) = platform
voie (vwah) = track
retard (ruh-tar) = delay
salle d'attente (sahl dah-tahnt) = waiting room
consigne automatique (kohn-seen auto-mah-teek) =
    storage lockers
première classe (pruhm-yair klahs) = first class
deuxième classe (duhz-yehm klahs) = second class

to other cities, called Grandes Lignes (major lines); and suburban service to outlying areas, called *Banlieue* or RER. Both *Banlieue* and RER serve outlying areas and the airports; the only difference is that *Banlieue* lines are operated by SNCF (France's train system) and RER lines are operated by RATP (Paris' Métro and bus system). Paris train stations can be intimidating, but if you slow down, take a deep breath, and ask for help, you'll find them helpful and efficient. Bring a pad of paper for clear communication at ticket/info windows.

Station Overview

Here's an overview of Paris' major train stations. Métro, RER, buses (BUS), and taxis are well signed at every station. When arriving by Métro, follow signs for Grandes Lignes-SNCF to find the main tracks and look for helpful *accueil* (information) booths.

Gare du Nord: This station serves cities in northern France and international destinations to the north of Paris (including London, Amsterdam, and Copenhagen). This is one of Paris' largest stations, offering the most services and confusion. Train information booths are opposite tracks 8 and 18, and blue-blazered information staff circulate around the station looking to help you. All rail staff are required to speak English at Gare du Nord. Information booths

TRAIN ROUTES

for Thalys trains are opposite track 8. All non-Eurostar ticket sales are opposite tracks 3 through 8. Passengers departing on the Eurostar (London via Chunnel) must check in on the second level, opposite track 6. (Note: Britain's time zone is 1 hour earlier than the Continent's; times listed on Eurostar tickets are local times.) Banlieue trains depart from tracks 19 through 21 and 30 through 36. A peaceful waiting area is provided on the upper level overlooking the tracks. Storage lockers, baggage check, and rental cars are at the far end, just opposite track 3 and down the steps.

Key destinations served by Gare du Nord Grandes Lignes: Brussels (10/day, 1.5 hrs), **Amsterdam** (10/day, 4 hrs), **Copenhagen** (3/day, 16 hrs), **Koblenz** (3/day, 7 hrs), **London** via Eurostar Chunnel (12/day, 3 hrs, tel. 08 36 35 35 39, www.raileurope.com, www.eurostar.co.uk). By Banlieue/RER lines: **Chantilly-Gouvieux** (hrly, fewer on weekends, 35 min), **Charles de Gaulle airport** (2/hrly, from 5:30–23:00, 30 min).

Gare de l'Est: This station serves eastern France and European points to the east of Paris. Much smaller than the Gare du Nord, this single-floor station (with underground Métro) is a snap. Train information booths are at tracks 1 and 26; ticket windows and the main exit to buses and Paris are opposite track 8; luggage storage is opposite track 12.

   Key destinations served by Gare de l'Est: Colmar (6/day, 5.5 hrs, transfer in Strasbourg or Mulhouse), **Strasbourg** (10/day, 4.5 hrs), **Reims** (8/day, 2 hrs), **Verdun** (5/day, 3 hrs), **Munich** (4/day, 8.5 hrs), **Vienna** (3/day, 13 hrs), **Zurich** (10/day, 7 hrs), **Prague** (2/day, 15 hrs).

Gare Montparnasse: This big and modern station covers three floors, serves Lower Normandy and Brittany, and offers TGV service to the Loire Valley and southwestern France. At street level you'll find a bank and Banlieue trains (serving Chartres); ticket windows are just to the right of the turnstiles in the center of this floor. (You can also reach the Banlieue trains from the second level). Lockers (*consigne automatique*) are on the mezzanine level between levels 1 and 2. Most services are provided on the second level, where the Grandes Lignes arrive and depart (ticket windows are to your left as you exit the escalators). Banlieue trains depart from tracks 10 through 19. The main rail information office is opposite track 15; another booth is near track 10.

   Key destinations served by Gare Montparnasse: Chartres (10/day, 1 hr), **Mont St. Michel** (2/day, 4.5 hrs, via Rennes), **Dinan** (7/day, 3 hrs, via Rennes and Dol), **Bordeaux** (14/day, 3.5 hrs), **Sarlat** (5/day, 6 hrs, transfer in Bordeaux), **Toulouse** (7/day, 5 hrs, possible transfer in Bordeaux), **Albi** (6.5 hrs, via Toulouse), **Carcassonne** (6.5 hrs, via Toulouse), **Tours** (14/day, 1 hr).

Gare de Lyon: This huge and confusing station offers TGV and regular service to southeastern France, Italy, and other international destinations. Banlieue trains serve Melun (near Vaux-le-Vicomte) and Fontainebleau. All trains arrive and depart from one level but are divided into two areas (tracks A-N and 5-23). They are connected by the long platform along tracks A and 5 and by the hallway adjacent to track A and opposite track 9. This hallway has all the services, ticket windows, banks, and shops. Banlieue ticket windows are just inside the hall adjacent to track A. Grandes Lignes (main lines) and Banlieue (suburban) lines share the same tracks. A Paris tourist information office and the main train information office are at track L. From the RER or Métro, follow signs for Grandes Lignes Arivées and take the escalator up to reach the platforms. Train information booths (*accueil*) are opposite tracks G and 13.

Key destinations served by Gare de Lyon: **Melun** (hrly/30 min), **Fontainebleau** (nearly hrly, 45 min), **Beaune** (8/day, 2.5 hrs), **Dijon** (13/day, 1.5 hrs), **Chamonix** (3/day, 9 hrs, transfer in Lyon and St. Gervais, 1 direct night train), **Annecy** (8/day, 4–7 hrs), **Lyon** (16/day, 2.5 hrs), **Avignon** (10/day, 4 hrs), **Arles** (10/day, 5 hrs), **Nice** (8/day, 7 hrs), **Venice** (5/day, 11 hrs), **Rome** (3/day, 15 hrs), **Bern** (5/day, 5 hrs).

Gare St. Lazare: This relatively small station serves Upper Normandy, including Rouen and Giverny. All trains arrive and depart one floor above street level. Follow signs to Grandes Lignes from the Métro to reach the tracks. You'll pass a mini-mall. Ticket windows and a Thomas Cook exchange are in the first hall on the second floor. The tracks are through the small hallways (lined with storage lockers). Grandes Lignes (main lines) depart from tracks 17 through 27; Banlieue suburban trains depart from 1 through 16. The train information office (*accueil*) is opposite track 15; the reservation office is opposite track 16. Baggage consignment and the post office are along track 27, and WCs are opposite track 19.

Key destinations served by Gare St. Lazare: Giverny (train to Vernon, 5/day, 45 min; then bus or taxi 10 min to Giverny), **Rouen** (15/day, 75 min), **Honfleur** (6/day, 3 hrs, via Lisieux, then bus), **Bayeux** (9/day, 2.5 hrs), **Caen** (12/day, 2 hrs).

Gare d'Austerlitz: This small station provides non-TGV service to the Loire Valley, southwestern France, and Spain. All tracks are at street level. The information booth is opposite track 17, and a Thomas Cook exchange and all ticket sales are in the hall opposite track 10. Baggage consignment and car rental are near Porte 27 (along the side, opposite track 21).

Key destinations served by Gare d'Austerlitz: Amboise (8/day, 2.5 hrs), **Cahors** (5/day, 7 hrs), **Barcelona** (3/day, 13 hrs), **Madrid** (5/day, 16 hrs), **Lisbon** (1/day, 24 hrs).

BUSES
Buses provide cheaper, if less comfortable and less flexible, transportation to major European cities. The main bus station is Gare Routière du Paris-Gallieni (avenue du General de Gaulle, in suburb of Bagnolet, Mo: Gallieni, tel. 01 49 72 51 51). Eurolines buses depart from here.

APPENDIX

French (and Parisian) History

Celts and Romans (52 B.C.–A.D. 500)

Julius Caesar conquered the Parisii, turning Paris from a tribal fishing village into a European city. The mix of Latin (southern) and Celtic (northern) cultures, with Paris right in the middle, defined the French character.

Paris Sites: Cluny Museum (Roman baths), Louvre (Roman antiquities), and Archeological Crypt near Notre-Dame.

Dark Ages (500–1000)

Roman Paris fell to German pirates ("Franks" = France) and later to the Vikings ("Norsemen" = Normans). During this turbulent time, Paris was just another island state ("Île de France") in the midst of many warring kingdoms. The lone bright spot was the reign of Charlemagne (A.D. 800), who briefly united the Franks, giving a glimpse of the modern nation-state of France.

Paris Sites: Cluny Museum artifacts and statue of Charlemagne near Notre-Dame.

Border Wars with England (1066–1500)

In 1066 the Norman king William ("the Conqueror") invaded and conquered England. This united England, Normandy, and much of what is today western France, sparking centuries of border wars and French-speaking kings of England. In 1328 a Norman-English king declared war on the king of France, leading to more than 100 years of Franco-Anglo wars (called the Hundred Years' War). Rallied by the teenage visionary Joan of Arc, the French finally united north and south, driving the English across the Channel in 1453. Modern France was born, with Paris as its capital.

Paris Sites: Notre-Dame, Sainte-Chapelle, Cluny Museum tapestries, Carnavalet Museum, Sorbonne, and the Latin Quarter.

Renaissance and Religious Wars (1500s)

A strong centralized France emerged, with French kings setting Europe's standard. Francois I made Paris a cultural capital, inviting Leonardo and *Mona Lisa* to visit. Catholics and Protestants fought openly, and 2,000 Parisians were slaughtered in the St. Bartholomew's Day Massacre.

Paris Sites: Louvre (palace and Renaissance art), pont Neuf, place des Vosges, and Fontainebleau.

Louis XIV, the Absolute Monarch (1600s)

Louis XIV centralized the power, neutered the nobility, and moved the capital to Versailles, which also became the center of European culture. France's wealth sparked "Enlightened" ideas. With these came the seeds of democracy.

Paris Sites: Versailles, Vaux-le-Vicomte, Les Invalides, paintings by Poussin and Lorraine.

Decadence and Revolution (1700s)

A financial crunch from wars and royal excess drove the French people to revolt. On July 14, 1789, they stormed the Bastille. Later they kidnapped and beheaded the king and queen. Thousands lost their heads—guillotined if suspected of hindering progress. A charismatic commoner rose amid the chaos, promising stability—Napoleon Bonaparte. Along with Napoleon, this was the age of Louis XV, Louis XVI, Marie Antoinette, Voltaire, Rousseau, and Robespierre.

Paris Sites: Versailles, place de la Concorde, place de la Bastille, Conciergerie, and paintings by Watteau, Boucher, Fragonard, and David.

Elected Emperors and Constitutional Kings (1800s)

Napoleon conquered Europe, crowned himself emperor, invaded Russia, and ended up defeated on the battlefields of Waterloo. The monarchy was restored, but a series of popular uprisings (1830, 1848, and 1870) forced rulers to toe the democratic line. Napoleon's nephew, Napoleon III, presided over a wealthy, middle-class nation with a colonial empire in slow decline. France's political clout was fading even as Paris remained the world's cultural center during the "belle epoque," or beautiful age.

Paris Sites: Arc de Triomphe, Haussman's wide boulevards, Eiffel Tower, Les Invalides and Napoleon's Tomb, pont Alexandre, Grand and Petit Palais, Montmartre, Opéra Garnier, paintings of Ingres and Delacroix at the Louvre, and Impressionist and Post-Impressionist paintings (Manet, Monet, Renoir, Degas, Toulouse-Lautrec, Cézanne, and so on) at the Orsay, Marmottan, and L'Orangerie (closed for renovation).

War and Depression (1900–1950)

France began the turn of the century as top dog, but the two World Wars with Germany (and the earlier Franco-Prussian War of 1870) wasted the country. France lost millions of men in World War I, sank into a depression, and was easily overrun by Hitler in World War II. Paris, now dirt cheap, attracted foreign writers and artists.

This was the age of Picasso, Ravel, Debussy, Satie, Stravinsky, Nijinsky, Hemingway, Fitzgerald, Stein, Pound, Sartre, Edith Piaf, and Maurice Chevalier.

Paris Sites: Picasso Museum, Deportation Memorial, Pompidou Center.

Postwar France (1950–Present)

Wartime hero Charles de Gaulle reestablished a democratic Republic. France's colonial empire dissolved after bitter wars in Algeria and Vietnam. Immigrants from former colonies flooded Paris. The turbulent '60s, progressive '70s, socialist-turned-conservative '80s, and the middle-of-the-road '90s bring us to the *début de siècle*, or the beginning of the century.

Paris Sites: Montparnasse Tower, La Défense, Louvre's pyramid, and Pompidou Center.

Contemporary Politics in France

The key political issues in France today are high unemployment (about 12 percent), a steadily increasing percentage of ethnic minorities, and a recognized need to compete in a global marketplace. The challenge is to address these issues while maintaining the social benefits the French expect from their government. As a result, national policies seem to conflict with each other (e.g., France supports the lean economic policies of the European Union but has recently reduced the French workweek to 35 hours).

The unification of Europe has been powered by France and Germany. The 15-member European Union, which is well on its way to becoming a "United States of Europe," is dissolving borders, freeing up trade, and establishing an all-European currency called the euro. Some stores already have prices marked in francs and euros (though euros won't appear as bills and coins until 2002).

French national politics are fascinating. While only two parties dominate American politics, France has five major parties. From left to right, these include the reformed Communists (PCF—Parti Communiste Francaise), the moderate Socialists (PS—Parti Socialiste), the aristocratically conservative UDF (Union pour la Democratie Francaise), the center-right RPR (Rassemblement pour la République), and the racist Front National. In general the UDF and RPR split the conservative middle ground and the Socialists dominate the liberal middle ground. But in France, unlike in the United States, coalitions are generally necessary for any party to "rule." At the fringes you'll read about the racist Front National party, led by Jean-Marie Le Pen. Le Pen's "France for the French" platform calls for the expulsion of ethnic minorities and broader police powers. As unemployment has gone up, so has the popularity of this far-right party. Garnering 15 percent of a recent national vote, Le Pen has been able to force center-right parties farther in his direction. On the far left, the reformed Communists, still recovering from the fall of the Soviet Union, have had to work more flexibly with the less radical Socialists and the environmental parties.

While the French president is elected by popular vote every seven years, he is more of a figurehead than his American counter-part. The more powerful prime minister is elected by the parlia-ment (every 3 years). With five major parties, a single majority is rare—it takes a coalition to elect a prime minister. Currently the left is working together better than the right, and France has a liberal prime minister (socialist Lionel Jospin) with a conservative president (Jacques Chirac). This "cohabitation," as it's called in French, is similar to an American president having to deal with a Congress controlled by an opposing party.

Let's Talk Telephones

Dialing Direct

Here are general instructions for making phone calls. (For infor-mation specific to France, see page 9). International access codes and country codes are listed below. Most European countries use area codes, but France is one of the exceptions (see "Europe's Exceptions," below).

Calling between Countries: Dial the international access code (of the country you're calling from), the country code (of the country you're calling), the area code (if it starts with zero, drop the zero), and the local number.

Calling Long Distance within a Country: First dial the area code (including its zero), then the local number.

Europe's Exceptions: Some countries, such as France, Italy, Spain, Portugal, Norway, and Denmark, do not use area codes. To make an international call to these countries, dial the international access code (usually 00 in Europe, 011 for the United States or Canada), the country code (see chart below), then the local number in its entirety (OK, so there's one excep-tion: for France, drop the initial zero of the local number). To make long-distance calls within any of these countries, simply dial the local number in its entirety.

International Access Codes

When dialing direct, first dial the international access code of the country you're calling from. For the United States and Canada, it's 011. Virtually all European countries use "00" as their international access code; the only exceptions are Finland (990), Estonia (800), and Lithuania (810).

Country Codes

After you've dialed the international access code, then dial the code of the country you're calling.

Austria—43	Finland—358	Norway—47
Belgium—32	France—33	Portugal—351
Britain—44	Germany—49	Spain—34
Canada—1	Greece—30	Sweden—46
Czech Repub.—420	Ireland—353	Switzerland—41
Denmark—45	Italy—39	United States—1
Estonia—372	Netherlands—31	

Calling-Card Operators

AT&T	**MCI**	**Sprint**
0800 99 00 11	0800 99 00 19	0800 99 00 87

Handy Phone Numbers

Directory assistance for Paris and France
    (some English spoken): 12
Lost property (Bureau des Objets Trouvés): open Tue and
    Thu 8:30–20:00, 36 rue des Morillons, Mo: Convention,
    tel. 01 55 76 20 20
American Church: 65 quai d'Orsay, tel. 01 40 62 05 00
Office of American Services (lost passports, etc):
    01 43 12 48 45
Sunday Banks: 115 and 154 avenue des Champs-Élysées

Emergency/Medical Needs

Police: 17
Emergency medical assistance: 15
American Hospital: 63 boulevard Victor Hugo, in suburb of
    Neuilly, Mo: Porte Maillot, then bus #82, tel. 01 46 41 25 25
American Pharmacy: Mo: Opéra, tel. 01 47 42 49 40
24-hour Pharmacy (called "Derhy"): 84 avenue des
    Champs-Élysées, tel. 01 45 62 02 41
Chiropractic Centers: tel. 01 43 54 26 25 or 01 43 87 81 62
SOS Doctors: tel. 01 47 07 77 77 or 01 48 28 40 04
SOS Help (English-speaking hotline): tel. 01 47 23 80 80

Consulates/Embassies
United States Consulate, 2 rue St. Florentin, tel. 01 43 12 48 45;
    Embassy, 2 avenue Gabriel, tel. 01 43 12 22 22,
    Mo: Concorde for both
Canadian Consulate and Embassy, 35 avenue Montaigne,
    Mo: Franklin-Roosevelt, tel. 01 44 43 29 00

Tourist and Transportation Information
Paris Tourist Information: tel. 08 36 68 31 12 (long menu), 01 43
    43 33 24 (live person, English spoken), or 01 49 52 53 10
Île de France Tourist Information (Paris area): tel. 01 42 60 28 62
Train (SNCF) information: tel. 08 36 35 35 35 (English spoken)
Bus and Métro (RATP) information: tel. 08 36 68 77 14
    (French only)

Travel Companies
The American Express Travel Company (11 rue Scribe, Mo:
Opéra, tel. 01 47 77 77 07) is a popular hangout for American
travelers, but you'll find cheaper flights at:
• Cash and Go (34 avenue Champs-Élysées, Mo: Franklin-
  Roosevelt, tel. 01 53 93 63 63)
• Voyageurs en Amerique du Nord (55 rue Sainte Anne, Mo:
  Pyramides, tel. 01 42 86 17 30)
• CTS Voyages (20 rue des Carmes, Mo: Maubert Mutualité,
  tel. 01 43 25 00 76)

Airports
Charles de Gaulle: tel. 01 48 62 22 80
Orly: tel. 01 49 75 15 15

Airlines
Aer Lingus: tel. 01 55 38 38 55
Air Canada: tel. 08 20 87 08 71
Air France: tel. 08 02 80 28 02
    (fee call)
Alitalia: tel. 08 02 31 53 15
American Airlines:
    tel. 08 01 87 28 72 (fee call)
British Airways:
    tel. 08 25 82 54 00
British Midlands:
    tel. 01 41 91 87 04
Continental:
    tel. 01 42 99 09 09
Delta: tel. 01 47 68 92 92

Iberia: tel. 08 02 07 50 75
KLM: tel. 01 44 56 18 18
Lufthansa: tel. 08 02 02 00 30
Northwest:
    tel. 01 44 56 18 18
Olympic: tel. 01 42 65 92 42
Sabena: tel. 08 20 83 08 30
SAS: tel. 08 01 25 25 25
Swissair: tel. 08 02 30 04 00
    (fee call)
TWA: tel. 08 01 89 28 92
United: tel. 08 01 72 72 72
    (fee call)
US Air: tel. 01 49 10 29 00

Classes

French-Language Classes
• American University of Paris (tel. 01 40 62 07 20,
   fax 01 47 05 34 32, www.aup.fr)
• France École Langue (tel. 01 45 00 40 15, fax 01 45 00 53 41,
   www.france-langue.fr)

Cooking Schools
These have demonstration courses:
• Le Cordon Bleu (tel. 01 53 68 22 50, fax 01 48 56 03 96)
• Ritz Escoffier École de Gastronomie Française
   (tel. 01 43 16 30 50)
• La Cuisine de Marie Blanche (tel. 01 45 51 36 34,
   fax 01 45 51 90 19)

Wine Classes
• Maison de la Vigne (tel. 01 47 20 20 76)

Paris Climate
First line, average daily low; second line, average daily high; third
line, days of no rain.

J	F	M	A	M	J	J	A	S	O	N	D
34°	34°	39°	43°	49°	55°	58°	58°	53°	46°	40°	36°
43°	45°	54°	60°	68°	73°	76°	75°	70°	60°	50°	44°
14	14	19	17	19	18	19	18	17	18	15	15

Numbers and Stumblers
• Europeans write a few of their numbers differently than we do.
   1 = 1 , 4 = 4 , 7 = 7 . Learn the difference or miss your train.
• In Europe, dates appear as day/month/year, so Christmas is
   25/12/01.
• Commas are decimal points and decimals commas. A dollar and
   a half is 1,50, and there are 5.280 feet in a mile.
• When pointing, use your whole hand, palm down.
• When counting with fingers, start with your thumb. If you hold
   up your first finger to request one item, you'll probably get two.
• What Americans call the second floor of a building is the first
   floor in Europe.
• Europeans keep the left "lane" open for passing on escalators
   and moving sidewalks. Keep to the right.

Metric Conversion (approximate)

1 inch = 25 millimeters   32 degrees F = 0 degrees C
1 foot = 0.3 meter   82 degrees F = about 28 degrees C
1 yard = 0.9 meter   1 ounce = 28 grams
1 mile = 1.6 kilometers   1 kilogram = 2.2 pounds
1 centimeter = 0.4 inch   1 quart = 0.95 liter
1 meter = 39.4 inches   1 square yard = 0.8 square meter
1 kilometer = .62 mile   1 acre = 0.4 hectare

French Survival Phrases

Hello (good day).	**Bonjour.**	bohn-zhoor
Do you speak English?	**Parlez-vous anglais?**	par-lay-voo ahn-glay
Yes. / No.	**Oui. / Non.**	wee / nohn
I'm sorry.	**Désolé.**	day-zoh-lay
Please.	**S'il vous plaît.**	see voo play
Thank you.	**Merci.**	mehr-see
Goodbye.	**Au revoir.**	oh vwahr
Where is...?	**Où est...?**	oo ay
...a hotel	**...un hôtel**	uhn oh-tehl
...a youth hostel	**...une auberge**	ewn oh-behrzh
	de jeunesse	duh zhuh-nehs
...a restaurant	**...un restaurant**	uhn rehs-toh-rahn
...a grocery store	**...une épicerie**	ewn ay-pee-suh-ree
...the train station	**...la gare**	lah gar
...the tourist info office	**...l'office du tourisme**	loh-fees dew too-reez-muh
Where are the toilets?	**Où sont les toilettes?**	oo sohn lay twah-leht
men / women	**hommes / dames**	ohm / dahm
How much is it?	**Combien?**	kohn-bee-an
Cheaper.	**Moins cher.**	mwan shehr
Included?	**Inclus?**	an-klew
Do you have...?	**Avez-vous...?**	ah-vay-voo
I would like...	**Je voudrais...**	zhuh voo-dray
...a ticket.	**...un billet.**	uhn bee-yay
...a room.	**...une chambre.**	ewn shahn-bruh
...the bill.	**...l'addition.**	lah-dee-see-ohn
one	**un**	uhn
two	**deux**	duh
three	**trois**	twah
four	**quatre**	kah-truh
five	**cinq**	sank
six	**six**	sees
seven	**sept**	seht
eight	**huit**	weet
nine	**neuf**	nuhf
ten	**dix**	dees
At what time?	**À quelle heure?**	ah kehl ur
Just a moment.	**Un moment.**	uhn moh-mahn
Now.	**Maintenant.**	man-tuh-nahn
today / tomorrow	**aujourd'hui / demain**	oh-zhoor-dwee / duh-man

For more user-friendly French phrases, check out *Rick Steves'
French Phrase Book and Dictionary* or *Rick Steves' French, Italian &
German Phrase Book and Dictionary.*

Road Scholar Feedback for PARIS 2001

We're all in the same travelers' school of hard knocks. Your feedback helps us improve this guidebook for future travelers. Please fill this out (or use the on-line version at www.ricksteves.com/feedback), attach more info or any tips/favorite discoveries if you like, and send it to us. As thanks for your help, we'll send you our quarterly travel newsletter free for one year. Thanks! **Rick**

Of the recommended accommodations/restaurants used, which was:

Best _____

       Why? _____

Worst _____

       Why? _____

Of the sights/experiences/destinations recommended by this book, which was:

Most overrated _____

       Why? _____

Most underrated _____

       Why? _____

Best ways to improve this book:

_____

_____

I'd like a free newsletter subscription:

_____ Yes   _____ No   _____ Already on list

_____
Name

_____
Address

_____
City, State, Zip

_____
E-mail Address

    Please send to: ETBD, Box 2009, Edmonds, WA 98020

Fax Your Hotel Reservation

Faxing is more accurate and cheaper than telephoning. Use this handy form for your fax (or find it online at www.ricksteves.com/reservation). Photocopy and fax away.

One-Page Fax

To: _____ @ _____
　　　　　　　　hotel　　　　　　　　　　　　　　　fax

From: _____ @ _____
　　　　　　　　name　　　　　　　　　　　　　　　fax

Today's date: ____ /_____ /____
　　　　　　　day　 month　 year

Dear Hotel _____,

Please make this reservation for me:

Name: _____

Total # of people: _____　# of rooms: _____　# of nights: _____

Arriving: ____ /_____ /____　My time of arrival (24-hr clock): _____
　　　　 day　 month　 year　(I will telephone if I will be late)

Departing: ____ /_____ /____
　　　　　day　 month　 year

Room(s):　Single___　Double___　Twin___　Triple___　Quad___

With:　Toilet___　Shower___　Bath___　Sink only___

Special needs:　View___　Quiet___　Cheap___　Ground Floor___

Credit card:　Visa___　MasterCard___　American Express___

Card #: _____

Expiration date: _____

Name on card: _____

You may charge me for the first night as a deposit. Please fax, e-mail, or mail me confirmation of my reservation, along with the type of room reserved, the price, and whether the price includes breakfast. Thank you.

_____
Signature

_____
Name

_____
Address

_____
City　　　　　　　　　State　　　Zip Code　　Country

_____
E-mail Address

INDEX

FREE-SPIRITED TOURS FROM

Rick Steves

Great Guides

Big Buses

Small Groups

No Grumps

Best of Europe ■ Best of Europe II ■ Eastern Europe ■ Turkey ■ Italy ■ Britain
Spain/Portugal ■ Ireland ■ Eastern France ■ Western France ■ Village France
Scandinavia ■ Germany/Austria/Switzerland ■ London ■ Paris ■ Rome

Looking for a one, two, or three-week tour that's run in the Rick Steves style? Check out Rick Steves' educational, experiential tours of Europe. Rather than seeing Europe as a spectator from a bus window, you'll be encouraged to dive into daily life. You'll have opportunities to meet the locals, see how local transportation and services work, and get comfortable wandering off on your own. By the end of the tour, you'll have the knowledge and confidence it takes to travel through Europe independently—which is what many of our tour members do before they return home.

Rick Steves' tours include much more in the "sticker price" than mainstream tours. Here's what you'll get with a Europe or regional Rick Steves tour...

Group size: Your tour group will be no larger than 26. **Guides:** You'll have two guides traveling and dining with you on your fully guided Rick Steves tour. **Bus:** You'll travel in a full-size 48-to-52-seat bus, with plenty of empty seats for you to spread out and read, snooze, enjoy the passing scenery, get away from your spouse, or whatever. **Sightseeing:** Your tour price includes all group sightseeing. There are no hidden extra charges. **Hotels:** You'll stay in small, characteristic, locally-run hotels in the center of each city, within walking distance of the sights you came to see. **Price and insurance:** Your tour price is guaranteed for 2001. Single travelers do not pay an extra supplement (we have them room with other singles). ETBD includes prorated tour cancellation/ interruption protection coverage at no extra cost. **Tips and kickbacks:** All guide and driver tips are included in your tour price. Because your driver and guides are paid salaries by ETBD, they can focus on giving you the best European travel experience possible.

Interested? Call (425) 771-8303 or visit www.ricksteves.com for a free copy of Rick Steves' 2001 Tours booklet!

Rick Steves' Europe Through the Back Door
130 Fourth Avenue North, PO Box 2009, Edmonds, WA 98020 USA
Phone: (425) 771-8303 ■ Fax: (425) 771-0833 ■ www.ricksteves.com

FREE TRAVEL GOODIES FROM

Rick Steves

EUROPEAN TRAVEL NEWSLETTER

My *Europe Through the Back Door* travel company will help you travel better *because* you're on a budget—not in spite of it. To see how, ask for my 64-page *travel newsletter* packed full of savvy travel tips, readers' discoveries, and your best bets for railpasses, guidebooks, videos, travel accessories and free-spirited tours.

2001 GUIDE TO EUROPEAN RAILPASSES

With hundreds of railpasses to choose from in 2001, finding the right pass for your trip has never been more confusing. To cut through the complexity, ask for my 64-page *2001 Guide to European Railpasses.* Once you've narrowed down your choices, we give you unbeatable prices, including important extras with every Eurailpass, *free:* my hour-long "How to get the most out of your railpass" video; your choice of one of my 16 country guidebooks and phrasebooks; and written advice on your one-page trip itinerary.

RICK STEVES' 2001 TOURS

We offer 16 different one, two, and three-week tours (160 departures in 2001) for those who want to experience Europe in Rick Steves' Back Door style, but without the transportation and hotel hassles. If a tour with a small group, modest family-run hotels, lots of exercise, great guides, and no tips or hidden charges sounds like your idea of fun, ask for my 48-page 2001 Tours booklet.

YEAR-ROUND GUIDEBOOK UPDATES

Even though the information in my guidebooks is the freshest around, things do change in Europe between book printings. I've set aside a special section at my website (www.ricksteves.com/update) listing *up-to-the-minute changes* for every Rick Steves guidebook.

Call, fax, or visit www.ricksteves.com to get your...

☑ FREE EUROPEAN TRAVEL NEWSLETTER
☑ FREE 2001 GUIDE TO EUROPEAN RAILPASSES
☑ FREE RICK STEVES' 2001 TOURS BOOKLET

Rick Steves' Europe Through the Back Door

130 Fourth Avenue North, PO Box 2009, Edmonds, WA 98020 USA
Phone: (425) 771-8303 ■ Fax: (425) 771-0833 ■ www.ricksteves.com

Rick Steves' Phrase Books

Unlike other phrase books and dictionaries on the market, my well-tested phrases and key words cover every situation a traveler is likely to encounter. With these books you'll laugh with your cabby, disarm street thieves with insults, and charm new European friends.

Each book in the series is 4" x 6", with maps.

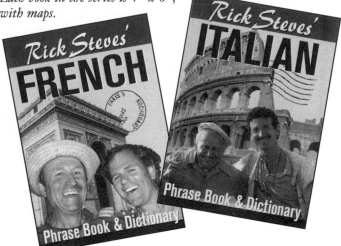

RICK STEVES' FRENCH PHRASE BOOK & DICTIONARY
U.S. $6.95/Canada $10.95

RICK STEVES' GERMAN PHRASE BOOK & DICTIONARY
U.S. $6.95/Canada $10.95

RICK STEVES' ITALIAN PHRASE BOOK & DICTIONARY
U.S. $6.95/Canada $10.95

RICK STEVES' SPANISH & PORTUGUESE PHRASE BOOK & DICTIONARY
U.S. $8.95/Canada $13.95

RICK STEVES' FRENCH, ITALIAN & GERMAN PHRASE BOOK & DICTIONARY
U.S. $8.95/Canada $13.95